THE BISHOP OF THE OLD SOUTH

THE PUBLICATION OF THIS BOOK IS DUE IN PART TO A GENEROUS GIFT BY THE WATSON-BROWN FOUNDATION.

The Bishop of the Old South

THE MINISTRY AND CIVIL WAR LEGACY OF LEONIDAS POLK

Glenn Robins

Mercer University Press
Macon, Georgia

ISBN 978-0-88146-038-4
MUP/H660

First Edition.

Books published by Mercer University Press are printed on acid free
paper that meets the requirements of American National Standard for
Information Sciences—Permanence of Paper for Printed Library
Materials.

Library of Congress Cataloging-in-Publication Data

Robins, Glenn.
The bishop of the Old South : the ministry and Civil War legacy
of
Leonidas Polk / Glenn Robins. –1st ed.
p. cm.
Includes bibliographical references and index.
ISBN-13: 978-0-88146-038-4 (hardcover : alk. paper)
ISBN-10: 0-88146-038-9 (hardcover : alk. paper)
1. Polk, Leonidas, 1806-1864. 2. Generals—Confederate States of
America—Biography. 3. Confederate States of America.
Army—Biography. 4. United States--History--Civil War, 1861-
1865--Biography. 5. Polk, Leonidas, 1806-1864—Religion.
6. Bishops—Louisiana—Biography. 7. Episcopal Church--
Clergy—Biography. 8. Southern States—Church history—19th
century. 9. Plantation owners—Louisiana—Biography. I. Title.
E467.1.P7R63 2006
973.7'3092—dc22
[B]
2006022090

CONTENTS

ACKNOWLEDGMENTS

Several years ago, I embarked on a journey of sorts. At that time, neither the University of Southern Mississippi nor Leonidas Polk figured in my plans, but the guiding hand of providence used them as a type of pathway toward the fulfillment of a lifelong dream. Throughout this journey, a number of people have lent their assistance and without their help none of this would have been possible.

All historians must acknowledge their dependence on archivists and librarians. The staffs at the United States Military Academy and the University of the South were gracious hosts. The personnel in the Manuscripts and Rare Books Department at Tulane University permitted me to continue working as they moved from one building to another. The Virginia Historical Society extended a similar courtesy by granting access to an unprocessed manuscript collection. Their goodwill was greatly appreciated.

One of the pleasures of college and graduate school is the forging of personal and professional friendships. I will always appreciate the companionship of former classmates John Wells, Gene Fant, Kathy Barbier, Tom Ward, and Eric Bobo. Despite my obnoxious antics and too frequent diatribes, they remained constant sources of support and encouragement. At Carson-Newman, Dr. James Baumgardner rekindled my passion for the study of history, Dr. Charles Moffat sharpened my love for the South, and professors Carolyn Blevins, Robert Shurden, and Ernest Lee exemplified everything that is noble and pure about the teaching profession. At East Tennessee State University, Dr. Margaret Ripley Wolfe trained me to think like a historian, introduced me to the historical profession, and challenged me to aim high. I may owe my greatest debts to the members of the history department at the University of Southern Mississippi. Dr. Orazio Ciccarelli has shown me that humbleness and gentleness are qualities worth emulating. Drs. Charles Bolton and Andrew Wiest reminded me that accomplished scholars could also enjoy basketball, softball, and golf. Dr. Jon Sensbach reshaped my view of Southern religious history. Dr. Brad Bond endured every infringement on his time, fielded mind-numbing questions, but still managed to help me distill my ideas. Special thanks go to Dr. William K. Scarborough. His encyclopedic knowledge of Southern history was never intimidating because he eagerly shared his expertise and, despite his own stature, respected my work. One day I hope to repay a portion of my debt to each of these individuals.

Finally, I wish to thank my parents, Marvin and Phyllis Robins. Their unconditional love and support have allowed me to pursue any and all opportunities. More importantly, they have allowed me just to be. And for that I will always be grateful.

PREFACE

"You damned Yankee sons of bitches have killed our old Gen. Polk," so wrote a Confederate infantryman in a note he left for William T. Sherman's Union soldiers as they marched mercilessly toward the city of Atlanta.[1] The requiem was not the usual tribute paid to deceased bishops of the Episcopal church, but then, Leonidas Polk was not the typical Southern prelate. Born into an aristocratic North Carolina family that had earned a reputation for valor during the American Revolution, Polk embraced the Southern way of life and accepted martial service as part of his sacred heritage. As a young cadet at the United States Military Academy, Polk embraced Christianity for the first time and suddenly found himself contemplating a call into the ministry. Indecision and self-doubt marked the early years of his ministry, but in 1838 he became missionary bishop of the Southwest and in 1841 he was named bishop of Louisiana. During this time, Polk also managed several impressive plantations and owned a large number of slaves. As the sectional controversy intensified, Polk defined himself as a Southern nationalist. After the firing on Fort Sumter, he accepted a generalship in the Confederate army. His controversial military career ended in tragedy on 14 June 1864, when he was struck in the chest by a Federal artillery shell. His spirit lived on though in the myths and romanticized truths of the Lost Cause. Unfortunately, the unmistakable image of "old Gen. Polk" has prevented religious historians as well as historians of the Old South from appreciating his significance as a Southern prelate. Even E. Brooks Hollifield, the distinguished historian of Southern religion who identifies Polk as one of the 100 gentleman theologians of the Old South, produced only one sentence on the "famed Episcopal bishop" in his study of the region's literary parsons.[2]

---

[1] Quoted in Steven Davis, "The Death of Bishop Polk," *Blue and Gray Magazine* 6/3 (June 1989): 14.

[2] E. Brooks Hollifield, *The Gentleman Theologians: American Theology in Southern Culture, 1795–1860* (Durham: Duke University Press, 1978) 20.

Leonidas Polk was one of the most important Episcopal leaders of the antebellum South. When he entered the ministry in 1830, evangelicalism had transformed the South into a distinctly Christian society, and religion functioned as the prism through which Southerners interpreted many life experiences, including social relations. Polk understood the religious culture of Southern society, and more importantly, he worked diligently to adapt Episcopalianism to the evangelical South.[3] To accomplish this goal, he had to consider two fundamental characteristics of Southern religious life. First, Southern Episcopalians competed against the extremely popular and successful Baptist and Methodist denominations. Second, Southern Episcopalians operated in a geographical region in which slaves represented a significant portion—and in some places a majority—of the Southern population.[4] Therefore, any effective Southern Episcopalian synthesis would by necessity have a strong sociological or cultural dimension and would differ markedly from the theologically oriented strategies employed by the high church and Northern traditions.[5] Regrettably, historians of Southern religion have understood poorly how the Episcopal denomination responded and related to the evangelical currents of the antebellum South, and even those scholars who have alluded to an evangelical Episcopal tradition have not focused sufficiently on Southern Episcopalians in general or Leonidas Polk in particular.[6]

---

[3] Christine Leigh Heyrman, *Southern Cross: The Origins of the Bible Belt* (Chapel Hill: University of North Carolina Press, 1997); Anne C. Loveland, *Southern Evangelicals and the Social Order, 1800–1860* (Baton Rouge: Louisiana State University Press, 1980); Hollifield, *The Gentleman Theologians.*

[4] Jerald Bauer, "Regionalism and Religion in America," *Church History* 54/3 (September 1985): 372–75.

[5] For an explanation of the Hobartian positions and the high church alternative to evangelical Protestantism, see R. Bruce Mullin, *Episcopal Vision/American Reality: High Church Theology and Social Thought in Evangelical America* (New Haven: Yale University Press, 1986).

[6] Donald Mathews, *Religion in the Old South* (Chicago: University of Chicago Press, 1977); Heyrman, *Southern Cross*; Loveland, *Southern Evangelicals*; Mitchell Snay, *The Gospel of Disunion: Religion and Separatism in the Antebellum South* (New York/Oxford: Oxford University Press, 1993); Robert W. Pritchard, *The Nature of Salvation: Theological Consensus in the Episcopal Church, 1801–73* (Urbana: University of Illinois Press, 1997); Diana Hochstedt Butler, *Standing against the Whirlwind: Evangelical Episcopalians in Nineteenth Century America* (New York/Oxford: Oxford University Press, 1995).

By 1830, as historian Allen Guelzo has noted, "The Episcopal Church had elbowed its way out of the margins of American Protestantism and claimed a place in the mainstream of Protestant evangelicalism." Based on this assertion, an argument can be made that Episcopalianism—if not in terms of numerical strength then in terms of its "ethos and purpose"—possessed the potential to become a powerful force in America's antebellum religious culture.[7] Southern Episcopalians maintained a discernible presence in the social and political spheres of their region, especially on the eve of the Civil War. Of the major Protestant denominations, the Old South's planter elite were most comfortable with the Episcopal tradition. By virtue of their elevated socioeconomic and political status, they played an especially prominent role in the development of the various strands of Southern nationalism. Of the known religious affiliations of the participants in Southern secession conventions, Episcopalians comprised 32 percent of delegates and represented the largest single religious group. Likewise, when the Confederate government began to take shape, Episcopalians occupied many of the most prominent positions. President Jefferson Davis, Secretary of the Treasury Christopher Memminger, and Secretary of the Navy Stephen Mallory were Episcopalian. Within the military, seven of the Confederacy's eight full generals were Episcopalian. The denomination also provided an inordinate number of chaplains in comparison to the number of churchmen serving in the ranks.[8] In summary, Southern Episcopalians expressed the values of the Southern slave society, and through their positions of leadership quite literally guided the Confederate quest for an independent republic. Moreover, the denomination deserves consideration as an important element in the religious life of the South as does Leonidas Polk.

This book will demonstrate how Polk attempted to adapt Episcopalianism to the evangelical South and to integrate the denomination into the mainstream of the region's religious life. Personally, Polk fit the profile of an evangelical. His emotional conversion, his emphasis on preaching the gospel, and his providential worldview reflected the typical

---

[7] Allen C. Guelzo, "Ritual, Romanism, and Rebellion: The Disappearance of the Evangelical Episcopalians, 1853–1873," *Anglican and Episcopal History* 62/4 (December 1993): 551.

[8] Jon L. Wakelyn, *Biographical Dictionary of the Confederacy* (Westport CT: Greenwood Press, 1977) 25, 307, 317, 362.

experiences and characteristics of evangelicals. Moreover, his martial heritage, aristocratic bearing, and patriarchal outlook were well suited to Southern evangelical culture. In addition, as a bishop and large slaveholder, Polk commanded the confidence and respect of both the religious and plantation communities and thereby influenced discussions about the peculiar institution. Also, comparisons will be drawn between Polk and other, more recognizable, prelates of the Old South such as Theodore Clapp, Charles Colcock Jones, James Hervey Otey, and Benjamin Morgan Palmer. Very little attention is devoted to Polk's family life for two reasons. Polk states on numerous occasions that for a bishop to be truly dedicated to the church he needed to be free of family obligations. For the most part, Polk led his live according to this mentality. He was separated from his family for long periods, and his "religious activities" consumed his time and attention. Furthermore, on a practical level, a study of Polk's family life proves problematic because the entire correspondence between Polk and his wife from their courtship days through the late 1850s was destroyed in a cabin fire.

The Civil War did not prevent Polk from continuing his mission. Despite the controversial nature of his military service, his actions during the sectional crisis represented some of his most aggressive attempts to make Episcopalianism relevant to the social and political concerns of the South. The bishop as general embodied the complementary nature of Southern Episcopalianism and Confederate identity, and within the army he symbolized Southern notions of honor and courage. Even in death, Polk became part of Southern explanations of the Old South and the Civil War. In fact, Lost Cause enthusiasts developed a positive image of Polk because he validated their claims that slaveholders were not immoral and that slavery was part of a sacred trust from God. As the Reformation scholar William J. Bouwsma has noted in his biography of John Calvin, the inquisitive mind should be "as much concerned to scrutinize the man in order to understand the time as to scrutinize the time in order to understand the man."[9] With that in mind, the story begins in North Carolina, Polk's birthplace and home of his substantial ancestors.

---

[9] William J. Bouwsma, *John Calvin: A Sixteenth-Century Portrait* (New York/Oxford: Oxford University Press, 1988) 4.

CHAPTER 1

A Martial Heritage

The Polks of North Carolina were one of the most prominent antebellum families in the Tarheel State, and yet their familial roots also included a link to the storied era of the English Civil War. Most genealogists trace the family history to Lanarkshire near Glasgow, Scotland. During the reign of James I, John Pollock, "an uncompromising Presbyterian," fled the religiously and politically troubled region of his nativity. He settled among "the new colony of Protestants" in Donegal, Ireland, and enjoyed the tranquil life of a country gentleman. Some of John Pollock's children, however, remained behind and yielded to the passions of the times. For example, his son Robert sided with Oliver Cromwell and the Parliamentary forces in their war against Charles I.[1] Following the failure of the Interregnum and the triumph of the Glorious Revolution, Robert, perhaps disappointed by the settlement that led to the constitutional monarchy, emigrated with his wife and children to the New World. He settled on the Eastern Shore of Maryland, changed his surname to Polk, and began a life as a simple farmer. Between 1687 and 1742, Robert, his sons, and grandsons, all received land grants from the Lords of Baltimore. For unknown reasons, Robert's grandson, William, moved to Carlisle, Pennsylvania, in the early 1740s, where he and his wife raised eight children. William's second son was Thomas Polk, the grandfather of Leonidas Polk. It was the ever-colorful Thomas Polk who provided the initial drama for the Polks' North Carolina odyssey.[2]

---

[1] William M. Polk, *Leonidas Polk: Bishop and General*, 2 vols. (New York: Longmans, Green, and Co., 1915) 1:2–3.
[2] Mrs. Frank B. Angellotti, *The Polks of North Carolina and Tennessee* (Easley SC: Southern Historical Press, 1984) 2–5.

Because he "could not bear the dull pursuits of a Pennsylvania farmer," Thomas Polk "left his parents about the year 1753 to seek his fortune in a country that furnished greater scope to his active mind."[3] Polk chose Mecklenburg County, North Carolina, as his destination, and established a residence on Sugar Creek, a tributary of the Catawba River. He soon married another Pennsylvania émigré, Susanna Sprat. Together they raised eight children and among that number was William Polk, the father of Leonidas.[4] Based on his success as a small planter and his aggressiveness as a land speculator, Thomas Polk earned the distinction as "one of the wealthiest and most prominent citizens" in Mecklenburg County. He played an important role in founding the city of Charlotte, served as a county magistrate, and was a member of the North Carolina colonial legislature for ten years. By 1771 Polk's political views had become "increasingly conservative," which was likely attributable to his disapproval of the Regulator Movement. When the backcountry men of the Piedmont challenged the colonial authorities Polk supported Governor William Tryon, and he actually aided the governor in dispensing punishments in the aftermath of the uprising.[5]

Although judged conservative by one political standard, Thomas Polk "from the beginning of colonial disturbances...boldly advocated a policy of uncompromising resistance to the encroachments of the British" government. In fact, he signed the Mecklenburg Declaration of 1775, which announced the county's intention to sever political ties with England and to erect a completely autonomous government. With the commencement of military hostilities between the Colonists and Great Britain, Polk received a commission as colonel of the Fourth North Carolina regiment. In the fall of 1776, his unit drew its first assignment and was part of the contingent that repelled the British at Charleston, South Carolina. From June 1777, to February 1778, Polk served under General Francis Nash and fought at the

---

[3] William H. Hoyt, ed., *The Papers of Archibald Murphey*, 2 vols. (Raleigh NC: E.M. Uzzell and Company, 1914) 2:400. This volume contains William Polk's brief autobiography.

[4] Angellotti, *The Polks of North Carolina and Tennessee*, 5–6.

[5] Norris W. Preyer, *Hezekiah Alexander and the Revolution in the Backcountry* (Charlotte NC: Heritage Printers, 1987) 127. Polk and Alexander were political rivals, and Preyer provides an excellent discussion of the roles these two men played in the political, economic, and social development of colonial North Carolina.

Battle of Brandywine. During the winter encampment at Valley Forge, the leaders of the Continental army decided to consolidate several brigades, causing Polk to lose his regimental command. Outraged that he had not been appointed to replace General Nash who had been mortally wounded at the Battle of Germantown, Polk informed George Washington, Continental commander and chief, that "such a flagrant demonstration of partiality and injurious preference...has determined me no longer to serve my ungrateful country in so painful and so hazardous a capacity." Offended by this apparent vote of no confidence, Polk returned promptly to North Carolina.[6]

Despite the disappointment, Polk remained committed to the Patriot cause and signed on as the Continental commissary agent in his adopted state of North Carolina. The job proved to be not only difficult but frustrating. Moreover, Polk found himself the target of vicious accusations leveled by General Horatio Gates, who had assumed command of the Continental forces in the southern theater in July 1780. Gates, whose army suffered from a lack of food and war materials, formally charged Polk with "doubtful and suspicious" conduct. According to historian Hugh Rankin, Gates "knew full well that there were not sufficient supplies" in central North Carolina, and the general should have realized that Polk "had done his best" although "his efforts had been unsuccessful." Most likely, Gates envisioned Polk as a potential scapegoat who could divert attention away from his own abysmal performance at the Battle of Camden. Angered that his patriotism and honor had been questioned, Polk contemplated resigning his post but reconsidered when General Nathanael Greene took command of the Southern army in December 1780.[7] Following a personal meeting with General Greene, Polk concluded that after only one day the new commander "better understood the situation of the country than Gates had in the entire period of his command." Greene expressed a similar confidence in Polk. He ordered the colonel "to succeed to the militia command held by the late General [William Lee] Davidson," and to muster out "five hundred riflemen to join the southern army."[8] Under Greene, Polk returned to the

[6]For Polk's early activities as a patriot and the letter to Washington see, Polk, *Leonidas Polk*, 1:10–19.

[7] Hugh F. Rankin, *The North Carolina Continentals* (Chapel Hill: University of North Carolina Press, 1971) 252–58.

[8] Ibid., 261, 286.

battlefield at Rugely's Mill, which in all likelihood was his final combat assignment, and the one that earned him the rank of general.[9]

Thomas Polk was not the only member of the Polk clan to enlist with the Continentals during the American Revolution. Thomas's three brothers—Charles, John, and Ezekial—each held a rank no lower than captain, and Thomas's eldest son was killed at the Battle of Eutaw Springs. However, Thomas's second son, William, the father of Leonidas, may have compiled the most impressive service record of any family member.[10] In 1775, at the tender age of sixteen, William Polk withdrew from Queen's College in Charlotte and accepted an appointment as a second lieutenant in the 2nd company of the Third South Carolina regiment. William's youthful exuberance most likely conditioned him to disregard his own mortality and to face grave danger with acts of personal bravery. During the Patriot assault on the British post at Ninety-Six (in Orangeburg District, South Carolina), Polk sustained a severe shoulder wound which required him "to lye on his back for nine months." The prolonged convalescence forced Polk to resign his first commission. Upon his recovery, Polk joined the 9th North Carolina regiment with the rank of major and campaigned under General George Washington at Brandywine and Germantown. At Germantown, Polk "was shot in the mouth...knocking out four Jaw teeth and shattering the Jaw bone." This injury did not require extended medical treatment, but Polk did transfer to North Carolina following the Valley Forge consolidation in order "to aid and superintend the recruiting service."[11] Polk's second tour of duty occurred in the South and introduced him to some of the Revolutionary War's most distinguished personalities. It was in his native region that Polk first met Andrew Jackson, and the friendship that they forged in war "lasted as long as the two lived." Polk also served with General Thaddeus Kosciusko and aided the famed Pole in the early stages of the climactic southern campaign against the British commander Lord Charles Cornwallis. After the Battle of Guilford Court House, Polk earned a

---

[9] Polk, *Leonidas Polk*, 1:34. The Continental Congress was extremely reluctant to grant promotions to anyone who had lost a command through regimental consolidations.

[10] Angellotti, *The Polks of North Carolina and Tennessee*, 6–8. Charles and John held the rank of captain; Ezekial was a lieutenant colonel. The son killed at Eutaw Springs was also named Thomas.

[11] Hoyt, *The Papers of Archibald Murphey*, 2:401–404.

promotion to lieutenant colonel that included the command of the 4th South Carolina regiment. Polk's finest hour came at the Battle of Eutaw Springs.[12] The official battle report singled out several state units, one of which was led by Polk, for fighting "with that gallantry & firmness which characterized the advocates for Liberty."[13] In awarding individual praise, General Nathanael Greene informed Thomas McKean, the president of the Continental Congress, that "Lieutenant-Colonels Polk and [Charles] Middleton [Myddelton] were no less conspicuous for their good conduct than their intrepidity, and the troops under their command gave a specimen of what may be expected from men naturally brave when improved by proper discipline."[14]

The Polks of North Carolina made the family name synonymous with the ideals of duty and patriotism by virtue of their impressive service records in the American Revolution. It was, however, William Polk who was most readily identified with this honorable military heritage. After the war, he became known by the simple appellation Colonel Polk and his public friendships with such luminaries as Andrew Jackson and Nathanael Greene only enhanced his celebrity. Polk was also an original member of the Order of Cincinnati, a club of Revolutionary war officers who identified themselves with the famed Roman citizen-general Lucius Quintius Cincinnatus. The zenith of his involvement in postwar patriotic organizations and celebrations occurred in 1825 during the "Triumphal Tour" of Revolutionary icon Marquis de Lafayette.

The Frenchman commenced his extended visit of America's twenty-four states in August 1824, arriving in North Carolina in March 1825, where

---

[12] Polk also had close ties to the political leadership of South Carolina; he received his lieutenant colonel commission from Governor John Rutledge and fought alongside Wade Hampton at Eutaw Springs. His total active war service was five years and two months. See Polk, *Leonidas Polk*, 1:41–45. For a brief account of Kosciuszko's role in the southern campaign see Miecislaus Haiman, *Kosciuszko in the American Revolution* (1943; repr., Boston: Gregg Press, 1972) 85–141. Polk assisted Kosciuszko in establishing fortifications on the Peedee River near Charlotte, North Carolina.

[13] General Greene's report is in Richard K Showman ed., *The Papers of Nathanael Greene*, 11 vols. (Chapel Hill: University of North Carolina Press, 1976–1999) 9:307.

[14] Nathanel Greene to Thomas McKean, 11 September 1771, in *The Papers of Nathanael Greene*, ed. Richard K. Showman, 11 vols. (Chapel Hill: University of North Carolina Press, 1976–1999) 9:328–38.

a coterie of state dignitaries received the "Nation's Guest." As one of four individuals comprising North Carolina's official welcoming committee, Polk had the privilege of private discussions with the esteemed visitor, and he occupied a conspicuous position on several local programs. In Raleigh, he delivered a memorable address to commemorate the French dignitary's visit to the capital city: "It is impossible to review the history of these times, and not dwell with delight on the name and services of Lafayette, who, animated with the purest love of liberty, relinquished what ordinary minds esteem the choicest blessings of life...quitting family, friends, fortune & country, to encounter the perils of military life, in an unequal and almost hopeless contest; and who, in the darkest period of the Revolution, instead of being appalled at the extent of danger, derived new ardor from the gathering storm." Following the honoree's rejoinder, a Raleigh *Register* correspondent commented that "the veteran Soldiers, Gen. Lafayette and Col. Polk rushed into each other's arms, and again wept their gratitude, that they who had borne the brunt of battle together in their joyful prime, had been spared to meet again on peaceful plains and in happier hours. It was a sight which warmed the cold heart of age, and made the youthful spirit glow with brighter enthusiasm, and a simultaneous expression of feeling burst forth in a lengthened huzza from the attendant crowd."[15] For many members of the Revolutionary generation, Lafayette served as an international symbol of their particular version of liberty and republican principles. William Polk's identification with the general cast him as a type of guardian of the spirit of 1776. From this position, he translated and transmitted the Revolutionary ideals of patriotism, bravery, sacrifice, and determination to the people of North Carolina, but in particular to his own family.[16]

The resourceful Polk capitalized on his popularity and took full advantage of the opportunities that accompanied American independence. In the reciprocal world of politics and wealth, Polk first used his political connections to amass a sizeable estate and then relied on his vested interests to extend his political standing. In 1783 the North Carolina legislature divided the Tennessee territory into three sectors and appointed William

---

[15] Edgar Ewing Brandon, ed., *A Pilgrimage of Liberty: A Contemporary Account of the Triumphal Tour of General Lafayette through the Southern and Western States in 1825, as Reported by the Local Newspapers* (Athens OH: Lawhead Press, 1944) 21–30.

[16] See Anne C. Loveland, *Emblem of Liberty: The Image of Lafayette in the American Mind* (Baton Rouge: Louisiana State University Press, 1971).

Polk as the chief surveyor of the "central" district, which encompassed the Nashville area. Although the statutes governing the distribution of land stipulated that one person could title no more than 5,000 acres in his name, historian Thomas Abernethy has suggested that district surveyors, "realizing the commercial possibilities" within their jurisdictions, circumvented the law in order to acquire enormous personal estates. The actions of William Polk confirm such conclusions. He accumulated roughly 100,000 acres in central Tennessee, which was five times the total of his counterpart Stockely Donelson, the eastern district surveyor, who registered an impressive 20,000 acres under his own name. It is clear that both Polk and Donelson abused the power of their offices for personal gain.[17]

Polk's role in the distribution of Tennessee lands, however, was not limited to the simple procurement of a sizeable personal fortune. In his capacity as a surveyor, Polk gained important friends and political allies by providing them with "information...from his fieldnotes." According to family tradition, he personally directed Andrew Jackson "in his selection of valuable tracts of land."[18] Jackson's career as a land speculator was much more complicated than the Polk family history suggests; in fact, his biographer Robert Remini does not even mention the North Carolinian in his discussion of Old Hickory's land dealings.[19] Nevertheless, because the land grab occurred in such a short period of time, the "choicest lands fell almost exclusively into the hands of a [few] politicians," and Polk often facilitated these transactions. As a result, he entered "a community of interests" that met no substantial challenges in the antebellum period, and this seat among the landed elite, in all probability, afforded him with the proper credentials for entering the political arena.[20]

William Polk was a loyal and partisan Federalist. As such, he benefited from political patronage as long as his party remained in power; however, Polk did not predicate his political allegiance upon the availability of party

---

[17]Thomas P. Abernethy, *From Frontier to Plantation in Tennessee: A Study in Frontier Democracy* (Chapel Hill: University of North Carolina Press, 1932) 44, 59. Both Polk, *Leonidas Polk*, 1:48 and Angellotti, *The Polks of North Carolina and Tennessee*, 15 estimate the size of William's estate at 100,000 acres.

[18] Polk, *Leonidas Polk*, 1:51.

[19] See Robert V. Remini, *Andrew Jackson and the Course of American Empire* (New York: Harper and Row, 1977).

[20] Abernethy, *From Frontier to Plantation*, 348.

favors. President George Washington selected Polk, in 1791, to be the supervisor of internal revenue for the district of North Carolina, a position he held for seventeen years. He also served as the director and president of the State Bank of North Carolina from 1811 to 1819.[21] His party loyalty was tested in the early 1800s when the Republicans gained control of the state legislature. Despite the decline of the Federalist Party, Polk was convinced that "Jacobinism" had reached its apogee in the Tarheel State and he refused to abandon his party. Furthermore, Polk declined an offer from Republican president James Madison to serve as a brigadier-general in the United States Army during the War of 1812. He based his decision in part on an ideological opposition to the war, but the intense partisanship of that day surely influenced his decision.

Polk supported North Carolina's "Peace Party" in 1812, which in addition to opposing the war, campaigned for changes to the system of selecting presidential electors in order to undermine the prospects of Republican candidates. Although many of Polk's political allies in the North Carolina legislature voted against war-related spending bills, his reputation suffered significantly for not answering the commander and chief's call to arms. Contributing to the public ridicule was United States congressman William Blackledge of North Carolina. Blackledge, who failed to win a sixth term in his reelection bid in 1812, believed that Polk would not accept a military appointment unless he could be stationed in Raleigh, where he could continue to profit financially from his position as president of the state bank. Such charges certainly embarrassed the Revolutionary War hero, but he refused to reverse his position. However, when the British forces sacked and burned the nation's capital in the summer of 1814, Polk ended his opposition to the war. "My objections are well known and in this communication it is unnecessary, if not improper, to state them," Polk informed North Carolina's pro-war governor William Hawkins, "it is enough to know...that danger does exist [and] it now behoves us to show the world" that the country is capable of extinguishing the British threat. Thus, even martial glory had limited appeal to the fifty-six-year-old Polk when the source of that fame necessitated a reversal of political allegiance.[22]

---

[21] Angellotti, *The Polks of North Carolina and Tennessee*, 15.

[22] Sarah McCulloh Lemmon, "Dissent in North Carolina during the War of 1812," *North Carolina Historical Review* 49/2 (April 1972): 103–18.

By 1824 the political pendulum had shifted significantly. Polk realized and admitted to himself that the Federalist Party had lost its national appeal and vitality and that Andrew Jackson represented the "best chance" for stemming the tide of Republicanism. Therefore, he teamed with Archibald D. Murphy in organizing support for Jackson throughout North Carolina.[23] Of the two tarheels, Murphy was clearly the more politically prominent. In fact, one historian of the Jacksonian period described him as "North Carolina's most thoughtful and original advocate of economic development." By supporting Jackson, Murphy and Polk hoped to secure federal aid for transportation projects and internal improvements in North Carolina, which they viewed as the best way to ensure long-term agricultural profitability. In addition, a transportation revolution that expedited a "westward expansion of commercial agriculture" would enhance land values, even into Tennessee. William Polk's heavy investment in railroad development seems to confirm an allegiance to this particular economic vision. For obvious reasons, Polk applauded the Jackson victory in 1828, and while not a high-profile member of the Jackson machine, his friendship and continued association with the new president capped a productive political career. In short, through lucrative land deals and political acumen, William Polk earned for himself and his family a place among the upper echelons of North Carolina society.[24]

Very little primary source material has survived regarding the childhood of Leonidas Polk, but it is reasonable to assume that the Polks represented the typical aristocratic family of North Carolina. Elite families have often been defined by such cultural indices as kinship networks, family wealth, religion, morality, and parenting philosophies.[25] An examination of

---

[23] Hugh Talmage Lefler and Albert Ray Newsome, *The History of a Southern State: North Carolina* (Chapel Hill: University of North Carolina Press, 1954) 285, 325. Polk died on 4 January 1834, during Jackson's second term, and was buried with full military honors.

[24] Harry L. Watson, *Jacksonian Politics and Community Conflict: The Emergence of the Second American Party System in Cumberland County, North Carolina* (Baton Rouge: Louisiana State University Press, 1981) 59, 49–52.

[25] Jane Turner Censer, *North Carolina Planters and Their Children, 1800–1860* (Baton Rouge: Louisiana State University Press, 1984). Although William Polk technically did not qualify for Censer's sample group, his father-in-law, Philemon Hawkins, and Leonidas's father-in-law, John Devereux, were among the 124 planters, which made the Polk family a viable component of the study.

these topics will provide useful insights into Leonidas Polk's early life. Leonidas Polk was born to William and Sarah Polk on 10 April 1806, in the capital city of Raleigh. Sarah was the daughter of Philemon and Lucy Davis Hawkins of Warren County, North Carolina. Hawkins was a successful planter in his own right and a large landholder who wielded significant political influence in the state. He was a member of the Continental Provincial Congress, served eleven terms in the North Carolina General Assembly between 1787 and 1818, and was a delegate to the state convention that ratified the Federal Constitution.[26] Sarah inherited from her father an affinity for large families and gave birth to thirteen children, nearly doubling the average number of offspring sired by North Carolina planters. The unusually high fertility pattern may have increased the chances of premature death among the Polk children. According to historian Jane Turner Censer, "An accurate measurement of child mortality among these North Carolina families is not possible, but a rough survey…suggests a rate of 230 [deaths] per 1,000 [births]." In simple terms, "at least one child in four did not reach its fifth birthday."[27] Unfortunately, the Polks experienced firsthand the tragedy of losing a child. Their first daughter died in infancy and their fourth son in childhood. Yet a truly painful chain of events occurred when three of William and Sarah's last five children died in infancy. Nonetheless, the Polks coped with their grief and by all accounts governed a warm, nurturing, child-centered household.[28]

Often, the North Carolina elite expressed their love for their children by honoring them with the name of a grandparent or close relative. This

---

[26] William S. Powell, *Dictionary of North Carolina Biography*, 6 vols. (Chapel Hill: University of North Carolina Press, 1979–1996) 3:75. Philemon's oldest son, William, served as governor of North Carolina from 1810 to 1814.

[27] Censer, *North Carolina Planters*, 24–25, 28. The average number of legitimate offspring for Turner's group was seven. Ironically, Sarah Polk came from a family of thirteen.

[28] Angellotti, *The Polks of North Carolina and Tennessee*, 14–17. The Polks' sixth child, Alexander Hamilton Polk, died of consumption in 1830, two days short of his twentieth birthday. It should also be noted that the Polks were a reconstituted family. William Polk first married Griselda Gilchrist on 15 October 1789. Griselda gave birth to two sons, Thomas Gilchrist Polk and William Julius Polk. She died on 22 October 799, whereupon William married Sarah Hawkins on 1 January 1801. There is no evidence to suggest that the stepsiblings ever displayed any animosity toward one another.

practice, which demonstrated the crucial role that kinship played in the households of planter families, was evident in some of the choices made by William and Sarah Polk. Of the thirteen Polk children, Lucinda Davis Polk received her maternal grandmother's maiden name, John Hawkins Polk his maternal grandparent's surname, Sarah Polk her mother's given name, Susan Spratt Polk her paternal grandmother's name, and Philemon Hawkins Polk his maternal grandfather's name. Clearly, the Polks followed in many cases the naming strategies of the elite families of their state, and the prevalence of maternal-based names confirms Jane Turner Censer's contention that women contributed significantly in the naming process.[29]

William and Sarah also adopted some of the more patriarchal naming customs of Southern aristocrats. Most notably, they followed the conventions of well-to-do South Carolina planters. Historian Michael Johnson, in his study of elite Charlestonian families, discovered that a given name was often selected in order to associate children with some individual "who had measured up to the [parents'] patriarchal ideal."[30] Certainly, William Polk revealed his admiration of Federalist icons when he named three of his sons, Alexander Hamilton Polk, Rufus King Polk, and George Washington Polk. Likewise, he displayed a strong affinity for political-martial heroes when he named a son Andrew Jackson Polk. Yet, William conferred the most interesting or distinctive name on his second son, Leonidas. Perhaps, the North Carolinian's reputation as a Revolutionary War hero convinced him to name his son Leonidas in honor of the Spartan warrior who had fought so valiantly at the Battle of Thermopylae. Notwithstanding the lack of direct evidence to support this assertion, historians have argued convincingly that "it gratified the vanity of southerners to identify themselves with the refined and cultured citizens" of classical Greece, and that southerners assumed "a spiritual kinship" with the ancient slave society.[31] But even if a given name was not an explicit reminder of a predetermined plan for a child's life, most fathers viewed their sons as "extensions of themselves." As historian Bertram Wyatt-Brown has argued,

---

[29] Censer, *North Carolina Planters*, 32–33.

[30] Michael P. Johnson, "Planters and Patriarchy: Charleston, 1800–1860," *Journal of Southern History* 46/1 (February 1980): 49.

[31] Edwin A. Miles, "The Old South and the Classical World," *North Carolina Historical Review* 48/3 (July 1971): 272, 258. Leonidas was the second son of William's second marriage, his fourth son overall.

"Duty to fathers came first. The future, even the present, rested on the past."[32] Throughout his life, Leonidas Polk found himself drawn to his family's, and in particular his father's, martial heritage, as well as his region's definitions of honor, duty, and patriotism.

With regard to religious affiliation, the majority of North Carolina planters aligned themselves with the Episcopal church. During the antebellum period nearly 58 percent of large slaveholders belonged to the Episcopal church, whereas the Baptists claimed only 16 percent, the Presbyterians 12 percent, and the Methodists 11 percent. The success of the Episcopal church in some North Carolina counties during the early part of the nineteenth century could have been a function of the denomination's cultural appeal to individuals of a "high socioeconomic status."[33] Yet, the Polks appeared to have held no official ties to an organized religious community.[34] Assuredly, William Polk neither cherished nor preserved in any manner the "uncompromising" Presbyterianism of his forefathers. Whatever concern he may have had for an afterlife he placed his faith in the redemptive quality of his own character and not the atoning sacrifice of a Christian messiah. On one occasion, William presented these very sentiments to John S. Ravenscroft, the Episcopal bishop of North Carolina.

"In a private conversation," Polk asked Ravenscroft "if a man of high morality and clean living would get to heaven by these means alone." The bishop replied, "No sir: he would go straight to hell." Polk accepted the answer without the appearance of despair or concern and gave no indication that he intended to join the church as a matter of spiritual necessity.[35] His

---

[32] Bertram Wyatt-Brown, *Southern Honor: Ethics and Behavior in the Old South* (New York/Oxford: Oxford University Press, 1982) 134, 122.

[33] Censer, *North Carolina Planters*, 5–6. Turner was able to determine the religious affiliation of 73 of 124 members of her sample group. See also table 2 of William K. Scarborough's, *Masters of the Big House: The Elite Slaveholders of the Mid-nineteenth Century South* (Baton Rouge: Louisiana State University Press, 2003). Scarborough found that 88 percent of North Carolina's largest planters were Episcopalian. His study, based on the 1850 and 1860 federal census, examined planters who owned 250 or more slaves. Of the seventeen North Carolina planters in his study, Scarborough was able to identify the religious affiliation of eight slaveholders.

[34] Polk, *Leonidas Polk*, 1:96.

[35] E. Clowes Chorley, *Men and Movements in the American Episcopal Church* (New York: Scribner, 1946) 164.

attitude toward religion was not unheard of in the Old South and in many ways resembled the sentiments of the independent-minded Edmund Ruffin. Although a life-long attendant of the Episcopal church and a committed moralist, the Virginia planter rejected outright the orthodox doctrine of atonement and insisted that character and conduct were the only logical means to salvation.[36] Ravenscroft's ministerial reputation could have soured Polk on the idea of church membership. The bishop, whose nickname was Mad Jack, "was the most unconventional person in the House of Bishops," according to one church historian, and he openly embraced "the theological positions of militant high churchmen."[37] For whatever reason, William Polk remained outside the confines of organized religion. Nevertheless, he and Sarah instilled in their children such ethics as honesty, hard work, self-control, and achievement.

Of the many values shared by the Polk family, education assumed a special importance. All of the Polk children, in the tradition of elite Southern families, attended private schools and Leonidas was no exception, studying at a small Raleigh academy. In addition, William Polk was an educator of sorts and served actively on the board of trustees at the University of North Carolina at Chapel Hill from 1792 to 1834, which explains in part why Leonidas matriculated at Chapel Hill in May 1821.[38] Although Leonidas spent only two years at the university, his correspondence reveals a young man cognizant of his aristocratic bearing, but not to the exclusion of a personable even compassionate temperament. Most indicative of Leonidas's fondness for high culture was an unmistakable fascination with fine fashion. In a letter to his mother, Polk detailed the visit of "Fowler, the little tailor from Raleigh." The clothier had traveled to Chapel Hill to meet with a client who had placed an order for a new coat

---

[36] There seems to be some disagreement over which religious tradition Ruffin embraced. Avery Craven considered Ruffin a Jeffersonian Unitarian where as David Allmendinger contends that Ruffin did not believe in heaven and "saw death in terms of an endless cycle of returning to earth." See Avery Craven, *Edmund Ruffin Southerner: A Study in Secession* (Baton Rouge: Louisiana State University Press, 1966) 26–35; David F. Allmendinger, Jr., ed., *Incidents of My Life: Edmund Ruffin's Autobiographical Essays* (Charlottesville: University Press of Virginia, 1990) 12.

[37] Chorley, *Men and Movements in the American Episcopal Church*, 159–60.

[38] Polk, *Leonidas Polk*, 1:63–64. In Tennessee, William helped secure the charter for Davidson Academy, which grew into the University of Nashville and was later renamed Peabody College.

only to find that the product had not satisfied the customer's tastes. Polk, acquainted with both the client and the garment, remarked that "it was in the tip of fashion, short tail and high collar, [but] the young man being a backwardsman [sic]" could not appreciate the quality of Fowler's work. Polk closed the letter with what would become a familiar benediction: "Very much in need of shirts and drawers…[please] have the ruffles on the shirts made pretty long." This attention to detail actually divulged how accustomed Leonidas had become to a high standard or quality of living.[39] Without question, the Polk children had grown to expect certain amenities and their father fully intended to cater to their wishes.

William also accepted this responsibility with regard to members of his extended family. For example, he accommodated the financial requests of his nephew Marshall T. Polk, the younger brother of future president James K. Polk and roommate of Leonidas at Chapel Hill. Marshall had borrowed more than $150 from his uncle to cover his living expenses. Somewhat embarrassed by the situation, Marshall asked his uncle to "pardon" the imposition and assured William that he had not been "lavish with [his] friends." The expenditures for "shoe accounts, [and] ball & society debts" were all part of "necessary" living expenses. Seemingly, William's generosity validated the children's understanding of parental obligations and confirmed the strong kinship ties that existed within the Polk family.[40]

During his days at Chapel Hill, Leonidas displayed a playful and compassionate nature. He often bantered with family members and injected humor into moderately serious situations. When he learned that his brother Lucius was struggling to secure a matrimonial partner, he quipped to his sister Mary that their brother had been unsuccessful because he had "not found any girl…who has all that is requisite to be the wife of a 'Polk,' for…they are choice" women. The good-natured ribbing was a small sign of the affection shared by the two brothers and indicated that the Polks perceived themselves as a special breed.[41] As part of that elite mentality,

---

[39]Leonidas Polk to Sarah Polk, 10 March 1822, Leonidas Polk Papers, Jesse duPont Library, University of the South, Sewanee, Tennessee (hereafter cited as Leonidas Polk Papers).

[40]Marshall T. Polk to William Polk, 1 August 1822, Leonidas Polk Papers. The exact amount of the debt is unclear. Upon receiving a note for $250 dollars, Marshall forwarded $155 to William.

[41] Leonidas Polk to Mary Polk, 10 February 1823, Leonidas Polk Papers.

Leonidas had a conscientious regard for the Southern practice of *noblesse oblige*. On one occasion at Chapel Hill, Polk "sat up" all night with Henry Potter, who had "taken sick" with what Polk first diagnosed as "Billious Fever" but later discovered was "Typhus Fever." This type of behavior may explain why Polk made friends so easily and how he sustained meaningful relationships. Shortly after leaving the university, Polk recalled with a "peculiar pleasure" the "indescribable feelings of satisfaction" that he held for his "old *clan* of *particulars*" at "the Hill."[42]

In early March 1823, Polk received word from his father that an appointment had been secured for him to attend the United States Military Academy at West Point. The slave economy of the Old South limited severely the employment opportunities for young males, especially those in large families. Aside from a military career, which was often a means to enter politics, the only other planter-professions of note were medicine and the law. According to one historian, the ministry was an option that appealed mainly to the "aspiring poor" not the well-to-do, although the latter could overcome the ministry's lack of social prestige by coupling their religious service with the secular profession of plantation ownership.[43] As expected, the young Polk erupted with excitement upon hearing the news and confided to his father, "You can imagine but few things which would have more highly gratified me." The junior Polk also immediately recognized that the fulfillment of their dream would produce a "vast...alteration in [his] career in life." In retrospect, these words contained both prophetic and ironic meanings.[44]

Many students, including Polk, acquired appointments as a result of political and social connections. Favoritism, however, ended with the appointment process. All cadets had to demonstrate their mettle in the classroom and many were unable to meet the challenge. Indeed, historian George McIver has established that only 35 percent of all North Carolinians admitted to West Point from 1802 to 1860 finished the academic program and graduated. McIver attributed the lack of success to poor scholastic

---

[42] Leonidas Polk to John William Watters, 14 September 1824, Leonidas Polk Papers.

[43] Wyatt-Brown, *Southern Honor*, 187–192.

[44] Leonidas Polk to William Polk, 10 March 1823, Leonidas Polk Papers.

"preparation" and the inadequacies of the Southern educational system.[45] In order for Leonidas to be adequately prepared for West Point, William Polk advised his son "to instantly turn [his] attention to acquiring a knowledge of arithmetic and Latin." Leonidas did not disagree with the recommendation to refocus his core curriculum, but he did believe that the current demands of his academic schedule "would not permit" him to expand his course load. He further explained that "society duties are to be attended to...weekly, which are of very great importance and require their portion of time." Committed to the aristocratic lifestyle, Leonidas often struggled to create an acceptable balance between academic demands and social desires.[46]

Leonidas realized that West Point would present a "most scrutinous examination" of his intellectual abilities. The young college student worried that he was "but imperfectly acquainted with" his current "studies," which he "imputed to [his] being badly prepared on entering college." Ultimately, he wanted more than "a mere knowledge sufficient to enable [him] to enter the Military Academy." Polk compared his situation to that of Bennett H. Henderson, a North Carolinian and former Chapel Hill student who had enrolled at the academy in 1822. After two years, Henderson stood sixth in his West Point class. Polk ascribed the high ranking to Henderson's proficiency in the French language. Thus, the idea of studying French appealed to him. An additional benefit, in Polk's mind, was that the language was spoken in the "best circles of society." As an alternative to his father's suggestions regarding intensive study in math and Latin, Polk

---

[45] George W. McIver, "North Carolinians at West Point before the Civil War," *North Carolina Historical Review* 7/1 (January 1930): 23–25. From 1802 to 1860, 67 of 193 North Carolinians graduated. During the same period Virginia had a 35 percent graduation rate, South Carolina 38 percent. Between 1845 and 1866, 43 percent of all (nationwide) appointed cadets graduated. McIver considered the superiority of New England schools as the primary factor in the higher graduation rates for northern states. See also James Morrison, Jr., *"The Best School in the World": West Point, the Pre-Civil War Years, 1833–1866* (Kent OH: Kent State University Press, 1986) 181. For the years 1833 to 1860, Morrison found that the cumulative graduation rate in the eleven states that would make up the Confederacy was 36.9 percent; in the border states of Kentucky, Maryland, Missouri, and the District of Columbia, 51.3 percent; in the Middle Atlantic states of New York, Pennsylvania, Delaware, and New Jersey, 56.4 percent; and in the New England States of Massachusetts, Rhode Island, Maine, New Hampshire, Connecticut, and Vermont, 64.1 percent.

[46] Leonidas Polk to William Polk, 10 March 1823, Leonidas Polk Papers.

proposed that he withdraw immediately from college and with his father's permission travel to Hillsborough, North Carolina and "study arithmetic, French, and geography under Mr. Rogers," a well-known "master of the French language." William rejected the plan, and his son remained at the university until the end of the term.[47]

In June 1823, Leonidas arrived at West Point, and despite all the consternation, he performed reasonably well on his entrance examinations. Typically, "the staff questioned" incoming cadets "very closely, & made them work many of the sums on the blackboard," but Polk received only two questions. "I answered quite readily," he reported to his father, and the review committee "dismissed me without arranging me before the board." Polk had begun his military career on a positive note, but his expectations remained high and greater challenges awaited him.[48]

Aside from the academic rigors, the initial experience at West Point demanded that each cadet also follow the academy's rigid code of conduct and endure a Spartan existence. Immediately after the entrance exams, Polk and his class received their first taste of military life when they bivouacked at Camp Scott, a training facility a short march from the West Point campus. In all likelihood, Polk experienced for the first time the habit of pitching tents and sleeping under the stars. He admitted freely that in the beginning he "was the fairest cadet in the corps."[49] With a hint of boyish enthusiasm (he was only seventeen) and an unmistakable sense of purpose, Polk instructed his loved ones on the conditions and routines of camp life. To brother Lucius, he remarked that "some of the effiminates [sic] complain" about the bucolic setting, "but to me it is a pleasure." Sarah Polk learned what future soldiers did to get a good night's rest. We use our "knapsacks for pillows," the cadet explained, and we "spread down one blanket and with the other...wrap it round [ourselves] Indian like."[50]

Polk viewed the two and one-half month encampment as a rite of passage to manhood. In this instance, he hoped that his father would recognize him as a part of the family's sacred military heritage. After the encampment, Polk boasted to his father that he was no longer "the fairest

---

[47] Ibid.
[48] Leonidas Polk to William Polk, 23 July 1823, Leonidas Polk Papers.
[49] Ibid.
[50] Leonidas Polk to Lucius Polk, 25 June 1823, Leonidas Polk Papers; Leonidas Polk to Sarah Polk, 17 July 1823, Leonidas Polk Papers.

cadet in the corps," and after completing two or three "tours of duty...was quite in uniform." Leonidas tried to convince his father that his previously held "disposition" and inclinations towards the military were "not mistaken." He promised that "no situation" in life suited him better, and he eagerly admitted that he enjoyed deeply "the uniformity & undeviating sameness" of the soldier's life.[51]

Polk appeared to have adjusted well to his new surroundings and passed the initial test of army life. These exercises, however, were hardly indicative of an authentic military experience. For instance, the cadets, instead of cooking their own food, "marched regularly to the mess hall & dine[d]...together." Although Polk had begun to think like a cadet, he had greater hurdles to face and had yet to prove whether he was willing to forfeit the conveniences and privileges of high society for the rigors and discipline of the United States military.[52]

As their youthful exuberance waned and the novelty of camp life subsided, cadets soon faced the monotony of academy life. Historian Walter Fleming described the West Point of the 1820s as "a secluded place little in touch with the outside world." The restriction of furloughs until the end of a cadet's third year contributed to the feelings of isolation and loneliness. Surely, the severity of a military program, which included long hours of drilling and marching, kept the boys in top physical condition, but cadets had difficulty finding constructive outlets for their pent-up energies. For the well-bred cadet, the closest thing to a cotillion or ball was an occasional stag dance.[53] Furthermore, the academy did not build its first gymnasium until 1846 and offered no intramural sports prior to the Civil War. Likewise, school officials limited the number of literary and debating clubs, fearing that such organizations would interfere with the regular duties of the cadets.[54]

Conformity became a hallmark of the academy. Indeed, as one historian has remarked, the "West Point [staff] made life hard for the cadets in order to turn out finished soldiers." For cadets accustomed to exorbitant living, the academy's pay scale and credit policy caused significant and

---

[51] Leonidas Polk to William Polk, 23 July 1823, Leonidas Polk Papers.
[52] Leonidas Polk to Lucius Polk, 25 June 1823, Leonidas Polk Papers.
[53] Walter L. Fleming, "Jefferson Davis at West Point," *Publications of the Mississippi Historical Society* 10/3 (1909): 247–61.
[54] James L. Morrison, Jr., *"The Best School in the World,"* 75–76.

unanticipated hardships. Although most cadets were fiscally responsible and spent their $28 per month salary at the commissaries "for such items as clothes, mirrors, razors, and other essentials," historian Stephen Ambrose has argued that "the monthly pay was never high enough to keep the cadets out of debt." Moreover, cadets could not have money deposited in their name or receive money from home.[55] Polk considered these policies unacceptable and intrusive. On several occasions, he explained the problem to his brother Lucius. He grumbled that his pay, "reduced as it [was], by so many deductions for clothing, books, board, & c.," could not provide all of his "wants." To offset the alleged inconveniences, Polk received "a small sum occasionally (though not solicited)" from his father. But this allowance was not sufficient. He felt that he deserved additional funds and "debated a long time with [himself] whether [he] should…write home" and request directly the money. After considerable deliberation, Polk confessed to his brother: "I have found my [prior] objections childish & henceforth I shall make no hesitation in drawing on my father whenever I shall need" financial support.[56]

Clearly, Cadet Polk had decided to ignore the academy's prohibitions against external sources of income. This decision would not escape the attention of the academy's superintendent, Sylvanus Thayer. Sometime in July 1825, Polk received a $50 note from his father that caused Thayer to take administrative action.[57] The superintendent apprised William Polk of the violation, explaining that it was a dismissible offense but offering to overlook this particular transgression in view of Leonidas's "general good conduct." Thayer expressed his belief that William had been unaware of the academy's policy when he sent the money to Leonidas, and the superintendent assumed that a warning from "General Polk" would resolve the matter.[58] Needless to say, the reprimand did not sit well with the young cadet. In fact, Leonidas accused Thayer of employing "emissaries…to spy"

---

[55] Stephen E. Ambrose, *Duty, Honor, Country: A History of West Point* (Baltimore: Johns Hopkins University Press, 1966) 147–49.

[56] Leonidas Polk to Lucius Polk, 18 October 1825, Leonidas Polk Papers.

[57] Leonidas Polk to Lucius Polk, 25 July 1825, Leonidas Polk Papers. In this letter, Leonidas mentions that he had received recently from "Pa" a note for fifty dollars.

[58] Sylvanus Thayer to William Polk, 26 September 1825, Leonidas Polk Papers. Interestingly, this letter and its envelope were addressed to General William Polk. Although incorrect, it is unmistakable testimony of William's military reputation.

on their fellow cades and report "all infractions of regulations." Cadet Polk theorized that "one of these ferrets...fashioned into the form of a postmaster" had exposed his private affairs to the superintendent. To his father, Leonidas quipped angrily: I leave "to you to judge of such conduct...of the head of an institution like this."[59]

When Thayer questioned Cadet Polk about receiving money from home, he "very unhesitantly answered that [he] had" and told the superintendent that the salary "paid by the government was...insufficient to satisfy [his] actual wants and moderate convenience." In elaborate detail, Polk outlined his expenditures and calculated that he actually controlled between $5 and $6 of his monthly stipend, which had to cover payments to "the tailor, shoemaker, and merchant" as well as other expenses. Polk estimated that "nineteen twentieths of the corps" was in the same predicament. He insisted that not even those individuals accustomed to the "rigid economy of the Yankees [could] withstand" such manipulation of wages. The objections and explanations proved futile, as William Polk assured Thayer "that such an infraction [would] not again occur." The news, coming in the dead of winter, distressed Leonidas even further because he was "in want of flannels and other things which only money [could] buy." All cadets languished under the academy's payroll system, but Polk's dilemma had been of his own making. Indeed, he and thirteen other cadets had each spent $2 per month to board with a local resident in order to avoid eating at the "mess-house." Polk also accumulated an additional debt of $2 per month for a personal attendant. By incurring these frivolous expenses, Polk had demonstrated that he was not ready to jettison the comforts of an aristocratic life style, and his criticism of Thayer revealed a type of paranoia, or, at least, the expectation that the privileged class was entitled to special treatment. Nevertheless, in the end Cadet Polk acquiesced to the superintendent's directive.[60]

Unfortunately for Leonidas Polk, the resolution of one problem simply gave way to a more serious controversy in January 1826. The case involved allegations that Polk and others had cheated on their drawing-class examinations. Prior to the incident, cadets—acting on adolescent impulses—had avoided difficult or time-consuming exercises by tracing their

---

[59] Leonidas Polk to William Polk, 4 December 1825, Leonidas Polk Papers.
[60] Ibid.

assignments, which angered the faculty because it violated the true spirit of learning. Consequently, Superintendent Thayer officially prohibited the practice. Nevertheless, Polk and several other students were willing to test the administration's resolve concerning the matter. To the cadets' chagrin, Thayer convened a committee to review the drawings and instructed them to censure the guilty individuals by lowering their respective scores in the drawing class. Believing that he had been unjustly penalized, Polk registered a formal complaint with Secretary of War James Barbour. At no point during the investigation did Polk deny that he had traced his assignments, but he did supply a ridiculous excuse for continuing to disregard Thayer's direct order. He maintained that no cadet gained an unfair advantage by tracing because "the practice was...so general that it might be called universal, and since they traced without the semblance of secrecy toward each other, its criminality was lessened to almost nothing, and their perfect openness seemed very little like a wish...to defraud" anyone. In addition, Polk asserted that the cadets "were willing to risk violating the order, and...abide by the consequences, provided each suffered in proportion to the magnitude of his offense."[61]

Polk's appeal to Secretary Barbour alleged that the investigating committee had refused to question every cadet in the drawing class while targeting "select individuals." In other cases, Polk claimed that the committee ignored the evidence.[62] For example, Cadet John Child, who eventually graduated second in the class of 1827, testified that "he executed his drawings unaided by other persons, but refused to say whether he had used means other than those permitted by his instructor." Similarly, Cadet James Bradford, who eventually graduated fourth in the class of 1827, admitted that "one drawing, which...was not among those exhibited [before the committee] had been unfairly executed" but the rest of his drawings were original pieces. During the investigation, the committee interviewed

---

[61] Leonidas Polk to James Barbour, 23 January 1826, Leonidas Polk Papers. Information regarding other cadets who filed complaints is in Leonidas Polk to William Polk, 8 February 1826, Leonidas Polk Papers. Cadet Lucien Bibb filed a complaint with United States Senator Richard M. Johnson of Kentucky, who "promised his aid, and observed that he had often thought that cadets were frequently unjustly oppressed" (Leonidas Polk to William Polk, 8 February 1826, Leonidas Polk Papers).

[62] Leonidas Polk to James Barbour, 23 January 1826.

eighteen cadets; of that number, Polk and eight others confessed their guilt, while Child, Bradford, and seven others denied any wrongdoing.[63] Obviously, Polk was certain that the committee had not cast its net wide enough and had permitted a number of guilty cadets to escape punishment. The greatest concern for him was the effect that the poor drawing score would have on his class standing not to mention the public humiliation of being branded a cheater.

Thayer acknowledged to Polk that some "oversight may have been made" when the committee moved hastily to close its investigation. Still, the superintendent rejected the idea of reconvening the committee.[64] He worried that further inquiries and guilty verdicts "might" necessitate amending "the published roll [of merit]...thereby setting a precedent dangerous to the future quiet of the institution."[65] In short, Thayer feared that a scandal might erupt and would create negative publicity for the academy. Nevertheless, he allowed Polk the opportunity to explore completely the appeals process and the various channels of military justice. Ultimately, the secretary of war informed the demonstrative cadet that he found no grounds for overturning the academy's decision and encouraged Polk to work "diligently" toward reclaiming his lost standing. Disappointed but not surprised, Polk ceased his protest and determined "to abide by the decision of the Secretary." He hoped that the passing of time would "obliterate" any memory of the four-month ordeal, and with a mind at "rest" he awaited "cheerfully" the remaining challenges of his West Point career.[66]

Although Polk enjoyed the academic competition at West Point, he was not satisfied with the focus of the institution's academic program, particularly its neglect of liberal arts. Superintendent Thayer upon his arrival had moved the West Point curriculum away from a classics-based approach that stressed Latin and Greek and guided the institution toward a science-based scheme that emphasized engineering and natural philosophy (or physics). Thayer's efforts convinced one historian that "for a time West Point was turning out better engineers than soldiers." Mathematics and

---

[63] United States Military Academy Staff Records, 1818 to 1835, 354–355, USMA Archives, West Point, New York.

[64] Leonidas Polk to William Polk, 8 February 1826, Leonidas Polk Papers.

[65] Leonidas Polk to James Barbour, 23 January 1826, Leonidas Polk Papers.

[66] Leonidas Polk to William Polk, 2 April 1826, Leonidas Polk Papers.

French represented the two most important components in the Thayer program. The former was the essential prerequisite for engineering and natural philosophy and a reading knowledge of the latter afforded cadets access to the "advanced texts" of their day.[67]

Accordingly, mathematics and French were the only courses that the cadets studied during their first three semesters. Polk excelled in mathematics and at the midpoint of his second year stood fourth in his class in that discipline. He failed, however, to achieve a similar outcome in French, falling from twenty-seventh at the end of his first semester to thirty-sixth one year later.[68] The poor showing in French frustrated Polk to the point that he became "indifferent [to] and almost disgusted" with the language.[69] On the one hand, Polk's French scores had prevented him from earning a spot on the academy's roll of merit, an honor reserved for the top five cadets in each class. On the other hand, Polk had hoped to acquire "knowledge of the French language [that] would enable [him] to speak it tolerably fluent," but the academy only required that cadets "read it sufficiently." Polk felt that Thayer's system made "it impossible to devote any [attention] to *literary attainments*," which he deemed a vital component of the educational development of a southern aristocrat.[70] Despite the less than stellar performance in French, Polk completed his second year ranked seventh in a class of forty-five. He achieved this standing as a result of the academy's weighted grading system. The formula that produced the aggregate merit favored mathematics over French by a two to one ratio.[71]

During his final two years at West Point, Polk compiled a remarkably consistent academic record. The midterm reports of 1826 listed him as fifth in both natural philosophy and chemistry. Similarly, the tabulations for 1827 placed him ninth in engineering. Also, Polk completed his final year tied with George W. Hughes for the highest score in rhetoric and moral philosophy, and he earned the second highest score in conduct.[72] Conduct

---

[67] Ambrose, *Duty, Honor, Country*, 87–90.

[68] USMA Staff Records, 1818–1835, 265, 308, USMA Archives.

[69] Leonidas Polk to Lucius Polk, 25 July 1825, Leonidas Polk Papers.

[70]Leonidas Polk to William Polk, 16 November 1825, Leonidas Polk Papers.

[71] Register of Merit, 1817 to 1835, n.p., USMA Archives. For an explanation of the weighted grading system, see *Regulations of the United States Military Academy* (West Point NY: USMA Printing Office, 1823) 15.

[72] USMA Staff Reports, 1818–1835, 350, 385, 391, USMA Archives.

scores were a significant percentage of a cadet's final standing and conduct, as a scholastic category, carried the same course value as engineering and science of war and natural philosophy.[73] Thayer and the academic board computed conduct scores by considering both subjective and objective variables. For his part, Thayer monitored the "progress" of cadets "through weekly reports from instructors" as well as his squadron of informants. Thayer also kept "in the hidden recesses" of his desk individual files on each cadet that the academic board used in determining conduct scores.[74] On a more empirical level, Thayer implemented the demerit system in 1825 as a way of systematically recording all violations of academy regulations. Under the new system, "a specific number of demerits would be given…for a particular deficiency" and "the number of demerits received in a year would be weighted" according to the seriousness of the offenses. Then, the academic board combined the demerit totals with Thayer's files to calculate the cadet's conduct score and published the results in the *Register of Cadets*.[75]

This complicated rating system has not been fully appreciated by historians, particularly those eager to make overly generalized assessments of cadet conduct. With respect to Leonidas Polk, the money fiasco and drawing scandal have emerged, somewhat erroneously, as the definitive statements on his character and personality as a cadet and have besmirched an otherwise impressive academic career. Of course, Polk was not the quintessential cadet. The *Record of Delinquencies* includes such charges as "absent from reveille," "using or permitting the use of tobacco in quarters," "bed not strapped," and "visiting during study hours."[76] During the first full year of Thayer's new system, Polk received 79 demerits, which ranked him 102 out of the whole corps of 222. This total was substantially worse than the zero demerits of first year cadet Robert E. Lee, slightly better than the 120 demerits of second-year cadet Jefferson Davis, but vastly superior to the 621 demerits of classmate Johnathan Clark. The next year Polk made an

---

[73] *Regulations of the USMA, 1823*, 15. The weight of each course for a first classman is as follows: conduct, 3; engineering and science of war, 3; mathematics, 3; natural philosophy, 3; practical military instruction, 2; geography, history, and moral science, 2; chemistry and mineralogy, 2; French, 1; and drawing, 1.

[74] James William Kershner, "Sylvanus Thayer: A Biography" (Ph.D. diss., West Virginia University, 1976) 186, 189.

[75] George S. Pappas, *To the Point: The United States Military Academy, 1802–1902* (Westport CT: Praeger, 1993) 159.

[76] Record of Delinquencies, 1822–1828, Archives, 239.

astonishing turnaround and was one of twelve cadets, along with Lee, who tallied no demerits. Jefferson Davis reduced his total to 70, and second classman Albert G. Blanchard replaced Clark as the least disciplined cadet in the corps by accruing 489 demerits.[77] Polk's conduct score, which included a subjective element, was even more impressive and suggests that Thayer viewed him in a favorable or positive light. Moreover, Polk avoided the pubescent acts of tomfoolery, such as the episodes associated with Benny Havens's tavern, and he learned the proper deportment of a cadet from his two exemplary roommates, Albert Sydney Johnson and Bennett H. Henderson. Finally, the symmetry of Polk's respective class standings—his class rank never fell below ninth and he graduated eighth in his class of thirty-eight—demonstrated that he was a very capable cadet.[78]

The notable improvement in Polk's conduct during his final year at the academy may have been attributable to the natural workings of the maturation process, but in all probability something more identifiable or specific refocused his attitudes and behavior. Interestingly, Polk made the life-changing decisions to embrace Christianity and to enter the gospel ministry while enrolled at West Point. The academy's chaplain and professor of ethics, Charles P. McIlvaine, was a key figure in his transformation. McIlvaine began his teaching and ministerial duties at West Point in the summer of 1825. From the beginning, the evangelist-at-heart complained strenuously that "the condition of the academy was very far from being encouraging" to a prelate "seeking the spiritual welfare of his charge." In fact, no cadet had ever made a public profession of faith at West Point. For almost a year, McIlvaine worked without "the slightest appearance of any" success. Cadets shunned him routinely for fear that their inquiries would be deemed as "some serious interest in religion."[79]

These conditions, however, changed abruptly in early April 1826, when a cadet, not Polk, visited McIlvaine as part of his father's "last injunction."

---

[77] *Official Registers of the USMA*, 1818–1850 (West Point: US Military Press, 1850) 4–6, 19–20.

[78] USMA Staff Records, 1818–1835, 365, 391, USMA Archives. Henderson and Johnston graduated seventh and eighth respectively in the class of 1826. Polk's respective class standings were eighth, seventh, ninth, and eighth.

[79] Charles P. McIlvaine, "Leonidas Polk: The Bishop-General Who Died for the South, Interesting Reminiscence of Life at West Point of the Gallant Churchman and Soldier," *Southern Historical Society Papers* 18/3 (1890): 371–72.

At the meeting, the chaplain gave the cadet two tracts, one "addressed to a person in affliction" and the other "addressed to an unbeliever." McIlvaine encouraged the cadet to read the former and to disperse the latter in a secretive manner somewhere on campus. Within a week, McIlvaine received another caller, a "stranger," and the young man identified himself as "Polk." McIlvaine offered Leonidas a chair and suspected that the cadet had violated some regulation and was now seeking advice. McIlvaine gently prodded Polk and encouraged him to unburden himself. Suddenly, there was a "burst of feeling and intense expression of a mind convinced of sin and literally and earnestly beg[ed] to be told what he must do for salvation," whereupon McIlvaine guided Polk in prayer and instruction.[80]

Explanations abound regarding the motivational forces behind Polk's conversion, which occurred during the same semester as the drawing scandal. Some have surmised that he was haunted by a recurring dream about the Day of Judgment and consequently sought out the academy chaplain. According to this theory, the emotional trauma of being branded a cheater prompted Polk to embrace Christianity.[81] Others have pointed to the power of McIlvaine's orations, which impressed many of the West Point residents. Crafts J. Wright recalled that "on the first day of Dr. McIlvaine's preaching at West Point the cadets went to chapel, as usual, some with books to read, and others hoping to sleep, but none expecting to take any interest in the sermon. Had a bugle been sounded in the chapel they could not have been more astonished. Books were dropped, sleep was forgotten, attention was riveted. There was general surprise and gratification." McIlvaine made a similar impression on Jefferson Davis. In regard to the chaplain, the Mississippian remarked that "he seemed to belong to the pulpit, and he had a peculiar power of voice rarely found elsewhere than on the stage." Davis appreciated especially McIlvaine's ability to extemporize his sermons. He recalled one blusterous and rainy day when the chaplain

---

[80] Ibid.

[81] Verification of this explanation is difficult because the author did not footnote the source of this story. Clement Eaton, *The Mind of the Old South* (Baton Rouge: Louisiana State University Press, 1967) 167.

incorporated into his homily the imagery of "a gathering storm…so that the crash of one fitted into a great outburst of the other."[82]

Although emotion was certainly one element of Polk's conversion, both the cadet and academy chaplain emphasized the rational and logical nature of the experience. After the fact, Polk related how he had stumbled inadvertently across a tract—the very one that had been planted by McIlvaine's first visitor—and had approached McIlvaine for an exegesis of its contents. It was during this investigative session that Polk made his fateful decision. He also admitted that McIlvaine's recent discourses on the "evidences of Christianity had made a certain measure of impression on his mind, which [to that point] had been in a degree skeptical." Furthermore, Polk had become familiar with Dr. Olenthus Gregory's *Evidences, Doctrines and Duties*, a work of Christian apologetics. McIlvaine had placed copies of this book with the quartermaster, and Polk had obtained the text on his own. Despite the obvious influence and interventions, McIlvaine accepted no credit for Polk's conversion. The graceful cleric believed that while Gregory's book "strengthened" Polk's understanding of the human condition; the tract was the decisive factor in the cadet's acceptance of Christianity.[83]

Polk's conversion touched McIlvaine personally and changed the religious culture at the academy. McIlvaine admired him for the courage he exhibited in becoming the first cadet in the history of the academy to come forward "as a follower of Christ." The chaplain marveled at the cadet's "docility and humbleness of spirit" as well as "his literal thirst" for religious instruction. In addition, McIlvaine cherished Polk's eagerness to demonstrate his new disposition without making "himself unnecessarily an object of observation." McIlvaine, however, did encourage Polk to display publicly his new-found faith. The cadet began subtly by kneeling prayerfully during portions of the chapel services, but the depth of the young convert's conviction soon placed him at the center of a campus-wide revival.[84] In many respects, Polk had initiated this revival. As one astonished cadet remembered, "The whole corps was roused as by a thunder-clap at the

---

[82] Wright quoted in Polk, *Leonidas Polk*, 1:89; Davis quoted in Varina Davis, *Jefferson Davis, Ex-president of the Confederate States of America; a Memoir*, 2 vols. (New York: D. Appleton and Co., 1890) 1:37.

[83] McIlvaine, "Interesting Reminiscence," 372–73.

[84] Ibid., 373–74.

announcement that Leonidas Polk and others had been 'converted,' and that Polk was to lead a 'praying squad' in...the barracks." Each day the number increased until "a veritable revolution [broke out] in the...corps of cadets."[85] As this description suggests, the winds of excitement were sweeping across the campus, and the use of the term revolution illustrated the intensity of the moment. Polk reported happily to his father that since his own conversion six others had "come forward after the same manner" and he expected a "further increase." Even the skeptical McIlvaine conceded that his study "was...occupied every evening with assemblies, composed...for prayer and the exposition of the Word of God; and a serious impression, more or less deep and abiding, was spread over a large part of the whole military community."[86] The religious fervor persisted as news circulated that Polk would be baptized in the academy chapel—another first at West Point. On 25 May 1826, McIlvaine baptized Polk and fellow cadet, William B. Magruder. At the end of the baptismal charge McIlvaine proclaimed: "Pray your Master and Savior to take you out of the world, rather than allow you to bring reproach on the cause you have now professed." Polk responded with a forceful "Amen."[87]

The cumulative effect of these events made a lasting impression on the entire corps of cadets. Several West Point graduates of this era went on to become ministers—Martin P. Parks even returned as the academy's chaplain—and others developed a reputable Christian character. Cadet Albert Church remembered the winter of 1826 as a time of "great religious excitement" in which daily "prayer and conversational meetings" stimulated a spiritual dialogue "among officers, professors, and cadets." After the revival, McIlvaine received visitors with increasing regularity and in most cases they first contacted Polk and requested that he make the introductions.[88] Despite the religiously charged atmosphere, historian James

---

[85] Quoted in Polk, *Leonidas Polk*, 1:89.

[86] Leonidas Polk to William Polk, 5 June 1826, Leonidas Polk Papers; Charles P. McIlvaine, *The Apostolic Commission. The Sermon Preached at the Consecration of the Rt. Rev. Leonidas Polk, D.D., Missionary Bishop for Arkansas in Christ Church, Cincinnati, December 9, 1838* (Gambier OH: G.W. Meyers, 1838) 36.

[87] McIlvaine, "Interesting Reminiscence," 375–76.

[88] For Davis and Johnston's reactions, see Fleming, "Jefferson Davis at West Point," 265. Parks, class of 1826, was chaplain and professor of geography, history, and ethics from 1840 to 1846. Interestingly, he converted from Methodism to Episcopalianism in 1836. See also Albert E. Church, *Personal Reminiscences of the*

Morrison has contended that "the corps of cadets remained largely unaffected by the waves of revivalism which swept the country in the antebellum" period. Certainly, the spiritual awakening at West Point had no direct connection to the burned-over districts or general climate of religious fervor in New York during the 1820s. But as historian Anne Loveland has shown, "college students [including cadets at West Point] were of an age and in a situation which made them particularly susceptible to religious experience." For Polk, West Point, although an unlikely venue, provided all of the essential ingredients necessary for a religious encounter. Indeed, Polk had access to a spiritual mentor and there was a certain degree of bonding among the religious-minded cadets, all of which were common denominators in any campus revival.[89]

The revival, however, had limits and not every cadet participated in the religious celebrations. Jefferson Davis, although mesmerized occasionally by McIlvaine's elocution, continued to participate in escapades of indiscretion such as the academy's infamous Christmas riot of 1826, which was a misguided assemblage of Southern boys gathered for the purpose of discussing the "mysteries of eggnog." Recent convert, William B. Magruder also collaborated in this festive colloquium.[90] Moreover, some cadets expressed a direct ambivalence toward Christianity. For example, Samuel P. Heintzelman noted drolly in his diary that McIlvaine's sermons typically "last 2 hours, from 11 to 1, our old parson used to keep us only about one hour."[91] Historian James Morrison accepted Heintzelman's assessment as the typical cadet reaction to religion, which led him to conclude that "except for introducing some cadets to Episcopalianism, West Point probably changed attitudes toward religion little if any...after all, the institution was a

---

United States Military Academy (West Point NY: USMA Printing Office, 1879) 70. Church, class of 1828, returned to West Point and taught mathematics from 1828 to 1878.

[89] Morrison, *"The Best School in the World,"* 86; Anne C. Loveland, *Southern Evangelicals and the Social Order, 1800–1860* (Baton Rouge: Louisiana State University Press, 1980) 6.

[90] Fleming, "Jefferson Davis at West Point," 264–65. This incident was quite serious. Davis's roommate, Walter B. Guion of Mississippi, was court-martialed and dismissed for attempting to shoot an officer. For more details see James Agnew, *Eggnog Riot: The Christmas Mutiny at West Point* (San Rafael CA: Presidio, 1979).

[91] Samuel P. Heintzelman, diary, 18 September 1825, USMA Special Collections, West Point New York.

military academy, not a seminary." Morrison adroitly and humorously points out the obvious—that West Point was not a monastic community populated by cerebral mystics—but his conclusions fail to capture the significance of the academy's first observable revival.[92]

As historian Stephen Ambrose has suggested, the Episcopal faith was "regarded as ideal for an officer and a gentleman," and comported with the academy's designs for producing "Christian gentlemen" as well as "Christian soldiers." To accomplish this goal, Thayer and McIlvaine worked incessantly to promote the Episcopalian form of Christianity. Thayer, in a rare departure from his scientific approach to education, added moral philosophy to the West Point curriculum. Moral philosophy, which at West Point was part of a course that included history, grammar, and geography, was taught by the academy's chaplain and ordinarily combined lectures on the evidences of Christianity with the other topics. In addition, chapel attendance became a mandatory requirement during Thayer's tenure at the academy. This policy encountered various forms of protest, including a formal charge by three instructors who claimed that mandatory chapel attendance "violated their constitutional rights." Undisturbed by the attempt to thwart religious activity at the academy, the superintendent simply referred their official complaint to the secretary of war. Here, Thayer had a powerful and sympathetic ally who explained to the aggrieved parties that he harbored no "desire to interfere in the least with their conscientious scruples, and would, therefore, send them where attendance upon Divine service would not be deemed necessary." The secretary of war then fulfilled his promise by transferring the three instructors to "frontier posts."[93] In the end, Thayer, who was not known to be a communicant of any church, granted chaplains a great deal of latitude in the execution of their ministerial duties, and his patronage of Episcopalianism and Christianity helped to foster a new attitude toward religion at the academy.[94]

McIlvaine played an equally important role in forging a discernable religious culture at West Point. The very selection of an Episcopalian to replace Presbyterian chaplain Thomas Picton signaled the academy's recognition that the Episcopal denomination was "most appropriate" to the

---

[92] Morrison, *"Best School in the World,"* 89.

[93] Ambrose, *Duty, Honor, and Country,* 151, 147, 96. The secretary is quoted in *Duty, Honor, and Country,* 152.

[94] McIlvaine, "Interesting Reminiscences," 371.

rules of discipline at the academy. Immediately before his posting to West Point, McIlvaine had served for five years as chaplain of the United States Senate, and Secretary of War John C. Calhoun was well aware of the clergyman's reputation as an ardent evangelical. McIlvaine's friendship with Calhoun proved to be an "unbeatable advantage" as he easily edged out his Episcopalian competitor, Thomas Warner of Connecticut, for the position at West Point. As chaplain, McIlvaine enjoyed the full support of the superintendent, and cadets were authorized to visit him at any time for counseling and religious instruction.[95] From the pulpit, McIlvaine espoused the highest standards of virtue and integrity. His "manner was pervasive...logical and convincing," and he confronted cadets in a matter-of-fact fashion.[96] Cadet Samuel P. Heintzelman recalled that when McIlvaine "passed through...camp...& heard some cadets swearing," he would take the opportunity to address the "impropriety" of profanity in his next chapel sermon.[97] By choosing McIlvaine, the academy and Thayer had endorsed, to a certain degree, the notion that the Episcopal faith was conducive to the academy's ideals of duty, loyalty, honor, and courage.[98] Aside from the societal perception that Episcopalianism was a gentleman's religion, the denomination appealed to the army because it was the only major Protestant denomination to avoid a major schism prior to the Civil War. The Presbyterians, Methodists, and Baptists all split over the slavery issue in the late antebellum period. Furthermore, although doctrinal strife manifested from time to time, the relative intellectual and philosophical stability within

---

[95] Quotes are from Edgar Denton, III, "The Formative Years of the United States Military Academy, 1775–1833" (Ph.D. diss., Syracuse University, 1964) 221–22, 224. For information on McIlvaine's pre-academy days see Diana H. Butler, *Standing against the Whirlwind: Evangelical Episcopalians in Nineteenth Century America* (New York/Oxford: Oxford University Press, 1995) 24–39.

[96] Church, *Personal Reminiscences*, 70.

[97] Samuel P. Heintzelman, diary, 17 July 1825, USMA Special Collections.

[98] Additional backing for the Christian tradition at West Point came from the Board of Visitors. After assessing the chapel facility in 1826, they reported that "the room now used for it was never intended for such a purpose and is entirely unfit for it, that its is wanted for other objects; that it never accommodated more than one half of the persons, who ought to be provided for; and, that in some seasons of the year, it will not contain even all the cadets." See Reports of the Board of Visitors, June, 1826, USMA Archives.

the Episcopal denomination comported well with the army's deep-seated social conservatism.

In many respects, Leonidas Polk's unprecedented actions provided Christianity, in general, and Episcopalianism, in particular, with a legitimacy and acceptability that were absent previously at the academy. Likewise, McIlvaine's orations convinced many cadets "of how naturally and how rationally the life of a soldier and that of a Christian harmonized." Within a generation of Polk's conversion, prayer meetings were no longer an anomaly. Cadet Morris Schaff believed that Christianity certainly contributed to the West Point identity and that the academy could not realize its "ideals [of] truth and honor and courage" without a Christian tradition.[99] On a personal level, Polk had redefined his family's martial heritage by adding a powerful new Christian dimension. In the process, he became part of a newly developing definition of Southern manhood, one that combined the heroic images of the cavalier knight with the righteousness of the Christian saint. Polk's decision was entirely of his own making and would propel him down an unusual path.[100]

Although Leonidas was aware that his father rejected the claims of Christianity on intellectual grounds, he still spoke confidently and boldly about his conversion. He regretted that his decision "had been the cause of uneasiness to the family," but he explained in uncompromising terms that he would endure "torture for centuries" rather than surrender "that hope which [now] cheers me in every duty."[101] Following his summer furlough in 1826, Leonidas returned to West Point to complete his final year. By all indications, including his academic record and conduct performance, he seemed destined for a successful career in the United States Army. Then, his father discovered, without the slightest warning, that he intended to abandon his martial calling. Distraught over his "radical deficiency" in the classics, Cadet Polk now informed his father that he wished to pursue his "education further." He now considered the military an obstacle to his new

---

[99] Morris Schaff, *The Spirit of Old West Point, 1858–1862* (Boston: Houghton-Mifflin, 1907) 70, 74. Schaff attended prayer meetings led by West Point instructor O. O. Howard. The usual attendance was fifteen.

[100] The theoretical framework for this assertion comes from Bertram Wyatt-Brown, "God and Honor in the Old South, *The Southern Review* 25/2 (April 1989): 283–96.

[101] Leonidas Polk to William Polk, 5 June 1826, Leonidas Polk Papers.

ambition. He investigated his "obligation" to the army and decided that while "the agreement" called for a service "term of five years" he could seek an early release or discharge. In particular, the cadet, with the encouragement of Superintendent Thayer, had his mind set on accepting a professorship of mathematics and physical sciences at a fledgling seminary in Massachusetts.[102] This news intensified William's skepticism regarding his son's emotional stability, and he interpreted the announcement as further evidence of his son's mercurial disposition. William lectured his son that the better "part of wisdom" was the avoidance of a "protracted period" of adolescent meandering. He also urged his son to settle on "a plan of Life" and "devote himself" to that end. Nothing could have been more shocking to William than when his son announced, "The ministry is the profession to which I should devote myself." After graduation and the traditional furlough, Leonidas Polk resigned from the United States Army and proceeded with his plans to enter the ministry.[103]

William Polk had raised his children according to the time-honored traditions of the Southern aristocracy with the full expectation that his son Leonidas would lead the life of a professional soldier and country gentleman. When the West Point graduate decided to forfeit a career in the military in favor of one in the ministry, his father experienced a mixture of anger and disbelief. Even as Leonidas made plans to attend the Virginia Theological Seminary, William's bewilderment continued to smolder and the smallest provocation aroused his displeasure. For instance, when President Andrew Jackson asked William, during a social event in Washington DC, where his son was stationed, the old Revolutionary War hero replied irritably, "By thunder he's stationed nowhere. He's down at the seminary in Virginia where they're ruining a good soldier to make a poor parson."[104] The family dream of martial glory, however, would only be deferred, for the lowly parson would one day emerge as a general in the

---

[102] Leonidas Polk to William Polk, 31 March 1827, Leonidas Polk Papers.

[103] Leonidas Polk to William Polk, 9 May 1827, Leonidas Polk Papers.

[104] William Dudley Gale, "Address delivered at the Centennial Celebration of Christ Church at Little Rock, Arkansas, on April 20, 1939," Leonidas Polk biographical file, Archives of the Episcopal Church USA, Austin, Texas. William Dudley Gale III, College of Arts and Sciences, class of 1920, the University of the South was Leonidas Polk's great-grandson and donated the Leonidas Polk Memorial Carillon to the University of the South in 1959.

Confederate army. In the meantime, Polk wrestled with his new identity and did so within the context of the Old South's evangelical religious culture.

CHAPTER 2

Evangelical Origins

Although Leonidas Polk was destined to influence a generation of Southern Episcopalians and become one of the foremost religious leaders of the antebellum period, his climb up the rungs of clerical achievement began inauspiciously. For more than ten years after his conversion, Polk's life lacked focus and direction, not in terms of his personal faith in God and Jesus Christ but in terms of his willingness to fulfill his ministerial calling. Shortly after graduating from West Point, he embarked on a search-for-self that began with an extended tour of the Northeast and ended with a lengthy stay in Tennessee. William Polk lessened the burdens of travel by covering his son's expenses and by providing him with letters of introduction to prominent citizens and politicians. Leonidas first traveled to New York City and then to Philadelphia and Boston. While in Massachusetts, he visited the town of Quincy and inspected the home of the late former president, John Adams. On the return trip to New York, Polk stopped in Albany and called on Governor Martin Van Buren. From there he journeyed down the Cumberland Road and eventually reached Maury County, Tennessee, where he reunited with his brother Lucius, a young but successful planter.[1]

In Tennessee, Polk continued to meet with influential people and on one occasion dined with General Andrew Jackson at the Hermitage. He also enjoyed spending time with Lucius, his closest and most trusted sibling. Impressed by what he observed in Tennessee, Leonidas expressed a modest interest in joining his brother as a Maury County planter. A more pressing concern, however, was the impending expiration of his furlough. To resolve

---

[1] For a detailed description of Polk's post–graduation travels, see Joseph Parks, *General Leonidas Polk, C.S.A.: The Fighting Bishop* (Baton Rouge: Louisiana State University Press, 1962) 41–42. The trip also included a stop in Montreal.

this problem, Polk drafted a letter of resignation that he forwarded to his father who in turn filed the notice with the academy. Thus, Polk ended, or so it seemed, any possibility that he would ever embark on a military career. But when he returned to North Carolina in the fall of 1827, he divulged no concrete plans for the ministry and for a time appeared content to enjoy the fruits of being the son of William Polk. During the winter of 1827 and part of 1828, business commitments drew the senior Polk from his Raleigh residence. As a gesture of confidence, he placed Leonidas in charge of his local affairs. William instructed his son to monitor the progress of crops, to oversee building and equipment maintenance, and to calculate the anticipated crop yields. Although the administration of a solvent, mature estate did not require the same expertise as building one from the ground floor, the experience caused the former cadet to consider investment options for the land and slaves that his father had given him. Before arriving at any substantive conclusions, Polk's restless spirit bested him. In October 1828, he departed abruptly for Brooklyn, New York, to study Hebrew under a renowned scholar.[2]

Once in New York, Polk developed a greater sense of urgency regarding his commitment to the ministry, but he decided to attend Virginia Theological Seminary in Alexandria and not General Theological Seminary in New York City, the only other Episcopal seminary. Polk based his choice on two factors: the "spirit" of the Virginia seminary and its geographical location. With respect to the latter, Polk hoped one day to draw a ministerial assignment in the South and opted "to study & become acquainted with those" seminarians who would become his colleagues and with those clerics who governed the Episcopal churches of the South. Even in the days of uncertainty and indecision, Polk demonstrated a love for and allegiance to his native region. In addition to being a significant distance from Raleigh and outside of the South, General Theological Seminary had earned a reputation as an enclave of high church Episcopalianism. Conversely, the Virginia Theological Seminary represented the low church or evangelical tradition. By selecting the Virginia seminary, Polk expressed a

---

[2] Polk revealed a curiosity concerning Lucius's affairs in Maury County while at West Point. See Leonidas Polk to Lucius Polk, 18 October 1825, 25 August 1826, Leonidas Polk Papers, Jesse duPont Library, University of the South, Sewanee, Tennessee (hereafter cited as Leonidas Polk Papers); Parks, *General Leonidas Polk*, 43–45.

tacit approval for the evangelical tradition and its emphasis on missionary societies, preaching the plan of salvation, and simple worship styles over the high church devotion to doctrinal distinctiveness and theological absolutes.[3]

The atmosphere at Virginia Theological Seminary was collegial. With only fifteen students and two full-time faculty members, student organizations were an important part of the educational experience. Students held informal prayer meetings on campus and met regularly in the homes of faculty members for the purpose of Bible study and fellowship. One of the seminary's first classes organized a missionary society that raised funds for various projects and cultivated a sense of "duty" toward missionary enterprises.[4] During his years at the seminary Polk assumed an active role in the society and contributed to its early successes. "Our little meetings in the neighborhood are pretty well attended, and occasionally much feeling and interest are manifested," Polk reported to his former West Point chaplain, Charles P. McIlvaine. His involvement in these activities had a profound impact on his spiritual development and led him to consider a call to the mission field. He turned to McIlvaine for advice: "And now my dear brother, I shall in an especial manner want your prayers and counsel. Your superior experience has already been of lasting benefit to me, and I earnestly hope it may not be withheld while we shall together labor in the cause of our beloved Martyr." Polk then remarked, "In looking about me, I find the field white with the harvest in every direction." Here, the seminarian had paraphrased John 4:35, a passage where Jesus Christ rebuked the disciples for their laxity in preaching the gospel. Apparently, Polk had gleaned a personal reprimand from this scripture, and intoned that he was "only solicitous to know [his] appropriate station" in the great harvest of souls.[5]

In comparison to his days at West Point where he had been very serious about his studies, had compiled an impressive academic record, and had advocated repeatedly the benefits of a classical education, Polk now demonstrated a much more casual attitude toward the academic portion of

---

[3] Leonidas Polk to William Polk, 7 October 1828, Leonidas Polk Papers.

[4] W. A. R. Goodwin, "Student Organizations," in *History of the Theological Seminary in Virginia and Its Historical Background*, ed. W. A. R. Goodwin, 2 vols. (New York: E. S. Gorham, 1923) 1:416, 410–11.

[5] Leonidas Polk to Charles P. McIlvaine, 2 February 1830, Leonidas Polk Papers. The King James Version of John 4:35 reads: "Lift up your eyes, and look on the fields; for they are white already to harvest."

seminary life. In short, he placed the onus for learning on the shoulders of the student. He also believed that most of what professors taught could "be found already published" in any number of texts. Polk did admit that "the course of study & manner of instruction, & the ability of the professor[s]" had some influence on the learning process.[6] Although the Virginia Theological Seminary had existed for only five years when Polk enrolled in the fall of 1828, he had no reason to assume that he could not obtain a quality education. Dr. Reuel Keith, a graduate of Middlebury College and Andover Seminary and former rector of Williamsburg, Virginia's famed Bruton Parish Church, became the seminary's first elected professor in October 1823. Keith was proficient in Hebrew, Greek, Latin, and German, and Episcopalians recognized him as a leading authority on Hengstenberg Christology. He embraced the Calvinist traditions of Protestant New England and often sided with the low churchmen of his denomination. Bishop John S. Ravenscroft, the militant high churchman of North Carolina, may have provided the most insightful description of Keith: "If there is a man in the world who lives close to God, it is Reuel Keith, but he knows no more of the church than my horse."[7] Considering Keith's scholarly reputation, his congenial personality, and his skill as a "fervent and impassioned speaker," one has to assume that the professor of divinity made some impression on Polk. In time, Polk would espouse a theological system and a view of the Episcopal church that were comparable to the beliefs of Keith.[8]

The close-knit environment at Virginia Theological Seminary accentuated Polk's talents and he earned the respect and admiration of his fellow seminarians. On the eve of his ordination, one classmate referred to Polk as "a superior man and much beloved...as holy and devoted a man as

---

[6] Leonidas Polk to William Polk, 7 October 1828, Leonidas Polk Papers.

[7] Quoted in W. A. R. Goodwin, "Rev. Dr. Reuel Keith," in *History of the Theological Seminary in Virginia and Its Historical Background*, ed. W. A. R. Goodwin, 2 vols. (New York: E.S. Gorham, 1923) 1:543–548. Keith became something of a pariah in his later years. He suffered from bouts of depression, which intensified after his wife's death in 1840. Many of his colleagues believed that his mind had been affected adversely by prolonged exposure to extreme Calvinist views. See Robert W. Prichard, *The Nature of Salvation: Theological Consensus in the Episcopal Church, 1801–73* (Urbana: University of Illinois Press, 1997) 53–54.

[8] Quoted in W. A. R. Goodwin, "Rev. Dr. Reuel Keith," in *History of the Theological Seminary in Virginia*, 1:546.

any we had." Some considered Polk "the most distinguished graduate" in the seminary's first decade of existence—a tribute based more on his achievements during his two bishoprics than his academic record, but somewhat reflective of the potential he displayed as a young seminarian. By the spring of 1830, Polk had completed his two years of ministerial training, but as he prepared for his ordination he was still uncertain about the exact nature of his calling, a predicament complicated by his aristocratic heritage.[9]

Like most elite Southerners, Polk maintained an interest in politics. While a student at the Alexandria seminary, he took advantage of his close proximity to the nation's capital and utilized his father's social connections to arrange a White House-visit with President John Quincy Adams and Secretary of State Henry Clay in November 1828. Although contrasting political ideologies were a significant part of the 1828 election cycle, Polk tended to view politics through the lens of personal character and style. Consequently, he regarded Clay as an engaging fellow and "a man of uncommonly imposing manners, tall, dignified, affable, & easy, & very intelligent looking." With respect to Adams, Polk found the president to be "as awkward as Mr. Clay is easy."[10] Polk employed a similar standard of assessment on Andrew Jackson when the Tennessean entered the White House in 1829. During the early days of his administration, Jackson terminated several employees of the Post Office Department as part of his general reform program to reduce corruption in government. Yet, Polk judged Jackson's "removal of petty postmasters" to be a purely partisan act and considered the firings to be unseemly "employment for the head of so great a nation." Instead of demeaning the presidency, Polk had hoped that Jackson would "furnish" the office with "a more elevated and altogether more useful character." His displeasure with Jackson's partisanship and his frequent use of the spoils system compelled him to remark to his father: "Were I a politician, I fear" the general tone of the president's first administration would be "enough to shake my Jackson principles." Unfortunately, the record is silent on the exact meaning of the phrase "my

---

[9] E. L. Goodwin, "The Contributions of the Seminary to the Domestic Missionary Work of the Church," in *History of the Theological Seminary in Virginia and Its Historical Background*, ed. W. A. R. Goodwin, 2 vols. (New York: E.S. Gorham, 1923) 2:396, 395. Polk's connection to the seminary was strong enough that he served as president of the alumni association from 1851 to 1857.

[10] Leonidas Polk to William Polk, 8 November 1828, Leonidas Polk Papers.

Jackson principles," but his rather condescending critique of the man his father had worked tirelessly to place in office proved that the seminarian was not a party loyalist.[11]

With respect to the slavery question, Polk followed intently the program of the American Colonization Society. The organization's official reports on such matters as available lands, inter-tribal cooperation, and the implementation of the "principles of self government" convinced Polk that the Liberian colony was making substantial progress. He maintained that the colonization plan seemed "feasible," but he believed that the two biggest obstacles to the program were the reluctance of slaveholders to emancipate their slaves and the lack of funding for transportation. Nevertheless, he predicted—based on his impressions of pro-colonization sentiment in Maryland and Virginia—that "in the course of not many years one State after another will be willing to abolish slavery." Despite his philosophical support for the American Colonization Society, neither Polk nor the members of his family made any effort to include their slaves in the repatriation crusade. Furthermore, Polk, at no time, deemed slavery as immoral, unchristian, or unconstitutional, although he would later voice certain reservations about the peculiar institution.[12]

When Leonidas Polk entered Virginia Theological Seminary in November 1828, he was steadfast in his Christian faith. Still, he had time to pursue worldly happiness. In May 1828 he had become engaged to Frances Ann Devereux, the daughter of John and Frances Pollock Devereux, who oddly enough was the granddaughter of the great Puritan theologian Jonathan Edwards. Polk wanted to marry right away, but with seminary studies ahead of him, Frances Ann insisted on a delay and the couple did not marry until 6 May 1830.[13] The Devereuxs ranked among the wealthiest and most influential families of North Carolina. The antebellum lawyer-journalist, Stephen Miller, paid the Devereuxs the ultimate compliment when he compared them to the Rothschilds of Europe. Although John Devereux inherited a great deal of wealth through his wife, he had a successful career as a planter and mercantilist, and at the time of his death his estate was valued in excess of $800,000. For Leonidas, the marriage

---

[11] Leonidas Polk to William Polk, 10 June 1829, Leonidas Polk Papers.

[12] Leonidas Polk to William Polk, 21 January 1829, Leonidas Polk Papers. Polk attended at least one meeting of the American Colonization Society.

[13] Parks, *General Leonidas Polk*, 45, 54.

essentially guaranteed his position among the South's social and cultural elite.[14] The courtship and marriage, however, did not divert Polk's attention from his clerical aspirations. Less than one month before his wedding, he received his ordination as deacon; then he interrupted his honeymoon to accept his first ministerial position as an assistant rector to Bishop Richard Channing Moore of Monumental Church in Richmond, Virginia.[15]

By accepting the Richmond assignment, Polk was entering one of the few areas of evangelical strength in the Southern Episcopal church. Historian E. Clowes Chorley credited Reverend Devereux Jarratt with lighting the "torch of evangelicalism" in Virginia and with developing a distinctly Episcopal form of evangelicalism. Jarratt, minister of Bath parish in Dinwiddie County, disapproved of the "loud outcries, tremblings, fallings, [and] convulsions" that characterized early revivalism. But, like Jonathan Edwards, Jarratt refused to ignore the pleas and confessions of repentant sinners. Jarratt labored "to disturb [the] carnal repose" of his listeners and to awaken in them "a sense of guilt and danger." To this end, he preached the depravity of man, the plan of salvation, and the necessity of spiritual regeneration. He criticized his ministerial colleagues who espoused "little else but morality and smooth harangues," and he traveled extensively within his district promoting Bible studies and prayer meetings, and in the process laid the foundation for an evangelical Episcopal tradition in Virginia.[16] For years, Richard Channing Moore, as rector of Monumental Church and as Bishop of Virginia, carried the mantle of Jarratt and by some accounts produced "spectacular results." Moore advanced a doctrinal synthesis that "opposed [Charles] Finney-style revivalism" but one that was

---

[14] William S. Powell, *Dictionary of North Carolina Biography*, 6 vols. (Chapel Hill University of North Carolina Press, 1979–1996) 2:58–59.

[15] Bishop Moore ordained Polk as deacon on 11 April 1830, and ordained him as priest on 22 May 1831.

[16] Devereux Jarratt quoted in E. Clowes Chorley, *Men and Movements in the American Episcopal Church* (New York: Scribner, 1946) 51. Chorley sees pockets of evangelical strength in Philadelphia, South Carolina, Massachusetts, Rhode Island, and New York. See also Donald Mathews, *Religion in the Old South* (Chicago: University of Chicago, 1977) 130. Mathews alludes to evangelicals in Virginia and on the southwestern frontier. See also Diana Butler, *Standing against the Whirlwind: Evangelical Episcopalians in Nineteeth Century America* (New York/Oxford: Oxford University Press, 1995). Butler points to Ohio as an evangelical stronghold because of Charles McIlvaine and Kenyon College.

sympathetic to heart-felt religious experiences. At the same time, he remained a loyal adherent to liturgical forms and Episcopal ecclesiology and episcopacy.[17] Under the successive bishoprics of Richard Channing Moore and William Meade, Virginia's diocesan conventions developed a discernible "evangelical tone."[18] The "evangelical tone" that Virginia's key Episcopal leaders created was an integral part of the ministerial training and religious education that Leonidas Polk received during his years in the Old Dominion state.

There were early indications that Polk was willing to follow these traditions. On 16 April 1830, he preached his first sermon at Richmond's Monumental Church and chose John 3:16 as his text. The following two Sundays, Bishop Moore was away on diocesan business, and Polk filled the pulpit in his absence. He based his next two messages on Hebrews 12:14 and James 2:18. Although the actual sermons have not survived, these three passages revealed the rudiments of Polk's theological orientation. The Johannine text has long served as the preeminent exposition on the offer of salvation, divine love, and eternal life. The reference from Hebrews focuses on the essential connections between personal holiness and Christian faith. The text from James carries the implication that genuine faith requires more than intellectual assent, and that faith, through supernatural agency, produces a lifestyle of good works. Therefore, in three successive weeks, Polk covered several of the major themes of evangelical preaching: personal salvation, piety, obedience, and spiritual regeneration.[19]

An additional sign that Polk had adopted an evangelical worldview was the uncompromising way in which he counseled mourners. While a student at Virginia Theological Seminary, he learned of the death of family friend Rachel Jackson, the wife of President Andrew Jackson. The terrible news afforded Polk an opportunity to share with his mother some reflections on mortality and suffering. Death, he warned, "must…teach [everyone of] the frailty of human existence, & the necessity for being at any moment ready to resign it." Polk hoped the tragedy might compel the president to appreciate fully the blessings already "conferred on him by Providence," to examine his

---

[17] Butler, *Standing against the Whirlwind*, 39, 78. See also Lawrence L. Brown, "Richard Channing Moore and the Revival of the Southern Church," *Historical Magazine of the Protestant Episcopal Church* 35 (March 1966): 3–36.

[18] Chorley, *Men and Movements*, 99.

[19] Leonidas Polk to Charles P. McIlvaine, 21 July 1830, Leonidas Polk Papers.

own spiritual state, and to ultimately accept Christianity. "It would be a noble spectacle to see" a man of Jackson's reputation and stature embrace the tenets of the Christian faith, Polk remarked to his mother. As events soon affirmed, Polk's admonitions and exhortations were not empty rhetoric. His beliefs were placed under a severe test when he lost two siblings in a painfully brief period in the fall of 1830.[20]

In September 1830, Polk traveled from Richmond to Raleigh to care for his twenty-year-old brother Hamilton, who had been stricken with consumption. Assuming the role of spiritual adviser, the young cleric answered Hamilton's questions concerning the afterlife, then baptized his own sibling and conducted the funeral service when his younger brother finally succumbed.[21] Before the grieving parents could recover from this tragedy, the family's youngest member, Charles Junius Polk, died in infancy. Leonidas extended his deepest sympathies to his father, and he attempted to reassure the family patriarch that while death diminished their number it could not destroy their love for one another. Of all the correspondence between Polk and his father, this letter of condolence was the most philosophical and the most poetic. Despite the severe emotional stress that accompanied these occasions of bereavement, Polk drew a sharp distinction between temporal happiness and eternal bliss. He reminded his father of his "very protracted old age, the certainty of death, [and] the immense and boundless eternity" that awaited him beyond the grave. Polk hoped that his father understood that the "inheritance" of eternal life required the "absolute necessity of a Christian character."[22] These candid discussions about mortality and personal salvation demonstrated that Polk's views were in accord with the great principle of nineteenth-century evangelical thought. Indeed, as historian Anne Loveland concludes, "The belief in the sovereignty and omnipotence of God…more than any other single element contributed to the distinctiveness of southern evangelical thought" in the nineteenth century.[23]

---

[20] Leonidas Polk to Sarah Polk, 10 January 1829, Leonidas Polk Papers.

[21] Parks, *General Leonidas Polk*, 55.

[22] Leonidas Polk to William Polk, 4 November 1830, Leonidas Polk Papers. Generally speaking, Polk's prose was cumbersome. He wrote best when giving testimonials of his own faith.

[23] Anne C. Loveland, *Southern Evangelicals and the Social Order, 1800–1860* (Baton Rouge: Louisiana State University Press, 1980) 265.

Although Polk accepted death and judgment as part of God's providential order, the certitude of an omnipotent, omniscient, omnipresent deity did not translate into personal confidence. In particular, Polk's pulpit performances left him less than satisfied, and his shortcomings became a source of irritation and displeasure. While he could sense the sustaining power of the Holy Spirit, he worried that his sermons were dull and uninspiring. He confessed to his dear friend, Reverend Charles McIlvaine, that he was "very much fettered by [his] notes, and could not help feeling that the congregation listened as to a written essay rather than to a spirited heartfelt appeal from the gospel." The "large" and "fashionable" congregation of Monumental Church presented a formidable challenge to any young cleric, even for one serving as the assistant to the rector. They exhibited "spirits of every grade and character," Polk discovered, and much to his dismay, he believed that most of the church's 130 communicants were not dedicated to an active pursuit of personal piety. Polk concluded that the congregation lacked "the bond of Christian fellowship," a "fault" he considered "common" to the Episcopal church. He also complained that Monumental's "kind and affectionate" rector, Bishop Richard Channing Moore, was hampered by old age and an overly "cautious" disposition towards "new plans" and ideas. For Polk the one outstanding feature of Monumental Church was its sponsorship of educational societies and foreign and domestic missions. Still, after only a few months at the Richmond church, Polk lamented that the "magnitude" of his work produced moments of distress and depression. His greatest fear was that he would become "ignorant of the way of salvation" and become "inadequate to the instruction" of the Monumental congregation.[24]

By mid-summer 1831, health problems compounded Polk's feelings of ineptness. To cope, he retreated to the familiarity of Raleigh. Various ailments had appeared not long after Polk graduated from West Point. Since that time, his condition, a persistent "cough and night sweats," had worsened, and he went to Philadelphia for a diagnosis and treatment. The first doctor advised Polk that "he had only a few months to live." A second opinion recommended convalescing in Europe. The diagnosis so alarmed Polk that he opted not to return to Raleigh but proceeded directly to New York, where he set sail for Europe on 8 August 1831. Incredibly, Polk made

---

[24] Leonidas Polk to Charles P. McIlvaine, 21 July 1830, Leonidas Polk Papers.

no effort to return to North Carolina, leaving his young bride and six-month old son, whom he had named Alexander Hamilton Polk in memory of his deceased brother, in the care of the extended Polk and Devereux families. At the age of twenty-five, Leonidas Polk had failed to demonstrate either the emotional or physical constitution requisite for success in the uncertain world of the Southern planter or the toilsome world of the Southern prelate.[25]

The voyage to Europe lasted twenty-one days. Polk landed in Le Havre, France, and traveled immediately to Paris, where doctors assured him that rest and relaxation would cure him. The news afforded him some consolation, and he wasted little time in preparing for a whirlwind tour of Europe that included stops in The Hague, Switzerland, Rome, Naples, and Nice. He spent most of his time visiting churches, colleges and universities, and the immortal sites of antiquity. His diary contained a mixture of acerbic social commentary and penetrating self-analysis. Of all the European locales, Polk found Paris to be the most objectionable. In evaluating the political climate in the French capital after the rise of Louis Philipe, Polk noted caustically: "We cannot be too grateful that so vast an expanse of water separates us from the broils and misrule of this region of crowned heads." He did not, however, limit his disdain for Paris to political barbs. In reference to Parisian culture, Polk remarked: "If we had no souls, if this world were the only theater of our existence, and if pleasure…were the sole object of life, Paris is the place to find it…. But if this life is the place to prepare for another, and if the Scriptures are true, one had better live anywhere else."[26]

On the surface, these comments appear hackneyed or pejorative, but irrespective of their merits, Polk's observations symbolized his extreme social conservatism. Toward the end of his European sojourn, Polk spent time at Cambridge and Oxford, England, a visit that elicited an interesting

---

[25] Parks, *General Leonidas Polk*, 57. Polk's maladies were not inventions of his imagination. The family had a history of tuberculosis, and the death of Hamilton Polk was a painfully fresh reminder that they was not immune to fatal diseases. In March 1836, Polk awoke one morning to find that he was partially paralyzed on one side and his speech was slurred. Miraculously, some might say, Polk exhibited no serious medical problems after 1840, except for a bout with yellow fever in 1854, even during the traumatic and demanding days of the Civil War.

[26] Diary excerpts in William M. Polk, *Leonidas Polk: Bishop and General*, 2 vols. (New York: Longmans, Green, and Co., 1915) 1:127–30.

exchange between himself and the wife he had left behind. He began by describing some local architecture and the pageantry of an annual stag hunt. Then, he turned to the lifestyle of the English country gentleman:

> I confess I am quite charmed with the neatness of the country houses…and when I think of our vast plantations, with our dirty, careless, thriftless negro population, I could, and do wish that we were thoroughly quit of them. The more I see of those who are without slaves, the more I am prepared to say that we are seriously wronging ourselves by retaining them,—but I am in no mood for entering into this subject.

In emphatic tones, Polk had derided the responsibilities and environs of the Southern planter. As he viewed it, the South lacked the "cultivation" and "comfort" of manorial life in England, which for most Southern elites epitomized conservative ideals and values.[27]

Throughout his trip, Polk's physical condition showed no signs of deterioration, and he maintained a constant and busy schedule. However, the self-doubt that haunted him during his days at Monumental Church resurfaced, and he appeared burdened by a melancholic disposition. There were days when he remained in his room avoiding all social interaction and acting like a "tired and half-asleep invalid." In December 1831 he reflected on a year of limited successes "with the keenest, [and] bitterest regret." To combat these feelings, Polk meditated on the grace and forgiveness of God. Whether convicted by the power of the Holy Spirit or the shame of inadequacy, Polk agreed to preach at a sailor's bethel in the Italian port city of Leghorn. The outcome disappointed him. The pulpiteering had taxed him physically, and he wondered if he would ever "be able to combat the…trials" of his ministerial calling. The feelings of despair did not, however, keep Polk from regular church attendance. Still, the services did little to improve his mood. After attending New College Chapel in Oxford, he sniped, "The music, certainly, was fine, but I can never be interested in a service designed wholly for effect…. And though I have attended church three times [today] I have not realized the solemnity and sanctity of this holy day." Polk left England in mid-June 1832 and toured Scotland and Ireland

---

[27] Leonidas Polk to Frances Polk, 30 May 1832, in Polk, *Leonidas Polk: Bishop and General*, 1:139–40. See also, Genovese and Fox–Genovese, "The Religious Ideals of Southern Slave Society," 1–16.

before sailing back to the United States. He reached North Carolina in October 1832.[28]

The fourteen-month European odyssey began with many questions but ended with few answers. Polk was reasonably healthy, and with a wife and young son, he felt obligated to provide a stable family environment. He had two choices. The Devereuxs had offered him a small, improved plantation and seventy slaves as an enticement to remain in North Carolina. Lucius Polk urged his brother to join him in Maury County, Tennessee, where he and his new bride, Mary Eastin, the grandniece of Rachel Jackson, were planning to raise their family. The idea of settling near his brother intrigued Leonidas, but he did not make a hasty decision. He and Frances wintered in North Carolina, spending time with both the Devereuxs and the Polks. Meanwhile, Leonidas was unable to overcome his fears and concerns about his ministerial abilities. Although he preached occasionally in Raleigh, he accepted no official position in any of the local churches. The status quo prevailed until the spring of 1833, when Leonidas and Frances left Raleigh and headed west.[29]

Tennessee became a place of new beginnings both for Leonidas Polk and James H. Otey. In 1834 Otey became the first bishop of the newly formed Episcopal diocese of Tennessee. As one of his first official acts, he convinced Polk to become the rector of St. Peter's Church in Columbia, Tennessee. Polk's commitment to St. Peter's, however, must be viewed in its proper context. When Otey became bishop, there were only 117 communicants of the Episcopal church in the entire state of Tennessee as compared to the 133 members of Monumental Church, the first and only place Polk had held a ministerial position. In addition, the Episcopalians of the Volunteer State could count only seven priests, including Otey and Polk, and three deacons. The small size and negligible demands of St. Peter's most likely comported with Polk's long-term plans. He could continue with his primary concern, building a profitable plantation, and fulfill technically his ministerial calling without the pressures of a large, cosmopolitan

---

[28] Diary excerpts in Polk, *Leonidas Polk*, 1:139–40, 133, 138, 142.

[29] Parks, *General Leonidas Polk*, 62–69. Lucius married while Leonidas was in Europe. The wedding was a grand affair and was hosted by President Andrew Jackson at the White House.

congregation.[30] As a result of Polk's return to the ministry, a close friendship emerged between himself and Bishop Otey. They traveled together on church business, and under Otey's prodding Polk became more involved in the affairs of the Episcopal church. Polk, for instance, served as a Tennessee delegate to the General Convention in 1835. In addition, he was "a zealous co-worker with Bishop Otey in all of his efforts on behalf of Christian education."[31] Partners they may have been, but Otey was clearly the dominant figure both in the Episcopal church and the diocese of Tennessee.

Otey was only thirty-four years old when he became bishop, but from the time of his confirmation twelve years earlier, he had supported the cause of high church Episcopalianism. According to one scholar, Otey's theological "trumpet had been attuned to that of Ravenscroft and so was in accord with those of Hobart, the Onderdonks and Doane; [that] when he put his lips to it, it gave forth no uncertain sound."[32] Harmonizing with high churchmen aside, Otey's ecclesiology served as incontrovertible proof of his high church credentials. He believed that the Episcopal church was "divine in organization, holy in character, catholic in extent, and apostolic in its ministry," and as such the historic succession of ordinations "validated" an individual's ministry.[33] Regarding the administration of the sacraments and the "other holy offices of the religion," Otey determined that it was the "obligation" of a clergyman "to comply with the directions which the church in her wisdom [had] prescribed in all these cases." A clergyman who acted otherwise would be "forgetful" and negligent "of the solemnity and binding force of his ordination vows."[34] For these reasons, the bishop of Tennessee became widely known as the defender of apostolic order.

---

[30] Donald S. Armentrout, *James Hervey Otey: First Episcopal Bishop of Tennessee* (Knoxville TN: Episcopal Diocese of Tennessee, 1984) 38–46.

[31] Arthur H. Noll, *History of the Church in the Diocese of Tennessee* (New York: J. Pott, 1900) 120. Otey announced in 1836 a threefold educational plan that included theological, classical, and professional training. Otey was a true educational reformer and an early advocate of the normal system. Polk, however, was an unconditional classicist.

[32] Noll, *History of the Church in the Diocese of Tennessee*, 85. Ravenscroft confirmed Otey on 8 May 1824.

[33] Armentrout, *James Hervey Otey*, 138, 144.

[34] James H. Otey, *The Duty of the Ministers of the Gospel, To Their People, Considered in Their Civil Relations: Set Forth in a Primary Charge to the Clergy of the Diocese of Tennessee* (Nashville: W.F. Bang and Co., 1837).

Otey's high church principles did not prevent him from exhibiting evangelical sympathies. For example, he subscribed to a Calvinist-like view of human nature that identified man as "corrupt," "inclined to evil," and trapped in a state of depravity where "natural strength and good works" could not free him. He held that "the whole purpose and object of the gospel [was] to save men by uniting them to Christ." Otey reasoned that preaching must impart "to man a knowledge of [God's] character and purposes, and of the worship and duty he expects from them."[35] The bishop, however, lamented in Jacksonian America what he called a profound "indifference to the preaching of the gospel." Otey considered this mindset to be a threat to social stability and "good and free government." Moreover, he believed that Christian instruction was the only way to reverse the spiritual malaise and remedy moral degeneracy. In outlining a mandate for the clergy of his diocese, Otey expressed, in unmistakable terms, the need to infuse civic life with Christian virtues. "Religion is the fountain which feeds the stream of public morals," the bishop proclaimed, "and if the fountain be impure or cease to send forth its waters, or if they be diverted from their proper channels, moral disease and infection will spread around and cast the pall of death over all the public and private relations of life."[36]

Otey also spoke passionately in defense of the missionary programs of the Episcopal church.[37] He understood the church to be "the appointed instrument of God...[for] instructing the ignorant, reclaiming the straying, comforting the wretched, relieving the distressed, warning the ungodly, and dispensing the light, hope, and salvation to repentant sinners."[38] By this definition, the church had a responsibility to take the gospel to every corner of the world including the sparsely populated regions of the United States. Despite the acceptance of certain evangelical principles, Otey remained a staunch high churchman, and the diocese of Tennessee, unlike the diocese of Virginia, never developed a so-called "evangelical tone."

---

[35] James H. Otey, *Preaching the Gospel: A Charge, delivered to the Clergy of the Protestant Episcopal Church in the State of Tennessee at the Twelfth Annual Convention of the Diocese* (Nashville: W.F. Bang and Co., 1840).

[36] Otey, *The Duty of the Ministers of the Gospel*, 7-19.

[37] See James H. Otey, *The Triennial Sermon, Before the Bishops, Clergy, and Laity, Constituting the Board of Missions of the Protestant Episcopal Church in the United States of America, Preached in St. Stephen's Church, Philadelphia, September 6, 1838* (Philadelphia: C. Sherman, 1838).

[38] Otey, quoted in Armentrout, *James Hervey Otey*, 108–109.

Otey's attentiveness to the missionary role of the church had specific consequences for his new friend, Leonidas Polk. In 1838 the Episcopal church elected the Tennessee planter to the position of missionary bishop of the Southwest. Interestingly, Polk was not the first choice. Reverend Francis Hawkins turned down the appointment prior to Polk's selection, which suggests that the post may not have been highly coveted. Polk did not even attend the General Convention of 1838, and no evidence exists to suggest that he campaigned for the post. In light of these circumstances Polk biographer Joseph Parks deduced that Bishops Charles P. McIlvaine and James H. Otey must have "promoted" the candidacy of the thirty-two-year-old planter-priest and that the General Convention accepted their recommendation. Parks's explanation seems to be the only logical conclusion, but his contention that Polk was admirably qualified is without merit, especially when Polk's limited experience and questionable commitment to the ministry is taken into consideration.[39]

McIlvaine and Otey knew Polk better than anyone else in the General Convention, and they both expected a great deal from the new missionary bishop. McIlvaine, who had left West Point and had become the bishop of Ohio, accepted the honor of preaching the sermon at Polk's consecration service, which was held on 9 December 1838, in Christ Church, Cincinnati, Ohio. His charge consisted of three themes: the nature of the office of bishop, the importance of the gospel ministry, and personal remarks to the candidate. By McIlvaine's definition, the office of bishop "was one of...*general supervision*...and embraced essentially the authority to preach the gospel; to administer the sacraments of the church; to preside over its government, [and] to ordain helpers and successors." These powers were not held collectively by the bishops of the church but "*individually*" in order to protect the church from the authority of a "singular Potentate." Included in the gospel ministry was the obligation "to teach, and disciple, and baptize all nations, and bring them into subjection to the commands of Christ...and be the instrument of creating anew the moral and spiritual character of all mankind." In fulfilling the Great Commission, bishops were "to be seen walking in the furnace of trial, and bearing the cross of heavy duty," even to

[39] Parks, *General Leonidas Polk*, 77.

the point of making "the most painful sacrifices of the sweets of home and family."[40]

McIlvaine believed that Polk was capable of meeting these challenges. He recalled with great fondness the days they spent together at West Point where they labored against the "almost universal indifference to religion." By McIlvaine's account, Polk's conversion sparked a "work of grace" that produced a "serious" and lasting impression on the entire West Point community. In the past, they had worked side by side. In the future they would walk separate paths. The one-time chaplain assumed they were traveling toward the same end. He compared his relationship with Polk to that between St. Paul and his youthful compatriot Timothy. Having once served as Polk's spiritual mentor, McIlvaine used the occasion of Polk's consecration to add a new dimension to their relationship: "I call you *Son*, in affectionate recollection of the past, I call you *Brother* now, in affectionate consideration of the present and the future." Just as St. Paul admonished Timothy, McIlvaine urged Polk to "endure hardness as a good soldier of Jesus Christ" (2 Tim 2:3) and remain committed to "the high vocation to which you are called."[41]

Although Bishop Otey did not attend the consecration ceremony, he explained the importance of the gospel ministry and enumerated the qualifications of a missionary in a sermon he delivered to the Board of Missions in 1838, the same year Polk was elected missionary bishop of the Southwest. Without the gospel, Otey argued, man could not avoid the "destruction of body and soul...which consummates the struggle of death." For the living, the gospel offered "deliverance" from the dominion of sin and provided for "the renewal of hearts" and "the sanctification of...purposes, desires, hopes and pursuits...without which all...other advantages and privileges" were meaningless. Those clerics appointed to the mission field were to be "men qualified by their learning, piety, talents and experience...men who shall go expecting to labor hard...men who shall possess a zeal according to knowledge, not an enthusiasm quickened by the spirit of romance." Above all, the missionary must overcome the "continued temptation to lower the standard of Christian attainment" and "lift the

---

[40] Charles P. McIlvaine, *The Apostolic Commission: The Sermon Preached at the Consecration of the Right Rev. Leonidas Polk, D. D., Missionary Bishop for Arkansas in Christ Church, Cincinnati, December 9, 1838* (Gambier OH: G. W. Meyers, 1838).

[41] Ibid.

standard of the blood-stained cross and proclaim [it] in...solemn and thrilling tones."[42]

At the time of his election as missionary bishop, Polk shared with McIlvaine and Otey a deep concern for the unsaved and an urgent desire to see the gospel preached. Moreover, since his days as a seminarian, Polk had supported conscientiously the missionary philosophy of the Episcopal church. But in the first eight years of his ministry, he had not demonstrated the confidence, determination, or the sacrificial qualities of a missionary bishop, which makes his decision to accept the position all the more interesting. For some reason, Polk was willing to enter a world vastly different from any he had ever known; in retrospect it was the turning point of his ministerial career.

The Episcopal church had placed a great deal of responsibility on the shoulders of a man with so little experience. Polk's jurisdiction included Arkansas, Mississippi, Louisiana, coastal Alabama, the Republic of Texas, and other southwestern territories designated ambiguously as the "Indian Territory." He embarked on his first missionary journey in February 1839, and visited Florence and Tuscumbia, Alabama; Memphis, Tennessee; Batesville, Fayetteville, and Little Rock, Arkansas; Shreveport, Natchitoches, and Alexandria, Louisiana; and Galveston and Houston, Texas. Of all these locations, Polk considered Texas the most intriguing. "The growing importance," he reported "of this Republic is daily becoming more manifest, and the influence for good over evil, on the future destiny of countless multitudes of our fellow man is equally certain."[43]

In particular, the cities of Galveston and Houston contained "friends of the church" who were "anxious" to establish local congregations and ultimately a diocese.[44] With uncharacteristic optimism, Polk commented that he was "satisfied" with what he had observed in Texas. Still, the new missionary bishop issued a call for more "pioneers," men "sound in the faith and full of evangelical zeal."[45] He cautioned, however, that "great discomfort must of course be counted upon, and no man should be encouraged to attempt such work, unless, he be willing to endure hardness, and labor with great singleness of purpose." The Board of Missions responded to Polk's

---

[42] Otey, *The Triennial Sermon.*
[43] Missions Report, *The Spirit of Missions* 4/3 (March 1839): 88.
[44] Missions Report, *The Spirit of Missions* 4/7 (July 1839): 198–99.
[45] Missions Report, *The Spirit of Missions* 4/3 (March 1839): 88.

request with a plea of their own that chided Episcopalians for squandering opportunities to plant "the Church in a destitute section" of the country and for effectively withholding "the means of salvation to perishing souls."[46] This first missionary journey lasted five months, and Polk estimated that he logged 5,000 miles, preached forty-four sermons, baptized fourteen, confirmed forty-one, and consecrated one church.[47]

Polk returned home and rested for a few months before departing on his second missionary journey on 30 November 1840. He covered much of the same territory, but this time he focused his attention on the region of Southwest Arkansas, Northwest Louisiana, and East Texas. "In no other part of my field of labor," Polk lamented, "have I seen a people of whom it may be so truly said that they are perishing for a lack of knowledge." The situation was so bleak that he regarded "the Indian tribes…better provided for than the whites who surrounded them." Consequently, he recommended that the church "do anything" to increase the supply of clergy to the area and to increase the flow of religious literature into the region. Polk even suggested that the church "introduce the system of itinerating" if no alternative could be discovered.[48] Overall, his experiences as missionary bishop translated into a deeper commitment to the ministry, and his endorsement of an itinerant ministry documented his evangelical impulses. His health problems, which just a few years earlier had compelled him to retreat to Europe, appeared inconsequential. He genuinely enjoyed his work. Reminiscent of the boyish enthusiasm that he had demonstrated during his first days at West Point, Polk informed his mother that his missionary adventures were exciting and that he traveled pioneer-like with a "buffalo robe and a supply of blankets." He also thanked her for his traveling companion, Folly, "the finest saddle-horse" he had ever ridden.[49] How ironic that a well-to-do Episcopal bishop was roving the hinterlands of the Southwest on a horse named Folly!

---

[46] Missions Report, *The Spirit of Missions* 4/5 (May 1839): 155. A specific charge was made to enlist support for the church's two domestic missionary bishops, Leonidas Polk and Kemper Jackson, missionary bishop of the Northwest.

[47] Parks, *General Leonidas Polk*, 85.

[48] Missions Report, *The Spirit of Missions* 6/5 (May 1841): 152.

[49] Leonidas Polk to Sarah Polk, 2 February 1841, in Polk, *Leonidas Polk*, 1:167–168.

Without question, the missionary bishopric marked the turning point of Polk's ministerial career. From this period forward, his personal confidence as well as his commitment to the ministry increased dramatically. He continued, as he had during his European travels, to use the beginning of each year as a time of introspection and evaluation. At the mid-point of his second missionary journey, he paused to consider his activities of the past year. He felt that he had "meditate[d] too little," bathed himself in prayer "too seldom," and failed to guard himself "against the intrusion of a worldly spirit."[50] These were harsh criticisms, but unlike the melancholy and confusion that hounded Polk in earlier days, these estimations reflected the thoughts of a determined man aspiring to greater spiritual productivity. During the first eighteen months of his missionary bishopric, he spent only four months with his family. By this time, Polk had three daughters and one son who ranged in age from one to nine. The schedule of the second missionary journey required that Polk be absent from his family during the Christmas season, an unavoidable conflict that he regretted deeply because he believed that the season could only be enjoyed fully in the presence of family and loved ones. Nevertheless, he confided to Bishop McIlvaine that a truly effective missionary bishop "ought not to have a family. He should be literally married to the church." He even ventured so far as to applaud the Roman Catholic doctrine of celibacy. In a letter to Bishop McIlvaine, Polk expressed his admiration of the Roman Catholic bishop of Ohio who frequently mocked Protestants for their prejudices against the doctrine of celibacy with such pithy lyrics as: "St. Paul [would] have cut a fine figure, while visiting the churches of Asia, with a wife and seven screaming children following in his train!"[51] As Polk began to reprioritize his life, it became clear that God and church took precedence and family came second.

As a result of this new-found devotion, Polk's star continued to rise, and he met and even exceeded the expectations of Otey and McIlvaine. In October 1841 the General Convention rewarded Polk with an invitation to become the first bishop of the diocese of Louisiana. He accepted without hesitation. During his second missionary journey, Polk had made several stops in Louisiana and was therefore fully aware of the task that awaited him. "There is no portion of the whole country so destitute…as Louisiana"

---

[50] Leonidas Polk to Sarah Polk, 18 January 1841, in Polk, *Leonidas Polk*, 1:166.
[51] Leonidas Polk to Charles P. McIlvaine, 10 August 1840, Leonidas Polk Papers.

was his earliest observation. "She has not, so far as I know, a single church west of the Mississippi River; and I find few or no Presbyterians, and only now and then a wandering Methodist." In Natchitoches, Polk once had postponed Sunday services until noon because local ordinances, which allowed residents to engage in routine business activity for the first half of the day, severely hampered church attendance. Polk deemed this violation of the Sabbath as reprehensible. He conducted a total of five services while in Natchitoches; each successive meeting increased in size and the fifth "was positively crowded." Natchitoches had a significant French Catholic population and Polk stereotyped them as setting "lightly by their religion." But he appreciated their attendance at his services, and he promised to "take steps" to meet the needs of the Francophones.[52] Louisiana presented a number of unique and interesting challenges, but with four parishes, six clergyman, and 238 communicants, Polk had reason for optimism.[53]

As bishop of Louisiana, Polk had a concentrated audience as opposed to a widely dispersed mission field, which required him to present his doctrinal positions in a clear and precise manner. The predominant themes of his inaugural address were unity in Christ and Christ crucified. "In pursuance of the example of the Apostles," Polk declared, "the chief work of our ministry, [is] to persuade men "to be found in Christ;" to be united to Him as the members to the body."[54] This phrase "united to Him as members to the body," communicated St. Paul's idea (Rom 12:4–10) that while the human body consists of a variety of parts, each appendage functioned in a system of "mutual dependence." The analogy connoted more than solidarity, it conveyed the "notion of corporate personality."[55] Indeed, Polk challenged his flock, in the tradition of St. Paul, to be of "one body...one mind and one heart." For him, the second theme, "Christ crucified," was the "ever-recurring" message of the apostles and "the source and end" of St. Paul's teachings. The centrality of Christ crucified to the

---

[52] Leonidas Polk to Sarah Polk, 5 April 1841, in Polk, *Leonidas Polk*, 1:169–170.

[53] Parks, *General Leonidas Polk*, 96.

[54] "Journal of the Fourth Annual Convention of the Protestant Episcopal Church of the Diocese of Louisiana, January 20, 1842," Historical Records of the Episcopal Church Collection, James Merrick Jones Hall, Tulane University, New Orleans, Louisiana, 22.

[55] J. A. Ziesler, *Pauline Christianity* (New York/Oxford: Oxford University Press, 1983) 55, 59.

theological orientation of Bishop Polk provides some insights into his Christology. Primarily, Polk understood the crucifixion, the resurrection, and the ascension, and not the miracles, parables, and teachings to be the essential nature and work of Jesus Christ.[56] This second Pauline principle implied a reliance, by the church and by individual believers, on the inspiration and illumination of the Holy Spirit rather than the teachings of Christ.[57]

In addition to expressing a commitment to the Pauline themes of unity in Christ and Christ crucified, Bishop Polk also pledged that his diocese would always tread "in the old paths of the Reformation and the early church." Specifically, Polk supported the doctrine of justification by faith, which he understood to mean "the condition of man after the fall of Adam is such, that he cannot turn and prepare himself, by his own natural strength and good works, to faith and calling upon God." Moreover, Polk argued that "without the grace of God by Christ" man has no ability to produce "good works (pleasant and acceptable to God)" or any claim to justification except through the atoning death of Jesus Christ.[58] Polk's views on justification by faith aligned him with the evangelical wing of the Episcopal church. Unlike many evangelicals who preferred "a neutrality sympathetic to Calvinism" or other Episcopalians who were either silent or ambivalent observers of the predestination debate, Polk defended an explicitly Calvinist view of human nature and the theology of reconciliation.[59]

The least developed aspects of Polk's theology were his interpretation of the sacraments and his doctrine of the church. For both evangelical and high church Episcopalians, assurance of salvation was a major theological issue, but the two groups sought assurance from different sources. On the one hand, high church Episcopalians emphasized "the baptismal covenant as a basis for assurance," arguing that the waters of baptism provided more assurance than the doctrine of predestination. On the other hand,

---

[56] "Journal of the Fourth Annual Convention," 23.

[57] Ziesler, *Pauline Christianity*, 22.

[58] "Journal of the Sixth Annual Convention of the Protestant Episcopal Church of the Diocese of Louisiana, April 30–June 1, 1844," Historical Records of the Episcopal Church Collection, James Merrick Jones Hall, Tulane University, New Orleans, Louisiana, 49.

[59] Robert Prichard also contends that high church Episcopalians displayed "a neutrality antagonistic to Calvinism." There were, of course, exceptions, and Prichard is concerned most with the ability of Episcopalians to tolerate both positions. See also Prichard, *The Nature of Salvation*, 57, 38–43, 62.

evangelical Episcopalians considered the doctrine of renewal or spiritual regeneration as the foundation of assurance.[60] Polk seems to have accepted both points of view. For example, he explained to the Episcopalians of his charge that the sacraments served "as certain sure witnesses and effectual signs of grace and God's will towards us...and confirm our faith in him." In this instance, the sacraments were a sign of the believer's faith or a seal of the covenant relationship between God and the believer. But Polk also warned that the sacraments were not to be worn "as badges of Christian profession." In his theology of the sacraments, he stopped short of defining baptism as the actual or fixed point of conversion. Like many evangelicals, he gained some assurance through the conversion experience, especially during the moments of decision when the intense feelings of sinfulness and forgiveness consumed the confessor. Polk also relied on the evidence of a transformed life for assurance of salvation. "The fruits of the faith...follow after justification," Polk asserted, and while good works "cannot put away our sins, yet are they pleasing and acceptable to God...and do spring out necessarily of a true faith."[61] Because assurance was a significant theological issue for Episcopalians, Polk appeared willing to accept elements from both high church and evangelical positions. However, his own conversion experience predisposed him to sympathize with the evangelical view of assurance, a position that boded well in the religious culture of the Old South.

With respect to his doctrine of the church, Polk accepted without reservation "the creeds, articles, homilies, and services" of the Episcopal church, and he expressed every confidence in their "truth and authority." Likewise, he affirmed the three sacred offices of the ministry: bishop, priest, and deacon.[62] But contrary to Bishop Otey, Bishop Polk preached rarely on ecclesiology, apostolic succession, or the history or practices of the Episcopal church. Curiously, Polk, on several occasions, made remarks that in a manner of speaking would have redefined the traditional offices of the ministry. As a missionary bishop, he encouraged the development of an itinerant program in order to increase the number of clergy working in the mission fields.[63] Then, as bishop of Louisiana, Polk petitioned the Episcopal

---

[60] Pritchard, *The Nature of Salvation*, 2–3.

[61] "Journal of the Sixth Annual Convention of the Protestant Episcopal Church of the Diocese of Louisiana, 30 April–1 June 1844," 49.

[62] "Journal of the Fourth Annual Convention," 22.

[63] Report in *The Spirit of Missions* 6 (May, 1841): 152.

church to adopt "by wise and temperate legislation" the means for "obtaining the services of a class of men suited to the instruction" of the slave population. These proposals did not seek to subvert the proper councils of the church or alter the qualifications necessary for ordination, but they did deflect the traditional evangelical criticism that the church was not responding to the needs of a changing society.[64] Although Polk never constructed a true systematic theology, he consistently held to the Pauline themes of unity in Christ and Christ crucified, and the Calvinist doctrines of the depravity of man and justification by faith. It could also be argued that his positions on the sacraments and the doctrine of the church, identified him as an evangelical Episcopalian.

For obvious reasons, most of the Episcopalian activity in Louisiana emanated from New Orleans, one of the South's largest, most diverse, and most cosmopolitan urban centers. Remarkably, the driving force behind the establishment of the first Episcopal church in New Orleans was the simple desire for an English-speaking Protestant church and not the advancement of a particular denomination. A committee of concerned citizens from divergent religious backgrounds met in June 1805 to weigh all options and cast their lot for a specific denomination. In convincing fashion, they voted—forty-five Episcopalian, seven Presbyterian, and one Methodist—to establish Christ (Episcopal) Church. On 13 November 1805, Philander Chase, a young cleric holding office in the diocese of New York, became the church's first minister. Christ Church progressed slowly. The congregation did not build the first church edifice and rectory until 1815, but by the time of Polk's election as bishop of the diocese, the communicants of Christ Church represented more than 30 percent of all Episcopalians in Louisiana.[65]

Despite the longstanding presence of Catholicism and the promising start of Protestantism, the Crescent City more closely resembled the City of Man than St. Augustine's City of God. Historian John Bettersworth has

---

[64] "Journal of the Fifth Annual Convention of the Protestant Episcopal Church of the Diocese of Louisiana, January 18–20, 1843," Historical Records of the Episcopal Church Collection, James Merrick Jones Hall, Tulane University, New Orleans, Louisiana, 34.

[65] Georgia Fairbanks Taylor, "The Early History of the Episcopal Church in New Orleans, 1805–1840," *Louisiana Historical Quarterly* 22/2 (April 1939): 432, 436–448, 466.

maintained that "nothing perhaps epitomized the essential divergence of
New Orleans from the moral pattern of the country…as its observance" of
the Sabbath.[66] Indeed, the Sunday spectacle "of revelry & mirth, of feasting
& dancing, of conviviality & pleasure" outraged more than one Christian
observer. "The Sabbath is openly desecrated in the worst manner by theater,
balls, circuses, cock fights & C," cried Henry B. Whipple, who visited the
city in 1844. Worse still, said Whipple, "Money is the God worshipped and
fashion & pleasure are followed by the giddy multitude with all the
eagerness & delight that there would be if there were no hereafter."[67] For
Bishop Polk, these conditions must have been a vivid reminder of the Paris
that he had condemned in the 1830s. While materialism and pleasure-
seeking contributed to the Orleanian ethos, religion enjoyed a respected
place among the city's wealthiest and most influential residents. New
Orleans did, however, produce some of the most unique religious and
intellectual traditions of the Old South.

"Unitarianism in antebellum New Orleans," according to historian
Timothy Reilly, "was among the most distinctive religious forces" in the
South. The progenitor of the movement was a former Presbyterian divine,
Dr. Theodore Clapp. As the undisputed "iconoclast" of New Orleans, Clapp
attacked Christian orthodoxy from virtually every perceivable angle. He
rejected outright the doctrines of the Trinity and predestination, and he
denied the existence of a literal hell. Clapp also denounced "the blind
emotionalism, anti-intellectualism, and general pandemonium" that
characterized revivalism in the South. Naturally, he opposed all efforts to
establish a revivalist tradition in New Orleans. In addition, he predicted that
if Southern churches did not respond to the plight of the poor, then
Southern cities were destined for chaos and collapse. Indeed, Clapp fired a
number of salvos against the breastworks of Christian orthodoxy and
Southern evangelicalism, but he refused to assault the South's hierarchical
social order or its divinely sanctioned institution of slavery. Nevertheless,
Reilly credited Clapp with stimulating a "free and open debate on a variety

---

[66] John K. Bettersworth, "Protestant Beginnings in New Orleans," *Louisiana
Historical Quarterly* 21/3 (July 1938): 831.

[67] Lester B. Shippe, ed., *Bishop Whipple's Southern Diary, 1843–1844* (New York:
Da Capo Press, 1937) 99, 111. At the time of his visit, Whipple was a Presbyterian,
but he converted to Episcopalianism shortly thereafter and later became the bishop
of Minnesota.

of social and intellectual topics."[68]

From agnosticism to hedonism, from Universalism to evangelicalism, New Orleanians accepted a plethora of religious and intellectual traditions. Philosophical diversity allowed various groups both to coexist and to recruit committed followers. Although the respective ideologues were able to carve out their own intellectual territory, they were all forced to explain and interpret one particular facet of Orleanian life, the constant barrage of disease and epidemics. By 1850 New Orleans had the highest death rate of any city in the nation. The constant presence and randomness of death had a profound effect on the theological and intellectual mind of the city. In order to understand fully the religious and intellectual mind of New Orleans, one must examine the reactions to and explanations of the two most dramatic pathological disasters of the late antebellum period—the cholera epidemic of 1848–1849 and the yellow fever epidemic of 1853.[69]

When an outbreak of cholera struck New Orleans in the winter of 1848, the editors of *The Daily Picayune* moved quickly to forestall any hysteria and offered a series of rational explanations for the epidemiological crisis in the city. "As a bugaboo," the editors opined, "the cholera is a monster, but stripped of its mystery it is a disease as manageable as any other." The paper advised its readers that the spread of the disease could be limited by early detection, "simple remedies," and "a little common sense." Similarly, the number of deaths could be reduced dramatically by observing "ordinary precautions" and by seeking such quality medical care as was being provided by the Howard Association, a type of Red Cross agency.[70] For all of his religious liberalism, Theodore Clapp did not concur with *The Daily Picayune*'s scientific interpretation of the cholera epidemic. The current drama, Clapp submitted, "should inspire us with a profound sense of our entire and absolute dependence on God, accompanied with an enlightened, unfaltering, and unlimited trust in his power and overruling providence." Regardless of whether "health, peace and prosperity" reigned or whether suffering, "sickness and death" prevailed, Clapp believed that the most important lesson to be learned was that God "directs the affairs of

---

[68] Timothy F. Reilly, "Parson Clapp of New Orleans: Antebellum Social Critic, Religious Radical, and Member of the Establishment," *Louisiana History* 16/2 (Spring 1975): 167, 176, 180, 189.

[69] Bettersworth, "Protestant Beginnings in New Orleans," 837.

[70] "The Cholera," *The Daily Picayune*, 27 December 1848.

mortals not in accordance with their vain, unhallowed desires, but in perfect subservience to their present and everlasting welfare."[71] It seems from these remarks that Clapp had not totally abandoned his Presbyterian heritage. His teleological view of history also comported with the prevailing currents of nineteenth-century Southern evangelical thought. However, the Unitarian did not see the cholera epidemic through the lens of the jeremiadic tradition.

The jeremiad, which frequently took the form of a treatise or sermon, was a type of cultural criticism. The ultimate intention of the jeremiad was spiritual renewal. Southern prelates often employed the jeremiad in the wake of natural disasters or social unrest and warned that the ensuing suffering and misfortune were results of spiritual infidelity and divine punishment. Relief, they intimated, could only be achieved through repentance and recommitment.[72] In contrast to the prophets of condemnation, Clapp alluded to the closeness of death "not for the purpose of inspiring...dark and melancholy feelings" but in order to convince believers that "a truly religious mind is calm, serene, unruffled, joyous," and full of "blessed desires, hopes and anticipations." Despite his optimistic tone, the Unitarian concluded that "a single sorrow renders" most believers "insensible to the countless blessings inscribed in the table of their life chronology." Clapp was certain that this "ingratitude is one of the most odious and aggravated forms of impiety."[73] Others who received Clapp's ire were those individuals who forecast that the cholera epidemic would "march forward to its destined goal, regardless of the chants or orchestras or the prayers of saints." He reminded them that in 1832 a cholera epidemic gripped the city and "a dark, damp, heavy, unelastic and muggy atmosphere" hung over it for twelve days until a storm appeared and breathed a "new, fresh, salubrious and life-giving spirit" into it. Clapp interpreted the weather change and the end of the epidemic as a miracle and honored God for saving the city "from calamity, in answer to the prayers of his children."[74] Clapp,

---

[71] See Clapp "A Sermon," *The Daily Picayune*, 14 January 1849.

[72] See Sacvan Bercovitch, *The American Jeremiad* (Madison WI: University of Wisconsin Press, 1978). For the application of the jeremiadic tradition in the South, see Startup, *The Root of all Evil*, 5–6.

[73] See Clapp, "A Sermon," *The Daily Picayune*, 14 January 1849.

[74] Clapp, "A Discourse," *The Daily Picayune*, 18 February 1849.

therefore, rejected notions of a vindictive or vengeful God and portrayed the Almighty as a loving father who was desirous of rescuing his children.

Unlike Clapp, Bishop Polk utilized the jeremiad to warn Louisianians about the consequences of unfaithfulness and an unrepentant heart. As part of the Episcopal church's liturgical tradition, Bishop Polk issued a special prayer to be used in all services during the Cholera epidemic.

> Oh Almighty and merciful God, to whom alone belong the issues of life and death; we thy servants, under a deep sense of our unworthiness, meekly acknowledge that we have grievously sinned, by thought, word, and deed, against thy Divine Majesty; and that by our sins, we have most justly provoked the infliction of that chastisement with which thou art now scourging us. But, Oh God, who desireth not the death of a sinner, but rather that he should turn from his wickedness and live, have mercy upon us thy unworthy servants, and give us grace that we may repent truly of our sins, and turn unto thee, the Lord our God, with full purpose of amendment of life. Spare us, good Lord, spare thy servants, and turn from us the ravages of the Pestilence with which thou art now visiting us; and grant that while this thy Fatherly correction may teach us to consider the uncertainty and frailty of life, and how entirely we are dependent upon thee, it may also lead us hereafter to put our whole trust and confidence in thy mercy, and to serve and please thee in newness of life through Jesus Christ our Lord. Amen[75]

This prayer clearly followed in the jeremiadic form, as did the remarks he delivered to the state diocesan convention of 1849. In his annual address, Polk evoked the language of the Old Testament prophets: "Our sins, national, social, and personal, have ascended up before God, and justly provoked [his] wrath and indignation." Only the prayers of the faithful, Polk maintained, and the mediation of Jesus Christ could avert "the anger of Almighty God."[76]

Polk's theology survived its first epidemiological test intact, but a greater challenge came in the summer and fall of 1853 when a yellow fever

---

[75] Leonidas Polk, "Form of Prayer in the Episcopal Church," *The Daily Picayune*, 7 January 1849.

[76] "Journal of the Eleventh Annual Convention of the Protestant Episcopal Church of the Diocese of Louisiana, April 18–19, 1849," Historical Records of the Episcopal Church Collection, James Merrick Jones Hall, Tulane University, New Orleans, Louisiana, 154. Polk also quoted Micah 6:9, "Hear the rod and who hath appointed it."

epidemic ravaged the city. In less than five months, the disease claimed the lives of approximately 11,000 people, roughly 11 percent of the city's population, and infected a total of 40,000.[77] As historian John Bettersworth posited, "The theological implications of death in New Orleans struck deep into the vitals of Calvinist theology" and caused many of its adherents to reconsider their beliefs.[78] Yet in the face of such a horrific scene, Polk once again offered a patently jeremiadic explanation. The prayer that he prepared for the Episcopal churches was almost an exact duplicate of the one he had issued during the cholera epidemic of 1848–1849. An inference, however, can be drawn from two key phrases in the second prayer that suggest that Polk was determined to prove that human sin and divine punishment had caused the yellow fever epidemic. "Our sins," Polk wrote in 1853, have "justly provoked thy wrath and indignation against us...and mercifully grant, that...this thy fatherly correction, may teach us...hereafter to be mindful of thy righteous judgement [sic]." The 1853 prayer substituted "wrath and indignation" in place of "chastisement," and the bishop also added "righteous judgement [sic]" in place of "the uncertainty of life." These were minor changes, but in the earlier version the image that Polk conjured was that of a father disciplining his children; in the second version he described a judge pronouncing sentence against the guilty.[79]

In the midst of these calamities, some contemporaries may have been tempted to accuse Bishop Polk of clerical detachment or sanctimoniousness. But they had only to look at his experiences during the catastrophes of 1848 and 1853 to realize that he feared God more than man and that he included his own sinfulness as part of the provocation of God's wrath. The cholera

---

[77] According to John Duffy, New Orleans had an annual death toll of 1,000 between 1825 and 1860. See John Duffy, *Sword of Pestilence: The New Orleans Yellow Fever Epidemic of 1853* (Baton Rouge: Louisiana State University Press, 1966) vii, 7, 167.

[78] Bettersworth, "Protestant Beginnings in New Orleans," 838.

[79] "Prayer," *The Daily Picayune*, 24 August 1853. For more analysis on the reaction and activities of the New Orleans press and Theodore Clapp during the yellow fever epidemic, see Duffy, *Sword of Pestilence*, 76–97. During this time the Presbyterian leadership in the city also remained loyal to its Calvinist orientation. Their prayer was "that God will be pleased to turn His anger away from us, and give us grace...to repent of all our manifold sins as a city and as a people, and incline the hearts of all men to learn righteousness when His judgements are abroad in the land." See "Prayer for the City," *The Daily Picayune*, 23 August 1853.

epidemic, which struck south Louisiana in the late 1840s, also visited Polk's Leighton plantation in LaFourche Parish, killing seventy slaves. Before he could recoup these losses, a tornado ripped through his property in the spring of 1850 causing an estimated $100,000 in damage to crops and buildings. Still, Polk stood firm. "I have done all that I could," he told his wife, "I must leave the future in God's hands. If he sends this trouble, it is his will. Let him do what seemeth to him good, but though he slay me yet will I trust him."[80] The future would include the scars of yellow fever. The epidemic of 1853–1854 claimed the lives of a number of slaves, and two of the bishop's daughters contracted the disease. They survived, as did Polk's faith in the justice and mercy of his God. Even after contracting yellow fever in 1854, Polk refused to jettison his Calvinist worldview. These afflictions "seem to be one of God's great agencies," he explained to Bishop Stephen Elliott of Georgia, "to keep himself visible before the world's haughty heart and to check it up in its forgetfulness."[81] Throughout his ministry, he sent a clear message to the Episcopalians of Louisiana: the sovereignty of God was not to be questioned and Christian duty required fervent repentance and zealous obedience.

One form of Christian duty or service stressed by Polk was involvement in benevolent agencies. The practices of New Orleans Episcopalians in these endeavors were both similar to and distinctive from the programmatic activity of other humanitarian groups in the Crescent City. In response to community concerns stemming from epidemics, Protestant and Catholic groups in New Orleans founded the Poydras Asylum for Girls (1817), the Asylum for Destitute Orphan Boys (1824), and St. Mary's Orphan Boy's Asylum (1835). These institutions, unlike many orphanages in the nation, did not implement a systematic program of custodial care or religious indoctrination. Instead, they were created to address the "practical," albeit tragic, problems of dislocation associated with extraordinary times of crisis. In other words, the orphanages were only temporary relief shelters and not agencies of social control.[82] Similarly, the Howard Association (1837), a

---

[80] Quoted in Parks, *General Leonidas Polk*, 111. When Polk became bishop of Louisiana, he sold Ashwood and purchased Leighton, a sugar plantation on Bayou Lafourche in Louisiana.

[81] Leonidas Polk to Stephen Elliott, 2 October 1856, Leonidas Polk Papers.

[82] Priscilla Ferguson Clement, "Children and Charity Orphanages in New Orleans, 1817–1914," *Louisiana History* 27/4 (Fall 1986): 338–39, 350. Protestants

group of male medical-social workers, was established to combat the yellow fever epidemic of 1837. The association was nonsectarian, operated on a volunteer basis, and cared for all indigents "regardless of race, color, or sex." From 1837 to 1878, the Howard Association tended to approximately 130,000 cholera and yellow fever patients. During the yellow fever epidemic of 1857, the association treated 4,554 patients in a one-month period. Aside from dispensing medical aid, the Howard Association "mended marriages" and assisted in the relocation of "rehabilitated prostitutes."[83]

There were a number of motivating forces behind the voluntary associations of New Orleans, but social conservatism was the strongest. The St. Patrick's Total Abstinence Society (1841), the Louisiana Division of the Sons of Temperance, and the Young Men's Christian Association (1852/53) based their programs on Christian values and adopted as their goals "the reformation of character, improvement of human relationships, and inculcation of simple virtues." These voluntary associations may have had strong Christian emphases, but they were "above denominationalism and ignored sectarian walls." Indeed, the New Orleans Bible Society (1841) consisted of representatives from each of the city's four major Protestant denominations: Presbyterian, Methodist, Baptist, and Episcopalian. Nevertheless, a number of benevolent societies operated under the supervision of a single religious group. For instance, the Jewish constituency of New Orleans formed the Hebrew Benevolent Society (1828) and the Israelite Society for the Relief of the Sick and Poor (1850s) to assist the city's indigent, immigrant, widowed, and orphaned population. This wave of religious-minded benevolent activity also inspired Episcopalians. Through the Ladies' Benevolent Society (1847), Episcopal women furnished employment for "poor and destitute females" by opening a "depository" and accepting "orders for plain and ornamental needlework, knitting, netting, and marking." Financial records for 1851 indicate that the Ladies' Benevolent Society paid $979.85 "to workwomen for 4,200 pieces and that $236.50 was donated to charity." In 1859 Reverend Amos D. McCoy, rector

founded Poydras and the Asylum for Destitute Orphan Boys, and Catholics founded St. Mary's.
[83] Peggy Bassett Hildreth, "Early Red Cross: The Howard Association of New Orleans, 1837–1878," *Louisiana History* 20/1 (Winter 1979): 49, 50, 51, 61. The 1857 figures are from *The Daily Picayune*, 24 August 1853. The report covers the period from 16 July to 20 August.

of St. Peter's Church, chartered the Children's Home of the Protestant Episcopal Church, a parochial asylum for "orphans and other destitute and defenseless children, who, by holy baptism, have been made members of Christ's Kingdom." Bishop Leonidas Polk endorsed McCoy's project and urged his Louisiana diocese to lend their financial support to the Children's Home. By 1860, forty-three children were in residence.[84]

Notwithstanding the support for the Ladies' Benevolent Society and the Children's Home, the benevolent organization that most clearly defined the reforming impulses of Bishop Polk and Louisiana Episcopalians was the St. Peter's Seamen's Bethel. While other Protestant and Catholic groups in New Orleans had established asylums for orphans and widows as well as agencies for the sick and poor, the seamen's bethel represented a truly unique undertaking and exceeded the endeavors of most humanitarian societies in the Crescent City. As early as 1825, Episcopalians had attempted, under Reverend James Hull, to establish a seamen's ministry in New Orleans. Their original efforts failed because of a lack of interest on the part of the sailors and a subsequent or corresponding lack of support by local Episcopalians.[85] Then in November 1846, the Young Men's Seamen's Missionary Society leased a small home on Esplanade Street and resurrected the campaign for a seamen's ministry. Six months earlier, Polk had announced his support for the idea at the state diocesan convention. "It gives me great pleasure," he remarked, "to bring to the notice of the Convention an effort...to supply the means of spiritual edification for the seamen of the port of New Orleans." In his appeal, Polk employed simple logic: "The seamen belong to two-thirds of the whole of the commercial marine of the United States, [and] find their way every year to New Orleans." These facts, he rationalized, make this ministry "both obvious and pressing." In addition to this blanket endorsement, Polk granted to Charles W. Whithall a license as lay-reader. An interesting character in his own

---

[84] Julianna Liles Boudreaux, *A History of Philanthropy in New Orleans, 1835–1862*, 2 vols. (master's of social work, Tulane University, 1961) 1:93–98, 99–105, 107, 170. The children's home's governing board consisted of ten women from local congregations and an all–male council served in an advisory role. See also Katharine S. Rice, "A Study of the Children's Home of the Protestant Episcopal Church of the Diocese of Louisiana" (master's of social work, Tulane University, 1937).

[85] Robert C. Witcher, "The Episcopal Church in Louisiana, 1805–1861" (Ph.D. diss., Louisiana State University, 1969) 228.

right, Whithall, a former seaman and Methodist minister, was a candidate for orders in the Episcopal church and considered by Polk "to be well fitted" for the assignment.[86]

The renewed interest in the seamen's ministry coincided with the expansion of the maritime industry in New Orleans. The catalyst for this explosive period of growth was the Mexican War. Briefly, the United States government intervened in this sector of the New Orleans economy, and its involvement was designed to eliminate such problems as high insurance rates, the limited number of ships, and currency and credit shortages. The result of Federal subsidies and regulation was that the volume of maritime traffic increased exponentially. In August 1846, for example, 163 vessels passed through New Orleans custom houses; only 43 vessels had passed through during the same month in 1845.[87] Hoping to establish inroads among the burgeoning maritime population, Chaplain Whithall altered his schedule to conduct three services each Sunday and one every Friday evening. The change paid immediate dividends. "The attendance on divine service is large," Whithall recounted, "and has increased more than four fold [sic], so that frequently the house is so crowded with hearers, that many for the want of room have gone away from the doors without hearing the blessed gospel" or "enjoying the precious ordinances." Whithall sensed "much interest in the mission...not only in this city, but also among the ship owners and masters of ships, five of whom are regular communicants of the [Episcopal] church." After five months of ministry, Whithall reported that thirty-three children and four adults had been baptized, eight people had been confirmed, and the chapel had a total of fifty-seven communicants. In addition, Whithall performed twenty-four marriages and thirty-nine funerals. Hence the scope of the seamen's ministry extended beyond the lone, wayfaring sailor to include the families of an entire social caste.[88]

---

[86] "Journal of the Eighth Annual Convention of the Protestant Episcopal Church of the Diocese of Louisiana, May 22–24, 1846," Historical Records of the Episcopal Church Collection, James Merrick Jones Hall, Tulane University, New Orleans, Louisiana, 98.

[87] Gene W. Boyett, "Money and Maritime Activities in New Orleans during the Mexican War," *Louisiana History* 17/4 (Fall 1976): 426–27, 429.

[88] Whithall report in "Journal of the Ninth Annual Convention of the Protestant Episcopal Church of the Diocese of Louisiana, April 14–16, 1847," Historical Records of the Episcopal Church Collection, James Merrick Jones Hall, Tulane University, New Orleans, Louisiana, 101–102.

In addition to pastoral care, religious education served as an important aspect of the seamen's ministry. During the first five months of operation, Whithall dispersed, through sales and gratuitously, ninety-six copies of the Bible; 109 copies of the New Testament in English, fourteen in German, four in Spanish, five in Danish, sixteen in French, and two in Italian. He also circulated, often by going aboard ship, another 15,000 pages of religious tracts, and forty-two Manuals of Prayer and thirty-one Books of Common Prayer.[89] For virtually every voluntary society as well as the denomination-controlled benevolent societies, the distribution of religious literature was a carefully planned activity; this was especially true of Episcopal programs. But within the Episcopal denomination, there were differences of opinion regarding the manner in which religious literature should be disseminated. On the one hand, the high churchmen believed that if groups only distributed the Bible and did not include Manuals of Prayer and Books of Common Prayer then the recipients might "misinterpret the Bible," which could "lead to theological anarchy and schism." On the other hand, evangelicals tended to place fewer—and in some cases no restrictions—on the distribution of Scripture and religious material. An examination of St. Peter's distribution records shows that Bible and New Testaments were distributed two to three times more often than Manuals of Prayer and the Book of Common Prayer. This ratio suggests that Louisiana Episcopalians adopted a distribution philosophy that was in accord with evangelical practices.[90]

In large measure, the early success of St. Peter's Seamen's Bethel was attributable to the efforts of Chaplain Charles Whithall. However, a number of concerned parties, including Bishop Polk and representatives from the shipping industry, made significant contributions. For example, Captain Charles C. Berry of the *Silas Homes* presented a "splendid communion service," and Captain William C. Berry presented a communion table on behalf of a Reverend Diller of Brooklyn, New York. For his part, Bishop Polk provided "a beautiful bethel flag." This symbolic gesture of support actually underscored Polk's deeper commitment to the local mission. "It is not that we ask you to part with your substance for distant heathen regions,"

---

[89] Ibid.

[90] Diana Hochstedt Butler, "The Church and American Destiny: Evangelical Episcopalians and Voluntary Societies in Antebellum America," *Religion and American Culture* 4/3 (Summer 1994): 204.

Polk told the state diocesan convention of 1847, "but we are called upon to aid in the spread of the gospel of truth and peace among our own brethren, bone of our bone, and flesh of our flesh." These people, Polk elaborated, "either by reason of their poverty, or in consequence of their ruinous habits of indifference and negligence...have lapsed into a spiritual blindness, grievously destructive to their present peace, and fearfully jeopardizing their everlasting salvation." How they reached this "perishing condition" was unimportant to Polk because he believed that the Episcopal church had a solemn responsibility "before God" to meet their spiritual needs. In addition, the bishop linked "the cultivation of the moral sense" of the seamen with the maintenance of "the purity and perpetuation" of the South's social order.[91]

By 1849 the St. Peter's Seamen's Bethel had become an integral part of the Episcopal influence in New Orleans. For the calendar year ending 18 April 1849, Whithall had baptized 233 infants and 6 adults and had performed 100 marriages and 210 funerals. The bethel's membership had grown significantly and now totaled 124 communicants. The most remarkable statistic, however, was the amount of religious literature flowing out of the seamen's bethel. That same year Whithall distributed 200,000 pages of religious tracts, 186 copies of the Bible, 300 copies of the New Testament, 257 Books of Common Prayer, and 294 Manuals of Prayer. Meanwhile, plans were underway to expand the scope of the seamen's ministry. Phase one had been completed in October 1848 when a reading room opened with a stock of several hundred "books, papers, and [other] religious" materials. Whithall confirmed that many seamen frequented the reading room "during the evenings, to read and pray."[92] Phase two entailed a proposal for a boardinghouse where seamen could escape the "temptations" of the city and find "a suitable place" for "leisure" and spiritual improve-

---

[91] Whithall report in "Journal of the Ninth Annual Convention of the Protestant Episcopal Church of the Diocese of Louisiana, April 14–16, 1847," 101, 108. There was a significant connection to New York. The bethel acquired "a small organ," and Holmes's packet shipping company delivered it from New York "free of freight" along with a $20 donation from the company's New York agent, John William Nelson.

[92] "Journal of the Eleventh Annual Convention of the Protestant Episcopal Church of the Diocese of Louisiana, April 18–19, 1849," 163. A Mr. Greenleaf had already donated a Sunday school library of 100 volumes and Captain Charles G. Berry and smaller one.

ment.[93] The boardinghouse idea became a topic of intense discussion throughout the city. The opinions of both Theodore Clapp and *The Daily Picayune* provide insights into the Episcopalian motives and strategies.

The boardinghouse plan combines "all the advantages of an enlightened, refined, and happy domestic circle," Clapp reasoned, and "the inmates do not subsist on charity" but "pay a full equivalent for their accommodations." Moreover, the boardinghouse offered seamen a place to find "protection, friends, congenial society, books, newspapers, periodicals...and all the means of happiness free from the danger of moral contamination."[94] The editors of *The Daily Picayune* also supported the sailor's home but believed too much emphasis was being placed on religious instruction during the developmental stages of the housing program. "We have already a "Bethel," or "sailor's chapel," they opined, "but we have begun at the wrong end—commenced at the apex instead of the base of the pyramid—in studying Jack's welfare. We should strive to meliorate his moral and social position; there would then be something solid to build up his spiritual concerns."[95] Although *The Daily Picayune* disagreed with the priorities the Episcopalians had established, it agreed with Episcopalians that social reform was the sole responsibility of voluntary associations and churches. "One of the greatest errors of the present age of reform," the editors bemoaned, "is undoubtedly that of seeking by legislative action to correct the derangements of the vast and complicated machinery of social life." Any reasonable person could see that "the mixing up of political and social questions...by specifying the duties of citizens to the Government and to one another, has been the bane of the French people since their revolution of last year." Furthermore, the editors concluded, "legislators have no right to meddle with the social condition of the people.... [their] true mission...is limited to political government, and its necessary agents to compel the refractory to obey its mandates." Thus, support for the boardinghouse was

---

[93] "Journal of the Tenth Annual Convention of the Protestant Episcopal Church of the Diocese of Louisiana, May 3–5, 1848," Historical Records of the Episcopal Church Collection, James Merrick Jones Hall, Tulane University, New Orleans, Louisiana, 137.

[94] *The Daily Picayune*, 1 April 1849.

[95] *The Daily Picayune*, 25 March 1849.

possible because religious benevolence and social conservatism shared a common goal.[96]

In reality this dynamic manifested throughout the South. According to historian Clifford Griffin, many of the region's leaders were unprepared for and alarmed by the socioeconomic and political changes that characterized Jacksonian America, but they quickly realized that evangelical Protestantism was an "excellent means of keeping the nation under control" through its emphasis on individual piety and its condemnation of worldliness. Moreover, as Lois Banner has suggested, "Many reformers came to view the voluntary society as the perfect means whereby benevolence could be institutionalized without granting additional and potentially dangerous powers to the central government."[97] Of all the Protestant denominations, "the connection between religious virtue and social cohesion" was especially appealing to Episcopalians. In her study of benevolence in Charleston, South Carolina, Barbara Bellows chronicles the Episcopalian approach to Christian charity and concludes that efforts were made to organize the masses within a religious structure that the denomination controlled. Illustrative of this mentality was a seamen's chapel on Charleston's famed Church Street. The chapel was basically an urban satellite station where baptisms, marriages, and funerals were performed for the less fortunate. There, Chaplain William B. Yates preached from a pulpit emblazoned with the mantra: "*He Taught Them out of a Boat.*" Some observers alleged that his audience included individuals that even the Methodists no longer tried to reach. The result was a type of Episcopal subculture within the more dominant evangelical religious culture of the Old South.[98]

---

[96] *The Daily Picayune*, 6 April 1849. This particular editorial was a response to "the attempt at regulating the price of labor." It should also be noted that Louisiana had no tax–supported poor relief until 1879.

[97] Clifford S. Griffin, "Religious Benevolence as Social Control, 1815–1860," *The Mississippi Valley Historical Review* 44/3 (December 1957): 423; Lois W. Banner, "Religious Benevolence as Social Control: A Critique of an Interpretation," *Journal of American History* 60/1 (June 1973): 39–40. The major difference between Griffin and Banner is that Griffin sees religious benevolence as an attempt to regain lost power and to hold back or turn back societal change whereas Banner sees it as an attempt to cope with or adjust to societal change.

[98] According to Bellows, Charleston was unique to the South in that it eventually supported benevolence "more [as] an instrument of public policy than personal salvation." See Barbara L. Bellows, *Benevolence among Slaveholders: Assisting the Poor in*

Although sharing a similar point of view, Episcopalians in Louisiana differed from their Charlestonian counterparts in that they embraced a more sophisticated vision for their seamen's ministry. The plan for the seamen's boardinghouse in New Orleans served as one example. In addition, increased attendance and interest in St. Peter's Chapel convinced New Orleans Episcopalians to construct a new building. The new facility with a capacity to hold 400 persons was completed in July 1849 at a cost of $16,000. The members then petitioned the Louisiana diocese to convert St. Peter's Chapel into a parish church, which would grant to the members the right to elect its own vestry. The original request was denied, but in May 1858 the diocese approved the conversion of the chapel into a church when the leaders at St. Peter's accepted a stipulation that seventy seats in the church be reserved for seamen. Although the financial expenditures associated with this project interrupted all progress on the boardinghouse enterprise, the comprehensive nature of the seamen's ministry in New Orleans marked a critical juncture in Southern Episcopalian history. Because of the codicil requiring the reservation of pews for sailors, two diverse elements of Southern society, the miscreant Jack Tar and the genteel cavalier, shared the same religious space. Whether this relationship produced a hegemonic advantage for the elites or symbiotic mixture of two different religious cultures cannot be determined from the extant record. To accomplish this unusual arrangement, New Orleans Episcopalians had pursued a pragmatic philosophy rooted in evangelical and conservative thought, and, more than any other Episcopal community in the South, they had created a formula for attracting a broad-based constituency. As the resident bishop and rector of a local congregation, Leonidas Polk not only approved each step of this process but championed the cause from a position of leadership and authority.[99]

Charleston 1670–1860 (Baton Rouge: Louisiana State University Press, 1993) 39–41, 116, 53–54.

[99] For more on the personnel changes and building programs of St. Peter's Church see Herman Cope Duncan, *The Diocese of Louisiana: Some of Its History, 1838–1888* (New Orleans: A. W. Hyatt, 1888)146–47. Unfortunately, the federal troops evicted rector R. A. McCoy in June 1863 and placed the church under military control. St. Peter's reopened in September 1864 but was unable to overcome the travails of Reconstruction and on 24 October 1869 conducted its last service. Apparently, the entire seamen's ministry collapsed with St. Peter's Church.

In New Orleans, Polk established himself as a formidable religious figure. During his tenure as bishop, the diocese of Louisiana grew from 238 communicants in 1842 to 1,859 in 1861, a record as impressive as any in the South.[100] Numbers and statistics, however, do not tell the full story. In the final analysis, Bishop Leonidas Polk shaped a vision for Louisiana Episcopalians that merged evangelical principles with social conservatism. "Our purpose," he stated categorically, "is not so much the establishment of the dogmas of a sect or faction, as to settle and make permanent those great truths [so] indispensable to the perfection of the common salvation."[101] Thus, Polk's significance as a religious leader was not based on a formal systematic theology but rather on his ability to plot a course for Southern Episcopalians so that they could not only survive but compete with the evangelical denominations of the Old South. The strongest indication of his desire to broaden the appeal and influence of Episcopalianism in the South came early in his Louisiana bishopric when he warned fellow Episcopalians to guard "less jealously…[their] intellectual reputation, and [demonstrate] more concern for the salvation of the perishing multitudes around her."[102] His evangelical zeal and social conservatism gave Louisiana Episcopalians a distinctly Southern as well as evangelical identity. These pillars of the ministry—when coupled with his views on slave management, his advocacy of the University of the South, and his controversial martial commitment to the Confederate cause—made Leonidas Polk a representative figure in the Southern quest for a Christian society.

---

[100] Duncan, *The Diocese of Louisiana*, 268. Although Bishop James H. Otey started with only 117 communicants in his Tennessee diocese, he began eight years earlier and in 1861 had 1,244 communicants. See Armentrout, *James Hervey Otey*, 46.

[101] "Journal of the Sixth Annual Convention," 49–50.

[102] "Journal of the Fifth Annual Convention," 34.

CHAPTER 3

The Planter as Priest

The agrarian lords of the Old South were a diverse group, but as priest and planter, Leonidas Polk held a unique position among the region's master class. During his respective tenures as missionary bishop of the Southwest and as bishop of Louisiana, Polk operated substantial plantations in Maury County, Tennessee, and in Lafourche Parish, Louisiana. In each case, his religious convictions influenced significantly his approach to plantation management. Although farming and the plantation lifestyle became an adopted part of his pedigree, wealth and aristocratic habits were synonymous with the Polk name. And Leonidas Polk pursued anxiously those avenues that would transport him to the highest levels of Southern society. However, as he matured in his Christian commitment, he became increasingly irritated with the culture of materialism and debt that plagued many Southern planters. This tension between the accumulation of personal wealth and the call to Christian service caused Polk to reassess his role as a spiritual leader in the Episcopal church.[1] Indeed, the planter-priest attempted, first in the Upper South and later in the Gulf South, to build a biracial Christian community within the bounds of the Episcopal tradition. In this regard, Polk's career was comparable to that of Presbyterian divine Charles Colcock Jones, a man who, according to Southern religious historian Donald Mathews, "exemplified" in his private life and espoused publicly "those assumptions of class hegemony and responsibility that were essential for supporting the slaveholders' worldview." Rather than advance a simple, biblical defense of slavery, Polk and others of his persuasion

---

[1] For a theological discussion of materialism and consumerism in the antebellum South, see Kenneth M. Startup, *The Root of All Evil: The Protestant Clergy and the Economic Mind of the Old South* (Athens: University of Georgia Press, 1997).

demanded that religious instruction of slaves become a standard convention of plantation culture.[2] For his part, Polk explained to Southern Episcopalians both the spiritual and social importance of their church's evangelistic mission to the slave population. His Ashwood and Leighton plantations served as the testing grounds for his bold agenda.

Polk first revealed a curiosity about the life of a Southern planter while enrolled at West Point. Lucius Polk, the eldest of Leonidas's brothers, moved to Tennessee in 1823 to manage the holdings of their father William. Lucius often corresponded with his younger brother regarding the economic opportunities in Maury County. In time, the eldest Polk son became a well-respected and successful planter. Understanding the basics of agrarian political economy, Leonidas quizzed his brother on the access and availability of navigable streams and the number of slaves he owned as well as their market value. Also, Leonidas wondered about the social life in Maury County and questioned Lucius about his "neighbors" and the "public spirit" in the community.[3] Generally, Lucius responded with confidence, optimism, and encouragement. The reports satisfied Leonidas and he predicted that several families of Polks would prosper in Tennessee once his father relinquished control of these lands.[4]

After Polk resigned from the military in the fall of 1827, he returned to North Carolina where his interest in commercial and agricultural enterprises continued to evolve. He gained first-hand experience in plantation management during the winter of 1827 and for part of 1828 when business commitments drew the senior Polk from his Raleigh residence and Leonidas was placed in charge of his father's local affairs.[5] At that time, Polk was not seeking an apprenticeship and he cared only about the earning potential of his assets, namely the land and slaves that his father had given him. In fact, he admitted to Lucius that he lacked "the smallest inclination to farm" in either North Carolina or Tennessee. Moreover, the

[2] Donald G. Mathews, "Charles Colcock Jones and the Southern Evangelical Crusade to Form a Biracial Community," *Journal of Southern History* 41/3 (August 1975): 316.
[3] Leonidas Polk to Lucius Polk, 18 October 1825, Leonidas Polk Papers, Jesse duPont Library, University of the South, Sewanee, Tennessee (hereafter cited as Leonidas Polk Papers).
[4] Leonidas Polk to Lucius Polk, 25 August 1826, Leonidas Polk Papers.
[5] Joseph H. Parks, *General Leonidas Polk, C.S.A: The Fighting Bishop* (Baton Rouge: Louisiana State University Press, 1962) 44.

"inconveniences" of plantation life were simply a means to an end in his opinion. Ultimately, Polk wanted to secure enough income so that he could live "decently & honourably" and be free "from apprehension and want." Whether the financial security came from the interest on his investments or resulted from plantation profits, Polk sought only to maintain the standards of his privileged upbringing.[6] He actually accomplished this objective when he married Frances Ann Devereux on 6 May 1830, thereby uniting two prominent and extremely wealthy North Carolina families. For Leonidas, the marriage essentially guaranteed his position among the Old South's aristocracy.[7]

In anticipation of the change from bachelor to husband, in the winter of 1829–1830 the young seminarian had instructed his father to liquidate his assets. William Polk obliged and actually purchased most of the holdings himself.[8] The money, of course, would put the newlyweds on a firm foundation, but, more importantly, Leonidas envisioned the ministry as an all-consuming endeavor that would require his undivided attention and he therefore had neither the time nor inclination to devote to the proper management of his assets. Indeed, Polk felt a special burden for the spiritual "welfare of [his] fellow creatures," and was committed to employ his "time and talents…in unfolding and explaining the scheme of redemption, and in urging its acceptance." Polk understood the preaching of the gospel to be his "obvious and unavoidable duty." Accordingly, he pledged to disregard "all other concerns" that might "interfere" with his calling, and promised "to concern" himself no longer with "worldly affairs" except for those that were absolutely "necessary." Polk realized that "this course" differed dramatically from the pursuits of his brothers. He regretted that he might "not see" his brother Lucius "for many years," and that their dream for an agrarian empire in Tennessee might dissipate under the cosmic manipulations of the "supreme Governor of the Universe."[9]

In retrospect, Polk's early reflections proved nothing more than the musings of a young man who was consumed with Christianity and somewhat naïve concerning the demands and stresses of the ministry. His personal

---

[6] Leonidas Polk to Lucius Polk, 22 August 1828, Leonidas Polk Papers.

[7] William S. Powell, *Dictionary of North Carolina Biography*, 6 vols. (Chapel Hill: University of North Carolina Press, 1979–1996) 2:58–59.

[8] Parks, *General Leonidas Polk*, 52.

[9] Leonidas Polk to William Polk, 3 February 1830, Leonidas Polk Papers.

confidence and enthusiasm for the ministry soon crumbled under the
pressures exerted by the congregation of Monumental Church in Richmond,
Virginia. Furthermore, the decisions he made following his return from
Europe in the fall of 1832 confirm that his heart was being pulled in several
different directions. With a wife and infant son, his family became a primary
concern, and once again the lure of Tennessee tempted his confused spirit.
Lucius urged his brother to join him in Maury County, where he and his
new bride, Mary Eastin, the grandniece of Rachel Jackson (Mrs. Andrew
Jackson), were planning to raise their family.[10] Another variable entered the
equation when Polk's father-in-law, John Devereux, offered the couple an
improved plantation and seventy slaves as an enticement to remain in North
Carolina. The proposition was more than a kind-hearted gesture.

The family patriarch was extremely eager to keep his daughter in
North Carolina. He worried that a prolonged separation from his darling
Fanny would be a "painful" prospect and would reduce dramatically his role
of promoting "her happiness." Perhaps Polk's impulsive fourteen-month
European escapade or his general state of indecisiveness heightened
Devereux's concern about his daughter leaving the physical boundaries of
his supervision. Also, Devereux worried whether his son-in-law's "health
and...constitution [would] enable him to endure such fatigue and exposure"
that were commonly associated with the construction and maintenance of a
profitable plantation. In fact, Devereux formally presented his proposal to
Polk's father hoping that the elder statesman might convince his son to
choose the "familiar and...abundant" comforts of the Devereux's Hills Ferry
plantation over the frontier conditions of Tennessee. Devereux explained
that the plantation had an estimated value of $75,000, possessed land of the
"first quality," and produced an annual income of $4,500. Although the 1831
crop year had not been a "favorable one" in Devereux's opinion, he had
harvested 2,000 barrels of corn, received one offer of $2 per barrel, and
speculated that he could earn as much as $2.50 a barrel by delivering the
corn directly to a local crib. In addition, Devereux had sold cotton for 11¢
per pound and had made a handsome profit. Thus, the Hills Ferry

[10] For details of Polk's post-Europe activities, see Parks, *General Leonidas Polk*,
62–69. Lucius married while Leonidas was in Europe. The wedding was a grand
affair and was hosted by President Andrew Jackson at the White House.

plantation was a generous offer, and the option presented as much security and earning potential as could be reasonably expected.[11]

Moreover, Devereux had every intention of adding to the original gift just as soon as he eliminated some personal debts and fulfilled certain obligations to his other children. Specifically, Devereux had one outstanding note of $11,000 due in four years and another $10,000 note due on demand. For a man of Devereux's wealth, these debts were not particularly troublesome, but they restricted his financial maneuverability. As a result, he proposed to William Polk that he assume the two debts, and in exchange, Leonidas would be given the Hills Ferry plantation free of "every encumbrance." Devereux also asked that he be given a portion of Polk's western lands as remuneration. Apparently, Devereux was only motivated by the desire to increase his liquidity so that together he and the senior Polk "might...add" to the size of their children's estate. In fact, Devereux felt that parents must compensate for the inexperience of their children, and must "prevent [them from] feeling degraded in their own situations." Despite his intervening, Devereux was convinced that his son-in-law had made up his mind to go to Tennessee in order to build "a new establishment...in his own style." If William could not or would not convince his son to accept the offer, then Devereux was willing to pledge $500 to help defray relocation expenses. He also promised to provide the couple with four trusted house servants and thirty slaves of the "family" variety, meaning Leonidas and Fanny would not be given thirty prime field hands. Having considered every possibility, Devereux resigned himself to trust God for personal blessings and prosperity "so that in a little while" he might provide his son-in-law and daughter with "thirty or forty more Negroes" and additional gifts. Devereux assumed that Leonidas "had enough to make a handsome beginning," and believed that his son-in-law was not "in haste to be rich." The senior Devereux was only correct on the first count.[12]

As expected, Leonidas opted to follow his brother to Tennessee. The young family departed Raleigh in late April 1833 full of optimism and excitement, but the three-week trip produced hardships and heartache. A pregnant Frances suffered a particularly difficult time and tragedy struck when she delivered a stillborn son near Knoxville, Tennessee. Their grief

[11] John Devereux to William Polk, 21 November 1832, Leonidas Polk Papers.
[12] Ibid.

subsided somewhat when they reached Hamilton Place, the home of Lucius and Mary Polk, in mid-May. The reunion stirred old memories and inspired new dreams. Most of all, Leonidas was happy to be among family. He informed his mother that he had been "very cordially received by Lucius and Mary" and had become "pleasantly situated…in two adjoining chambers" of Lucius's home. The grandchildren also appeared to have adapted well to the new arrangements. Hamilton, the two-and-a-half-year-old son of Leonidas and Frances, was fit and "lively." Likewise, "Hamy's" cousin Sarah, the namesake of the Polk family matriarch and daughter of Lucius and Mary, had charmed the entire clan, and they all regarded her as a "sweet, good tempered little baby."[13]

Leonidas was always at ease around family members, and the smooth transition and comfortable surroundings allowed him to concentrate on personal affairs. First, he negotiated a settlement with his tenant Mr. Fleming and assumed immediate control of and responsibility for the crops that Fleming had planted. In the transfer, Polk received a very functional four-room house, and despite the hospitality of Lucius and Mary, he decided to move his family to his own property in order to supervise more closely the farming operations and to begin the construction of a new home.[14] The priest settled quickly into his second profession and as a planter he soon became engrossed with tending his crops and improving his land and buildings. The frenzied activity on Polk's plantation bewildered some of his new friends and neighbors. A few of them even accused him of peculiar habits. In fact, when his father visited in mid-1833, he drew similar conclusions but tempered his scrutiny with fatherly love and a bit of humor. Indeed, the aging colonel remarked that if his son rebuilt, changed, and accomplished all that he intended then his millstones would need to grind out gold dust. If nothing else, William's observations indicated that his son was definitely intent on doing things his own way and was determined to succeed on a grand scale. Not surprisingly, Leonidas predicted that by the time his mother made her first visit to Tennessee she could expect to see a fenced and landscaped estate with large herds of milch cows while "the

---

[13] Leonidas Polk to Sarah Polk, 28 May 1833, Leonidas Polk Papers.
[14] Leonidas Polk to Sarah Polk, 17 August 1833, Leonidas Polk Papers.

woods [would be] teeming with young mules and their mammies."[15] Polk had good reason for such optimism.

Between 1820 and 1860, agriculture flourished in Middle Tennessee, and both yeoman as well as the few planters of the region capitalized on a number of opportunities. Not only in Middle Tennessee but throughout the state, corn reigned as the premier cash crop. Tennesseeans, in fact, produced nearly 45 million bushels of corn in 1840, a total that exceeded the output of any other state in the union. Most Tennessee farmers, including those in Middle Tennessee, earned their living in a corn and livestock economy. Middle Tennessee's favorable growing season and diverse soil types, however, did lead to the cultivation of other crops. As early as the 1790s, the decade of Tennessee's statehood, the region discovered cotton as a viable cash staple, and farmers in Maury and Lincoln counties raised it in significant quantities. Tobacco, Tennessee's second largest cash crop in 1840, was also important, especially in the Nashville Basin counties of Davidson and Montgomery. In addition, some farmers in the state's heartland produced appreciable amounts of hemp, and all farmers, of course, grew timothy, red clover, rye, and oats as the principal feeds for their livestock.[16]

According to historian Stephen Ash, the political economy of Middle Tennessee represented a type of "third South," one noticeably different from both the Southern highlands and the Deep South. "Broad prosperity, a large slave population, and widespread slave holding" characterized the region, but its "agricultural wealth" rested primarily "in the hands of middle-class farmers" who owned few or no slaves.[17] There were, however, exceptions to this rule. For instance, Mark Cockrill, the planter-breeder of the 5,000-acre Robertson's Bend plantation in Davidson County, amassed a sizeable fortune as a wool producer. He first introduced Merino sheep to Middle Tennessee in 1824, and his wool products won a medal at the 1851 London Exposition. By 1860 his stock of 3,500 sheep yielded 10,000 pounds

---

[15] Leonidas Polk to Sarah Polk, 15 September 1833, Leonidas Polk Papers.

[16] Chase C. Mooney, *Slavery in Tennessee* (Bloomington: Indiana University Press, 1957) 128, 139; Lewis C. Gray, *History of Agriculture in the Southern United States to 1860*, 2 vols. (Gloucester, Mass.: Peter Smith, 1933) 2:687; Stephen V. Ash, *Middle Tennessee Society Transformed 1860–1870: War and Peace in the Upper South* (Baton Rouge: Louisiana State University Press, 1988) 16–18.

[17] Ash, *Middle Tennessee Society Transformed*, xi, 15.

of wool.[18] Equally impressive was Robertson County tobacco baron, George A. Washington, the second largest slaveholder in Tennessee in 1860. With 274 slaves and 5,000 improved acres, Robertson's workforce produced 50,000 bushels of wheat, 22,000 bushels of corn, and an astounding 250,000 pounds of tobacco in 1859.[19] Although no one in the Polk family ever rivaled the power and success of Mark Cockrill or George A. Washington, the family more closely resembled these exceptional figures than the middle-class yeomen and husbandmen who dominated Middle Tennessee's agricultural economy.[20]

Clearly, an industrious planter with imagination and a keen business mind could succeed in Middle Tennessee. Unfortunately, virtually no information has survived regarding Leonidas Polk's plantation affairs in that region. Having operated in Maury County prior to 1850, census records before that date do not include detailed analyses of crop yields or livestock holdings. Moreover, his personal correspondence contains little more than vague references to the actual productivity on his plantation. Yet, contemporary observers and subsequent generations of agricultural and economic historians have developed a number of land and labor ratios for calculating agricultural output. The evidence derived from these models is a reasonable substitute for the lack of documentary evidence. In his *History of Agriculture in the Southern United States*, Lewis Gray concluded that in the "very hilly portions" of South Carolina, Georgia, Alabama, and Mississippi one hand could produce approximately three acres of cotton. A higher production ratio existed in portions of the Southwest where planters

---

[18] Mooney, *Slavery in Tennessee*, 199. Cockrill also owned a Mississippi cotton plantation with 135 slaves. For more on Cockrill, see "Editorial Miscellany," *De Bow's Review* 29/4 (July–December 1860): 248–56; George H. Stueckrath, "Incidents in the Early Settlement of the State of Tennessee, and Nashville," *De Bow's Review* 27 (July–December 1859): 84–94.

[19] Washington's 5,000 acres of improved land was sixty-seven times the regional median. See Robert Tracy McKenzie, *One South or Many? Plantation Belt and Upcountry in Civil War-Era Tennessee* (New York: Cambridge University Press, 1994) 21.

[20] In 1850, three Polk brothers, Lucius, Andrew J., and George W., farmed in Maury County. Together their respective farms were valued at $192,000. By combining their individual records from the 1850 census, they owned 260 slaves and 3,470 improved acres, produced 32,500 bushels of corn and 1,400 pounds of wool, held 1,250 swine worth $28,980, and Andrew J. produced 230 bales of cotton on his own. Figures adapted from Mooney, *Slavery in Tennessee*, 165–66.

typically harvested ten acres of cotton and six acres of corn per hand. But in areas such as Middle Tennessee with "rolling" terrain and where farmers placed "considerable attention...[on] animal husbandry," cotton yields averaged from five to seven acres per hand. Gray also stated that less than six acres of corn per hand did not adequately provide for "laborers and work stock."[21]

The census of 1840 indicates that Leonidas Polk owned 111 slaves, which made him the largest slaveholder in Maury County and one of only two people in the county with more than 100 slaves. Of Polk's slave total, thirty-seven were under age ten, and five were between the ages of fifty-five and a hundred, leaving forty-six males and twenty-three females between the ages of ten and fifty-five.[22] Yet, the sixty-nine slaves between the ages of ten and fifty-five cannot be properly designated as full field hands. By using the variant figure of fifty field hands and land and labor ratios of six acres of corn and six acres of cotton per hand, one might estimate that under ideal conditions Polk's slaves could have tended 300 acres of corn and 300 acres of cotton. Such output figures would have been unlikely because Polk employed slaves in other capacities such as growing and processing hemp as well as on construction details for his new home. Generally speaking, a cotton farmer of Polk's class could have expected an annual yield of no more than 100 bales, which after the subtraction of freight, storage, insurance, and brokerage fees netted roughly $3,000 on the New Orleans market in 1839.[23] By contrast, corn yields typically fared better than cotton yields. An annual

[21] Gray, *History of Agriculture*, 2:707–708.

[22] The Maury County population consisted of 17,900 whites, 11,000 slaves, and 94 free blacks. I. [?] P. Bayley was the second largest slaveholder in the county with 102, and Polk's brothers, Lucius and Rufus, owned 68 and 62 slaves respectively. See United States Census Office, *Sixth Census of the United States*, 1840. *Population Schedule, Maury County, Tennessee* (Washington DC: Government Printing Office, 1843).

[23] On one of his Tennessee plantations with a total slave population of 132, William Polk produced 111 bales in 1829. In 1839, Lucius Polk sold 102 bales through M. D. Cooper and Co. of New Orleans for $3,801.19 but received $3,351.85 after fee and service deductions. Andrew Jackson Polk, a committed cotton planter, produced only 270 bales in 1849 with a total slave population of 168 and 1,800 improved acres. All examples from Mooney, *Slavery in Tennessee*, 163–64.

output of 10,000 bushels would not have been unusual for planters of Polk's class.[24]

Regardless of the productivity and profitability of Polk's agricultural enterprises, he deemed it necessary to pursue additional investment opportunities. For instance, he joined regional efforts to promote railroad development in the Nashville area. His interest in such projects stemmed in part from his support of technological progress and his desire to improve the transportation systems of the South. But, the Polks also viewed railroads as sound investments. As a stockholder in a North Carolina railroad company, Polk's mother had earned a 300 percent return on her original investment. Polk hoped that he could duplicate his mother's financial success. However, the economic turmoil in the mid-1830s that culminated in the Panic of 1837 prevented rapid or consistent headway on the project and no remaining evidence suggests that he reaped a windfall from railroad investments.[25]

Nevertheless, wealth and economic prosperity continued to hold a significant place in Polk's immediate plans and his general outlook on life. During the summer of 1837, he moved into a new home, which he called Ashwood. The furnishings confirmed his rich tastes and appreciation for luxurious living. From W. W. Chester's of New York, Polk received quotes on two "handsome maple setters with cane bottoms & backs," one dozen mahogany chairs, and curtains and windows for the parlor, dining room, and bedrooms. Eventually, family friend William S. Johnson made several purchases from New York firms on behalf of Leonidas and Lucius Polk. The quantity of dishes and tableware that Leonidas Polk ordered from Baldwin Gardiner's gives the impression that the planter-prelate expected to entertain guests on a grand scale. One china dining and dessert set consisted of approximately 200 assorted dishes, plates, and bowls. An additional two dozen tea cups and saucers and two dozen coffee bowls and saucers complemented the china set. Interestingly, the $480.72 that Leonidas spent

---

[24] According to Lewis C. Gray, farmers in regions similar to Middle Tennessee produced thirty-five to fifty bushels of corn per acre, see Gray, *History of Agriculture*, 2:2:816. In 1849, Lucius Polk, with a total slave population of sixty-one and 900 improved acres, produced 10,000 bushels of corn as well as 800 pounds of tobacco, suggesting that he was not simply a grain producer. See Mooney, *Slavery in Tennessee*, 165.

[25] William M. Polk, *Leonidas Polk: Bishop and General*, 2 vols. (New York, 1915) 1:149–50.

on china, tableware, and cutlery fell well short of the $1,149.61 that Lucius spent on an order that included two sets of china and $600 worth of silver serving pieces. Clearly rural Tennessee would not dampen the Polks' fashionable and genteel spirit.[26]

Polk's agricultural interests and financial dealings easily identified him with the aristocratic class of the Old South, and he readily supported the region's patriarchal social order. The strongest evidence of his class-consciousness appears in the correspondence between Polk and his youngest sister Susan. Since the death of his father in January 1834, Polk—although not the eldest male in the family—had on occasion assumed the role of family patriarch. He routinely offered family members a mixture of practical as well as pastoral advice, and he expressed a particular interest in Susan's affairs. In October 1835 Polk sent his sister $400 so that she could assemble a fall and winter wardrobe and retire several small debts that she had incurred during a recent tour of Europe.[27] The fatherly attachment reached its apogee in August 1839 when Susan received a marriage proposal from a distant relative, whose surname was Dickinson. Marriage, Polk counseled, possessed the power "to affect...worldly happiness" and quite possibly the potential to "determine...[one's] lot for eternity." Therefore, a "marriage connection" should only be made after careful deliberation. Indeed, Polk suspected that "nine-tenths of the unhappy marriages of the world [arose] from want of thought, and [were] founded on the most frivolous possible pretences." Still, he believed that marriage, when initiated under the proper conditions, represented the surest way for Susan to attain a safe, secure, and enjoyable future. The proper conditions included a reliable source of wealth.[28]

Money, Polk acknowledged, was not the "chief good" in life, nor was the ability to achieve financial success the requisite quality of a "suitable" marriage partner. Nevertheless, Polk wittily remarked, "People can't live on the wind, they must have something more substantial." He further contended that "money...[was] positively necessary both to happiness and respectability, and it would be a hazardous enterprise to attempt life without it." He also insisted that "the means of living don't just grow...without

---

[26] Receipts and invoices in Miscellaneous Papers, Leonidas Polk Papers.
[27] Leonidas Polk to Susan Polk, 23 October 1835, Leonidas Polk Papers.
[28] Leonidas Polk to Susan Polk, 16 August 1839, Leonidas Polk Papers.

effort" but was only acquired through dedication and hard work. In the bishop's estimation, Dickinson was "a mere drone." He considered the suitor's lack of "an avocation, a destitution" that would prove "fatal to the pretensions of any man." Consequently, he advised Susan to reject the marriage proposal of Mr. Dickinson. How Susan reacted to her brother's advice is not known, but she obviously pleased her brother when she rebuffed Dickinson's hand in marriage.[29]

In addition, Polk viewed Dickinson's personal shortcomings as emblematic of a type of ethical laxity prevalent among certain classes of Southerners. Specifically, Polk expressed dissatisfaction with the moral ambiguity exhibited by some social elites and accused them of lacking integrity and character. "A man of unexceptionable principles," Polk explained, was not guided by "an inflated, boastful talking of "my honor," and "high minded and honorable men" and "high toned character" and such matters. These traits were "perfectly compatible with deception, bad faith, lack of moral courage, bad temper and blasphemy." In contrast, men of principle "fear to do wrong, because to do wrong is mean, hurtful to conscience, and displeasing to God."[30] The timing of this critical outburst coincided with the turning point of Polk's ministerial career. Just eight months earlier in December 1838, Polk had been consecrated missionary bishop of the Southwest, and he completed his first missionary journey in mid-summer 1839. From these experiences, he gained a deeper appreciation for both his personal faith and the ministry, which translated into a greater resolve to preach against the excesses of materialism and avarice. Shortly thereafter, Polk heard the echoes of his own sermons when he became mired in a financial quagmire that pitted his Christian patience against the standard operating habits and practices of Southern businessmen.

Sometime in the mid-1830s, the Polk brothers, Leonidas and Lucius, backed a business venture by family friend A. D. Harris of Columbia, Tennesseee, and his associate Mr. Caruthers. The ties between the Polks and the two entrepreneurs dated back to 1833. At that time, William Polk, who already had a business relationship with Caruthers, loaned Harris

---

[29] Ibid. Susan eventually married Kenneth Rayner of North Carolina, a prominent Whig politician who served in the United States Congress from 1839 to 1845.

[30] Ibid.

$5,000 to invest in a New Orleans commission business.[31] Somewhat later, Leonidas established a friendship with Harris based on their mutual involvement in the Episcopal church; Polk called Harris his "right arm in every good work" that they accomplished for the church. Harris, in fact, served as a vestryman and warden in Polk's church in Tennessee, and when Harris asked for a business loan the prelate regarded the request as a sound business prospect and an opportunity to assist a fellow churchman. Regrettably, for both Leonidas and Lucius who co-signed the note, Harris's new venture folded. The collapse saddled the two brothers with an enormous debt. For his part, Leonidas hoped to "escape" with a $15,000 loss. With hindsight as a clear guide, Polk admitted that he had been "indiscreet" in making the original decision, but he did not hold Harris personally responsible, citing the "reverses of the times" as the main culprit. Moreover, Polk stated that if given the opportunity he "would do again what [he] did" because he believed he "was doing a good work."[32] Leonidas appeared ready to follow the dictates of Christian forgiveness and turn the other cheek. Lucius, however, viewed the situation in a different light.

Apparently, Lucius contemplated some form of retaliation against Harris and Caruthers and possibly considered challenging Harris to a duel. In the midst of their troubles, Leonidas warned his brother that "nothing but harm can result from either attacking them by language or action." Moreover, the bishop advised that "violence…never yet answered any good purpose" and might force Harris to become "reckless & desperate." The prudent response, according to Polk, would be for the two brothers to "quietly" pocket their losses, pay their "liabilities," allow Harris "a fair chance to act the gentleman & man of honor," and inform him that they expected to be reimbursed for their losses. "This is the sensible course," the bishop argued, and "Christian forbearance demands that we should obtain & keep mastery over ourselves & maintain an attitude of courtesy toward" those who offended or aggrieved us.[33] Although Polk disapproved of violence as a solution to his financial woes, he confessed to his friend, Bishop Charles P. McIlvaine of Ohio, that "of all human ills, debt to a clergyman is, perhaps, as grievous as any." Polk resented the time and attention he had to

---

[31] Parks, *General Leonidas Polk*, 88.
[32] Leonidas Polk to Charles P. McIlvaine, 10 August 1840, Leonidas Polk Papers.
[33] Leonidas Polk to Lucius Polk, 2 April 1840, Leonidas Polk Papers.

devote to "arranging and running" his financial affairs because the distractions lessened his "usefulness." For the moment, Polk stopped short of washing his hands of the South's aristocratic notions of wealth, but he clearly expressed a concern over the growing conflict between his own clerical obligations and the material excesses and culture of debt that ensnared many members of his own social class.[34]

Despite some misgivings, Polk still considered the agrarian, country-gentleman ideal to be a proper avenue to wealth and respectability. Accordingly, in an effort to align his clerical duties more closely with his familial responsibilities and planter aspirations, in mid-1841 Polk purchased a sugar plantation in southern Louisiana. The decision rested in part on Polk's desire to establish a residence closer to the "geographical center" of his ecclesiastical jurisdiction and thereby reduce the lengthy periods of separation from his family that occurred during his missionary travels.[35] Not long after Polk purchased the Louisiana plantation, he received word that he had been elected bishop of Louisiana, which made relocation a matter of practical necessity. Polk and his brother Lucius agreed that sugar planting in Louisiana presented more opportunities for financial advancement than cotton farming and husbandry in Middle Tennessee, especially in the aftermath of the Panic of 1837 when cotton prices plummeted. Thus, a number of factors influenced Polk's decision to embark on yet another endeavor, one that required patience, dedication, and large sums of capital, and one where miscalculation, misfortune, or lack of commitment could spell disaster.

After carefully weighing his options, Polk purchased Leighton plantation from James Porter for $100,000. The well-developed tract, which covered 2,500 arpents including 1,000 to 1,100 arpents of arable land, rested on the right bank of Bayou Lafourche about 1 mile above Thibodaux and some 60 miles southwest of New Orleans. To acquire Leighton, Polk borrowed heavily and entered into financial agreements with several parties; evidently the losses he suffered at the hands of A. D. Harris had not impaired his ability to secure credit. He signed two notes with Union Bank of Louisiana that totaled $27,945. With Porter, he agreed to pay on demand

[34] Leonidas Polk to Charles P. McIlvaine, 10 August 1840, Leonidas Polk Papers.
[35] Polk, *Leonidas Polk*, 1:176.

one note of $5,220 and negotiated a seven-year contract for an additional fourteen payments of $5,313.77.[36]

Although the acquisition of Leighton represented a serious investment in terms of money and time, Polk did not liquidate his Tennessee holdings. To solidify his financial footing, he activated an option on an inheritance obtained by his wife Frances, who had become a beneficiary in the settlement of the estate of her uncle, George Pollock. Under the terms of the agreement, the Polks could receive their $100,000 gift in land, slaves, or installment payments. If Polk intended to operate Leighton at an optimum level, more slaves would be needed. Therefore, he accepted 161 slaves valued at $50,132 and the remainder of the inheritance in deferred payments. Less than a year later, Polk found himself strapped for cash and asked his mother for a $10,000 loan. Sarah Polk had sufficient resources to assist her son, but son-in-law Kenneth Rayner, the Whig congressman, had her assets tied up in investments. Consequently, with limited liquid capital she was unable to fulfill her son's request. Polk did, however, find a creditor, possibly James Porter, and he secured a $25,000 advance on his anticipated sugar crop. Polk concealed the identity of his creditor feeling that it was "hardly worth while [sic] for these affairs to be much before the public." Reassured by the new line of credit, he relayed a message to "Brother Rayner" that if he managed to keep the tariff low, then Polk himself would have money to lend.[37]

Notwithstanding the indebtedness that Polk had acquired, Leighton itself was a sound investment. As cotton prices declined sharply throughout

---

[36] The financial transactions are discussed in Parks, *General Leonidas Polk*, 93–94. The physical descriptions of Leighton are based on an 1848 assessment made by Solon Robinson. See H. A. Keller, ed., *Solon Robinson, Pioneer and Agriculturalist*, 2 vols. (Indianapolis: Indiana Historical Bureau, 1936) 1:201. According to J. Carlyle Sitterson, an arpent was a French unit of measure that was locally defined and varied from .84 acres to 1.28 acres, see J. Carlyle Sitterson, *Sugar Country: The Cane Sugar Industry in the South, 1753–1950* (Lexington: University of Kentucky Press, 1953) 11.

[37] Leonidas Polk to Sarah Polk, 9 June 1843, Leondias Polk Papers. As late as 1850, Polk still owed Mrs. James Porter, the heir of the Porter estate, $20,000. Since Polk's original agreement of fourteen payments to Porter expired in 1848 it is possible that the $20,000 he owed Mrs. Porter in 1850 was the remaining balance of a second loan. See discussion of Polk's finances in A. McWilliams to Charles P. Leverich, 20 June 1850, in Leverich Correspondence, Louisiana and Lower Mississippi Valley Collections, Hill Memorial Library, Louisiana State University, Baton Rouge, Louisiana.

the 1840s, sugar planting became an attractive alternative, particularly in Louisiana. According to historian J. Carlyle Sitterson, Louisiana produced as much as 95 percent of the South's entire antebellum sugar crop. The most productive sugar lands in Louisiana bordered on Bayou Lafourche, which stretched some 120 miles from the Mississippi River to the Gulf of Mexico and encompassed parts of such parishes as Plaquemines, Lafourche, Terrebonne, St. Mary, Assumption, St. James, Ascension, and Iberville. Although the sugar industry "was in dire financial straits" from 1838 to 1841, higher sugar prices in the 1840s and 1850s bolstered the sagging industry and placed it on a steady course to recovery. The potential for and realization of greater profits enhanced the commercial value of sugar plantations, and sugar planters enjoyed an ever-increasing social stature throughout the region. Thus, Polk found himself entering the sugar business at an opportune time, and Leighton's location placed the bishop in the social and economic center of Louisiana's sugar culture.[38]

Polk's career as a sugar planter, which lasted from 1841 to 1854, paralleled the sugar industry's period of general prosperity. Despite his original inexperience with the basic operations and methods of sugar planting, famed agriculturalist Solon Robinson classified Polk as "an experimenting and improving planter" when he visited Leighton in 1848. Robinson's review came at the conclusion of Polk's seventh full year of sugar planting. By then, he had become well acquainted with the work routine and scheduling problems that confronted every sugar planter.[39] But the nature of sugar production demanded that planters be receptive to agricultural experimentation and demonstrate a familiarity with scientific principles. Indeed, "sugar," as one historian has noted, "was unique among southern staples in that the boiling of cane juice constituted a manufacturing process, and it therefore stood to benefit more from the proliferation of scientific knowledge in the mid-nineteenth century than did any other commercial crop produced in the slave states."[40] While Polk was clearly not in the class of such scientific planters as Edmund Ruffin, John S. Skinner, Pierre Rost, John Wesley Monette, James Hamilton Couper, or Dr. Martin W. Philips,

---

[38] Sitterson, *Sugar Country*, 13, 177, 164.

[39] Keller, *Solon Robinson, Pioneer and Agriculturalist*, 1:202.

[40] William K. Scarborough, "Science on the Plantation," in *Science and Medicine in the Old South*, ed. Ronald L. Numbers and Todd L. Savitt (Baton Rouge: Louisiana State University Press, 1989) 82.

Robinson reported that Polk utilized progressive or innovative techniques in the cultivation and processing of sugar. Some of the improvements that captured Robinson's attention were of a simplistic nature. Whereas most planters, for example, elevated their cane on a carrier during the manufacturing process "so as to pitch it down in the mill," Robinson was impressed that Polk constructed a "level" transporting system that fed the cane into "the mill in a very regular manner." The intent of this new method was to prevent the accidental waste of cane juice at the beginning of the extracting process.[41]

In other ways, Polk departed from the restraints of conservative management and embraced the latest trends or technology of the sugar industry. Perhaps the most disputed aspect of cane cultivation was the rule of thumb used to determine the distance between cane rows. Prior to the 1840s, planters set rows anywhere from 2 1/2 to 4 feet apart, arguing that narrow rows generated the greatest yields. By the 1850s, a shift toward wider rows appeared. Most cane planters settled on a standard of six-foot rows, claiming that the increased width allowed slaves to weed cane plants with two-mule plows thereby reducing the labor intensive practice of hoeing by 75 percent.[42] Polk, along with Valcour Aime of St. James Parish, was part of a small group of progressive planters who advocated eight-foot rows as a way to prevent mules or horses from trampling on the cane during the heavy plowing months of May and June. Another question with which sugar planters wrestled concerned the advantages and disadvantages of using oxen, mules, or horses as plowing teams. Some planters preferred horses over mules, contending that "horses cost about half as much as mules, [did] more work, and live[d] nearly as long," which made them the more economical choice. Polk seemed undecided on this issue, as he owned a few oxen and an equal distribution of mules and horses.[43] Like most sugar planters who owned herds of livestock and farm animals, Polk did not appreciate fully the soil-enhancing properties of animal manure.[44] Instead, he followed the advice of his overseer, Mr. Boatner, who recommended vegetable fertilizers. Boatner, described by Robinson as a "very intelligent overseer," preferred

---

[41] Keller, *Solon Robinson, Pioneer and Agriculturalist*, 1:202–203.

[42] Sitterson, *Sugar Country*, 114–15.

[43] Polk owned a total of seventy-five horses and mules. Keller, *Solon Robinson, Pioneer and Agriculturalist*, 1:203.

[44] Sitterson, *Sugar Country*, 126.

rotted bagasse to green bagasse on the theory that the latter "injures the land" while the former was simply "the best manure in the world." Polk also deferred to Boatner on plowing techniques. The overseer was skeptical of the efficiency of deep or "subsoil" plowing, which Robinson favored, and preferred instead the Beranger or Jacob plows "in stiff land."[45]

As the price and maintenance of slaves rose in the late antebellum period, planters searched for ways to reduce labor costs. Most experts agreed that the plow was an extremely valuable labor-saving device.[46] At Leighton, Polk's slaves manufactured a variety of agricultural implements ranging from hoes and spades to carts and wagons. The quality of the equipment impressed Robinson. In fact, he remarked that Polk possessed "one of the best fluke plows...I have seen anywhere. The [plow's] beam is 5 1/2 feet long, 17 inches high." Generally speaking, most of Polk's equipment was of a high caliber—especially the mill.[47] During the grinding process, the average sugar planter expressed fifty to fifty-five pounds of juice from 100 pounds of cane. On rare occasions, a planter expressed as much as sixty-five pounds of juice from 100 pounds of cane, but even under optimal conditions as much as 28 percent of the juice was not collected.[48] Polk's grinding operations, however, produced exceptional results that varied from a low of sixty-two pounds to a high of sixty-seven pounds of juice per 100 pounds of cane. "To do this," Robinson surmised, "the mill must be first rate." In addition, Polk attempted to reduce expenses and increase profits through other means. For example, he conducted a limited experiment on seven acres of land by "stripping the cane of [its] leaves, to give it a better opportunity to mature." Slave children, "whose labor was not of much value at that season or for any other purpose," stripped the cane, and even if their labor "had been valuable," Polk thought that the stripping "greatly facilitated" the work of the cane cutters and was therefore a practical or time-saving step. The results of the experiment—"21 hogsheads of good sugar from seven acres"—exceeded the production yields of the larger fields. Polk believed that the technique held great promise, but Robinson was not

---

[45] Keller, *Solon Robinson, Pioneer and Agriculturalist*, 1:204.

[46] Sitterson, *Sugar Country*, 127–28.

[47] Keller, *Solon Robinson, Pioneer and Agriculturalist*, 1:203–204.

[48] Sitterson, *Sugar Country*, 139.

totally persuaded because the experiment had been conducted on first-year rattoons, which generally produced high yields.[49]

Robinson displayed greater skepticism concerning Polk's decision to raise swine and cure his own pork. Conceived as a cost-cutting measure, the plan called "for every mouth" at Leighton to receive half a pound of pork per day, which, calculated over the course of a year, was approximately 73,000 pounds. The incredible expense caused Robinson to "doubt the policy," and he offered several objections to its implementation. First, he did not consider the hot, humid climate of southern Louisiana conducive to curing pork. In the second and strongest objection, Robinson maintained that if the labor were invested in cane production rather than corn production, the resulting profits would "buy more pork than the corn [would] fatten." In short, it was cheaper to buy pigs than to raise them.[50] The question of cost-effectiveness has been examined by economic historians, and Polk appears to have embraced a strategy at odds with most sugar planters. Increases in the price of grains, the cost of transporting grains to market, and the price of pork, which rose about 60 percent at New Orleans during the 1850s, convinced small farmers and sugar planters to engage in an "intra-regional trade pattern," whereby "small farmers sold off surplus swine to planters who used their grain supplies to fatten pigs." Under the agreement, planters avoided the expense of shipping their surplus corn to market, developed a more efficient use of their labor since corn could be grown in the months leading up to the hectic rolling season, and benefited politically and economically by incorporating the small farmer into the "plantation regime."[51] Apparently, Polk declined to participate in this trading alliance, opting instead for self-sufficiency. Despite some philosophical differences with the planter-prelate, Robinson concluded his report by praising Polk as a man of "high character, both as a gentleman, an

---

[49] The expression data is based on two separate extractions. The first, which included a reground, netted 168 gallons of juice that weighed 8 1/2 pounds per gallon from 2,300 pounds of cane. Only the final ratio was provided for the second case. Keller, *Solon Robinson, Pioneer and Agriculturalist*, 1:202.

[50] Ibid., 1:203.

[51] Mark Schmitz, *Economic Analysis of Antebellum Sugar Plantations in Louisiana* (New York: Arno Press, 1977) 234–39.

improving agriculturist, and a kind master to those whom Providence has placed" under his care.[52]

Clearly, Polk made a favorable impression on Robinson, but ultimately a sugar planter had to be judged by his ability to produce sugar and turn a profit. Among Louisiana's 762 sugar plantations in 1844, Leighton ranked as the largest in Lafourche Parish and among the more productive in the state. During ten growing seasons from 1844–1845 to 1853–1854, Polk produced an average of 692 hogsheads or 761,200 pounds of sugar per season. In comparison, Duncan Kenner of Ascension Parish and Valcour Aime of St. James Parish, two of the most prosperous planters in the entire South, averaged 973 hogsheads (1.07 million pounds) and 964 hogsheads (1.06 million pounds), respectively. Issac Osgood of Plaquemines Parish and William J. Minor's Waterloo plantation in Ascension Parish, whose operations more closely resembled Polk's in terms of size and production capability, averaged 672 hogsheads (739,200 pounds) and 452 hogsheads (497,200 pounds) respectively, for the same ten-year period.[53]

For most Louisiana sugar planters, success depended to a large degree on their ability to cope with and adjust to "the unpredictable and uncontrollable forces of nature." Despite their close proximity to the Gulf Coast, surprisingly few sugar planters suffered significant financial loses as a result of direct damage from hurricanes or tropical storms. A more constant and severe threat came in the form of freezing weather, which could strike either in the spring when the cane was barely above ground or in the fall before the harvest was completed. Similarly, sugar planters feared the destructive power of flooding rivers and broken crevasses.[54] During the 1851–1852 season, for example, William J. Minor lost his entire crop at Waterloo, and production at Judah P. Benjamin's Belle Chase plantation in Plaquemines Parish dropped 65 percent from the previous year's total.[55]

---

[52] Keller, *Solon Robinson, Pioneer and Agriculturalist*, 1:204.

[53] It should be noted that William J. Minor owned two additional plantations, Southdown and Hollywood, in Terrebonne Parish, and the combined output of the three plantations placed Minor in the same category as Kenner and Aime. But the Waterloo operation is a fair comparison to Leighton. Pierre. A. Champomier, *Statement of the Sugar Crop Made in Louisiana* (New Orleans, 1844–1862) passim.

[54] Sitterson, *Sugar Country*, 13–20.

[55] Champomier, *Statement of the Sugar Crop Made in Louisiana*, passim.

Although never victimized by inundated sugar fields, Leighton experienced its share of natural disasters.

In the spring of 1849, a cholera epidemic swept through Louisiana and Mississippi leaving in its path a demoralized population and a staggering death toll. From Natchez, Mississippi, cotton planter Stephen Duncan, who monitored the epidemic with great interest, reported that a third outbreak of cholera on his five plantations in Issaquena County, Mississippi, had raised the death toll to ninety and he expected the figure to climb to a hundred before the epidemic subsided. Duncan, a nominal Episcopalian, also reported that at Leighton Bishop Polk had lost eighty slaves to the cholera outbreak.[56] The nabob's information was fairly accurate. Although a precise death toll at Leighton was not recorded, final estimates place the total number of dead "above 70," including twenty-five children and twenty-eight field hands.[57] One historian has opined that "the death of valuable slaves" and the "weakened and disorganized" state of the survivors immediately reduced the sugar production at Leighton to a financially disastrous level.[58] The evidence suggests otherwise.

Indeed, Polk produced 605 hogsheads of sugar in 1849–1850, the same year of the epidemic, which was five more than he produced in 1845–1846 and just 87 hogsheads below his ten-year average. In actuality, a greater crop disaster occurred in 1850–1851 when an early frost and a tornado wreaked havoc on Polk's plantation. The tornado destroyed the sugar house, valued at $75,000, several slave cabins, and damaged the Polks' personal residence. His wife estimated the total loss in property and crops at $100,000. The sugar production that year dropped to a mere 250 hogsheads. While these successive disasters weighed heavily on Polk, he recovered, and sugar production doubled to 500 hogsheads in 1851–1852. Over the course of the next two years, Polk made astounding progress. In 1852, he produced 920 hogsheads, and during the state's banner year of 1853–1854 he produced 1,200 hogsheads, which for that one season placed him in the company of Duncan Kenner (1,370 hogsheads) and Valcour Aime (1,409 hogsheads) and well ahead of rival William J. Minor (650 hogsheads at Waterloo).

---

[56] Stephen Duncan to Charles P. Leverich, 18, 23 June 1849, Charles P. Leverich Papers, Mississippi Dept of Archives and History, Jackson, Mississippi.

[57] Keller, *Solon Robinson, Pioneer and Agriculturalist*, 1:201.

[58] Parks, *General Leonidas Polk*, 109.

Notwithstanding this notable recovery, the down years exacted a heavy toll on Polk's personal finances.[59]

Life at Leighton, however, consisted of more than sugar production and in some ways the plantation's social world resembled the environs of the romanticized South. The palatial grounds, which were maintained by a full-time gardener, were decorated by a perimeter hedge of Cherokee roses, orange trees, and a garden of Picayune roses. This colorful setting served as the backdrop for the Polk's nineteen-room residence. Visitors frequented Leighton in search of good conversation, tea parties, and the perquisites of aristocratic life. Despite the ornate landscaping, the bishop apparently had a practical side when it came to his living quarters. One of his guests, Mrs. Isaac H. Hilliard of Arkansas, who visited Leighton in February 1850, noted in her diary that the residence was "not a fine house nor sumptuously furnished" and that "comfort and convenience seem to be the object instead of pomp and show." When Polk's guests needed additional entertainment and recreational activities, they often made the relatively short trip to New Orleans. During her tour of Louisiana, Hilliard shopped in the finest boutiques in New Orleans, purchased French translations of *Les Confidence de Lamatre Raphael* and *Marie Antoinette*, and intended to partake in Mardi Gras festivities only to have her plans altered by torrential rains. Without question, Mrs. Hilliard had exquisite tastes, and although she dispensed praise sparingly, she raved over Polk's "extensive and rare library," particularly the books and prints that had been collected from Italy.[60] Other guests at Leighton included church leaders who came to the plantation to discuss ecclesiastical matters or to debate theological issues as well as the famed agriculturalists Solon Robinson and Frederick Law Olmsted.

Polk thrived in this type of social setting, which if not the rule was at least the ideal coveted by members of the planter class. Yet, Polk broke from convention on occasion and he seemed particularly committed to establishing new patterns of conduct regarding the master-slave relationship. The exact number of slaves Polk owned has been a source of confusion. As slave holding became an ever-increasing component of social prestige, some contemporary observers often exaggerated individual slave parcels, and the

---

[59] Champomier, *Statement of the Sugar Crop Made in Louisiana*, passim; Polk, *Leonidas Polk: Bishop and General*, 1:206.

[60] Mrs. Issac H. Hilliard Diary, 2, 4, 7, 8, and 11 February 1850, Louisiana and Lower Mississippi Valley Collections.

holdings of some planters, including Polk, reached mythical proportions. For example, when British military attaché Arthur Lyons Fremantle met Polk during the Civil War he was under the mistaken impression that Polk was "very rich" and owned 700 slaves. The most useful evidence regarding Polk's slave holding spans a five-year period from 1849 to 1853, beginning with the report of agriculturalist Solon Robinson who visited Leighton in February 1849, shortly before the cholera epidemic. At the time of his visit, Robinson set the total number of slaves at 370, which included "upwards of 30 entirely superannuated [and] upwards of 70 children under ten years of age." Less than one-third of the total was field hands. Before the publication of his notes, Robinson was able to add that "above 70" slaves had died during the cholera epidemic, leaving approximately 300 slaves for the start of the 1849–1850 crop season. However, the well-informed cotton baron, Stephen Duncan, estimated the pre-cholera slave population at 200 and believed that the epidemic caused a loss of eighty slaves. The usually reliable federal census of 1850 indicated that Polk owned 215 slaves. Four years later, in 1854, the renowned traveler, Frederick Law Olmstead, identified Polk as the owner of 400 slaves. Polk biographer Joseph Parks accepted the authenticity of Robinson's claims and added that in 1852 the Polks received slaves valued at $20,000 upon the death of Mrs. Polk's mother, Mrs. John Devereux, which would have added between twenty and thirty more slaves. Thus, it is unclear how Polk could have acquired as many as 400 slaves when Olmsted visited in 1854; furthermore the discrepancies are acute.[61]

Regardless of the exact number, a conservative estimate of 215 slaves placed Polk among the seventeen largest slaveholding clergymen in the entire South.[62] In terms of slave management, Polk followed a model that afforded slaves more responsibility and greater autonomy than on most

[61] Arthur Lyons Fremantle, *Three Months in the Southern States: April–June, 1863* (New York: J. Bradburn, 1864) 139; Keller, *Solon Robinson, Pioneer and Agriculturalist,* 1:201–202; Stephen Duncan to Charles P. Leverich, 23 June 1849, Charles P. Leverich Papers; United States Census Office, *Seventh Census of the United* States, 1850; *Slave Population, Lafourche Parish, Louisiana* (Washington DC: Government Printing Office, 1853); Frederick Law Olmsted, *The Cotton Kingdom: A Traveller's Observations on Cotton and Slavery in the American Slave States* (New York: Dix & Edwards, 1856) 460; Parks, *General Leonidas Polk,* 107, 111–12.

[62] Adapted from Larry E. Tise, *Proslavery: A History of the Defense of Slavery in America, 1701–1840* (Athens: University of Georgia Press, 1987) 172. Tise's figures are based on the 1850 and 1860 censuses.

plantations in the South. At Leighton, slaves not only manufactured a number of agricultural items, but they made clothing as well. The duties of spinning thread and weaving cloth fell to the "old people...mothers, just before and after giving birth to children,...invalids, [and] convalescents, who [were] unable to go to the field." Surprisingly, one slave supervised the entire operation. In fact, he received the bales of wool and cotton, determined the work assignments, and dispensed the clothing "without ever troubling his master, or overseer, about the matter."[63] There were additional times when Polk trusted his slaves with an unusual amount of discretion. Frederick Law Olmsted reported that when church business drew Polk away from Leighton he "left his whole estate, his keys, & c. in the sole charge of one of his slaves, without the slightest apprehension of loss or damage."[64] The decision to grant discretionary power to trusted slaves was a function of Polk's religious convictions. He also allowed religious convictions to interfere with the routine operations of his sugar plantation. Although Polk was in the sugar business to make money, he suspended all work on the Sabbath even during the critical rolling season.[65] Polk's son, William, remembered that his father's neighbors feared that their slaves "when required to work on Sunday, would become dissatisfied and discontented" when they compared their situation to life at Leighton. Moreover, "his overseer predicted" that by reducing the work week by one day Polk's "sugar-making would be so diminished that his reputation as a practical man...would necessarily suffer." Nevertheless, Polk disregarded all criticisms and insisted that he was simply following his Christian conscience.[66]

The one area in which Polk made the most significant strides toward redefining plantation culture was in his aggressive promotion of religious instruction for slaves. As a bishop and planter with over 200 slaves, Polk commanded the respect of the master class. From his unique position he articulated a plan that harmonized with the evangelical traditions of the Old South, but one that incorporated basic Episcopalian forms and traditions. To appreciate fully the vision that Polk espoused, one must first consider the

---

[63] Keller, *Solon Robinson, Pioneer and Agriculturalist*, 1:203.

[64] Olmsted, *The Cotton Kingdom*, 460.

[65] Kellar, *Solon Robinson, Pioneer and Agriculturalist*, 1:203–204.

[66] Polk, *Leonidas Polk*, 1:183.

dynamics, motives and objectives of all denominations in regard to the religious education of the slave population.

Beginning with the Great Awakening and the work of the Grand Itinerant George Whitefield, Southerners were forced to consider the idea of promoting Christianity among their slaves. A serious debate ensued over the wisdom of this course of action. Critics warned that slaves who could read the Bible and who heard the message of spiritual equality would be predisposed to rebelliousness, especially if black preachers were part of the process. Advocates countered that religious instruction would render the slaves more docile and obedient, and it was at the very least an inescapable Christian duty. On those plantations where masters exposed their slaves to Christianity, a system of "bargaining" emerged between the master and slave that marked the initial "step in the development of a paternalistic relationship." By expressing an interest in religion, a slave, for example, might exchange church attendance for work reductions or the opportunity to meet other slaves.[67] On a more substantive level, Christianity afforded slaves the ability to resist dehumanization and self-hatred. Also, the religious dimension of the master-slave relationship could serve as "a measuring rod with which to hold slaveholders to a standard of behavior appropriate to their own professions of Christian faith." On the other side of the paternalistic equation, slaveholders congratulated themselves when they obeyed the dictates of the Great Commission. Moreover, slaveholders pointed to the conversion of slaves to Christianity as a central component of the "positive good" defense of slavery, which claimed that the peculiar institution produced a civilizing effect on the inferior black race.[68]

The effort to convert slaves to Christianity was a multi-denominational movement. Each of the major denominations vied for the souls of black folks, but the Methodists and Baptists achieved the greatest results. Illustrative of the Methodist and Baptist triumphs was South Carolina. In the Palmetto State, roughly one-sixth, or 54,908, of the state's 327,038 slaves affiliated with an organized church body by 1840, and of that total, 77 percent were Methodists or Baptists, and only 5 percent, or 2,500, were

---

[67] Alan Gallay, "Planters and Slaves in the Great Awakening," in *Masters and Slaves in the House of the Lord: Race and Religion in the American South, 1740–1870*, ed. John B. Boles (Lexington: University Press of Kentucky, 1988) 35.

[68] Eugene D. Genovese, *Roll, Jordan, Roll: The World the Slaveholders Made* (New York: Vintage Books, 1972) 280–84, 132–33.

Episcopalian.[69] The Episcopalians fared even worse in Virginia and North Carolina. Convention reports from the Old Dominion indicate that in 1848 Episcopalians baptized only 219 blacks in a state that boasted a slave population of nearly 400,000.[70] Numbers and statistics, however, do not tell the full story. According to historian Richard Rankin, "a few" Episcopalians in North Carolina supported plantation chapels and missionary efforts among their slaves, but those planters "left no evidence that their slaves' Christianity affected them personally." Thus, even in those cases where Episcopalians organized missionary enterprises, a level of detachment existed between master and slave. Similarly, John Hope Franklin contends that the Episcopal church touched "only a small minority" of blacks in North Carolina, and even in those pockets of contact "the Negro was first of all a Negro and then a Christian."[71]

Several factors hampered the Episcopal mission to the slaves, but the most important obstacles were the absence of a denominational spokesman, the lack of a comprehensive strategy, and the hostility or ambivalence of Episcopal planters. Episcopalian Thomas R. Dew, professor and later president of the College of William and Mary, established himself as one of the foremost proslavery theorists of his day, but he tended to discuss slavery from the perspective of a political economist. Moreover, as two historians have noted, Dew "wore his Episcopalianism lightly" and hence did not qualify as a denominational voice.[72] South Carolina Bishops Theodore

---

[69] J. Carleton Hayden, "Conversion and Control: Dilemma of Episcopalians in Providing for the Religious Instruction of Slaves, Charleston, South Carolina, 1845–1860," *Historical Magazine of the Protestant Episcopal Church* 40/2 (June 1971): 150.

[70] G. Maclaren Brydon, *The Episcopal Church Among the Negroes of Virginia* (Richmond: Virginia Diocese Library, 1937) 6.

[71] Richard Rankin, *Ambivalent Churchmen and Evangelical Church Women: The Religion of the Episcopal Elite in North Carolina, 1800–1860* (Columbia: University of South Carolina, 1993) xii; John Hope Franklin, "Negro Episcopalians in Ante-Bellum North Carolina," *Historical Magazine of the Protestant Episcopal Church* 13/3 (September 1944): 230, 232.

[72] Elizabeth Fox-Genovese and Eugene Genovese, "The Divine Sanction of Social Order: Religious Foundations of the Southern Slaveholders' World View," *Journal of the American Academy of Religion* 55/2 (Summer 1987): 226. For more on Dew and his works on moral philosophy and the idea of progress, see Eugene D. Genovese, *The Slaveholders' Dilemma: Freedom and Progress in Southern Conservative Thought, 1820–1860* (Columbia: University of South Carolina, 1992) 13–20.

Dehon and Nathaniel Bowen were early advocates of religious instruction for slaves and advanced their agenda through the Society for the Promotion of the Instruction of Negroes in South Carolina, an agency that sought to place Episcopal catechists or missionaries among the slave population. Most of the proselytizing took place in the South Carolina low country, where the four counties of Beaufort, Colleton, Charleston, and Georgetown claimed 90 percent of all Episcopal communicants in the Palmetto State. The figures included both black and white members and the total represented one-third of all Episcopal communicants in the Southern states.[73] Because South Carolina had the highest percentage of black inhabitants of any state in the South, slavery influenced every aspect of religious, economic, and political life and produced some atypical patterns of benevolence and evangelistic activity in the South Carolina low country. One scholar has theorized that Charleston's elite reached out to both the urban poor and the slaves in order to retain "Anglicanism's comprehensive social vision of the organic unity of public life."[74] If this contention is accepted, then South Carolina must be regarded as a truly unique enclave of social, religious, and political thought in the Old South.

Episcopalians in Virginia and Georgia provide a clearer, more accurate image of the denomination's mission to the slaves. From time to time, Episcopal clerics such as Bishop William Meade of Virginia and Bishop Stephen Elliott of Georgia published pastoral letters urging slaveholders to make Christianity part of plantation culture. In 1834 Meade circulated "The Duty Affording Religious Instruction to Those in Bondage," a rather straightforward pastoral plea that reiterated basic notions of Christian obligation to the slaves.[75] Shortly thereafter, Meade released *Sermons, Dialogues and Narratives for Servants*, but he was not satisfied that an adequate supply of tracts, catechisms, and sermons existed for use with the South's slave population. At one point, he "considered a set of sermons for servants the greatest desideration in the Christian Church of [the] southern

---

[73] Hayden, "Conversion and Control," 150; R. E. Hood, "From Headstart to Deadstart: The Historical Basis for Black Indifference toward the Episcopal Church, 1800–1860," *Historical Magazine of the Protestant Episcopal Church* 51/3 (September 1982): 275–77.

[74] Barbara Bellows, *Benevolence among Slaveholders: Assisting the Poor in Charleston, 1670–1860* (Baton Rouge: Louisiana State University Press, 1993) 27.

[75] Hood, "From Headstart to Deadstart," 274.

country," and far more important "than a composition of a large volume of the most learned and eloquent sermons which could only be appreciated by the more educated" members of Southern society.[76] Meade's interest in the religious education of slaves was not reciprocated by most Episcopalians under his charge. The Virginia diocese did not organize an official committee to address this pressing concern until 1859.[77] A strong case can be made that the anti-slavery activities of Bishop Meade's sister, Ann Page, overshadowed much of his own work and created a general climate of suspicion among Virginia's Episcopal planters.[78]

From his Georgia bishopric, Stephen Elliott refuted conventional notions that the liturgical character of the Episcopal church was unappealing to the slave population. He insisted that "there [was] no arrangement of worship so well qualified" as Episcopalianism "to meet the needs of [the] colored" race. Elliott viewed the religious education of slaves as part of the church's divine mandate, but he also perceived certain practical advantages to what he considered a sacred responsibility. Primarily, Elliott believed Episcopalianism posed a reasonable alternative to "the religion of excitement" that was within the "reach" of most slaves. In Georgia, the Methodist church had made significant inroads among the slave population. As a result, Elliott recommended that Episcopal clergymen concentrate on slave children and baptize and catechize them with the same fervor that they devoted to the "white children" of their congregations. Elliott contended that this strategy of "attaching the [slave] children" to the Episcopal form of worship was the only way to prevent "the servants of Episcopal families" from "wander[ing] off into other folds," ones that allowed black religious leadership and encouraged more democratic notions of spiritual equality. Thus, Bishop Elliott believed that the Episcopal mission to the slaves was both a means for ensuring social control on Southern plantations and for expanding the denomination's influence in the region.[79]

---

[76] "Religious Instruction of Slaves," *Southern Churchman*, 22 March 1844, 33.

[77] Hood, "From Headstart to Deadstart," 283.

[78] For a brief sketch of Ann Page's activities, see Arthur Dickens Thomas, Jr., "O That Slavery's Curse Might Cease," *Virginia Seminary Journal* 45/4 (December 1993): 56–61.

[79] Elliott quoted in "Sermons for Servants," *Southern Churchman*, 15 August 1845, 118. For an excellent treatment of the Methodist success in Georgia, see Christopher H. Owen, *The Sacred Flame of Love: Methodism and Society in Nineteenth-Century Georgia* (Athens: University of Georgia Press, 1998).

Elliott's philosophy resonated with some Episcopalians. They responded by creating Sunday schools and plantation chapels specifically for slaves. However, the Episcopal church's subordinate position to the other denominations of the South forced it to expend the majority of its energy and resources on efforts to reach the white population. In Georgia, for instance, the Episcopal church seized the initiative when the removal of the Cherokee nation in 1838–1839 opened the state to additional white settlement. Bishop Elliott welcomed this opportunity and remarked that "after a tedious struggle of sixty years" Georgia was finally poised to be "the mistress of her fine domain."[80] During the twenty-year period following the Cherokee removal, the Diocese of Georgia grew from six parishes to twenty-three and from 300 communicants to 2,000.[81] Still, a significant number of Episcopalians in Georgia and throughout the South remained committed to spreading the gospel among the slaves. Not surprisingly, these missions-minded Episcopalians reacted favorably when the Presbyterian divine, Charles Colcock Jones, published *The Religious Instruction of the Negroes* in 1842.

Indeed, the *Spirit of Missions*, the journalistic arm of the Episcopal church's Board of Missions, hailed the book as one of the most "valuable works" on the subject of the religious instruction of slaves. "We know not one" single volume, the editors opined, that "we should covet the authorship [of] more earnestly." Curiously, the *Spirit of Missions* claimed no knowledge of Jones's religious affiliation and professed that it had "been too much absorbed by [the book] to inquire." Part of Jones's appeal to Episcopalians was the complementary, albeit overstated, fashion in which he heralded the Episcopal mission to the slaves. "In this day of rebuke and depreciation of our Church," the editors wrote, Jones "may rest assured that [Episcopal] churchmen know how to appreciate the kindness and courtesy with which he has spoken of their efforts." If nothing else Jones soothed the consciences of sensitive Episcopalians. But there was more. Episcopalians also

---

[80] Stephen Elliott, *A High Civilization: The Moral Duty of Georgians, a Discourse Delivered Before the Georgia Historical Society on the Occasion of the Fifth Anniversary, Monday, 12th February 1844* (Savannah: The Society, 1844).

[81] Henry Thompson Malone, *The Episcopal Church in Georgia, 1733–1957* (Atlanta: Protestant Episcopal Church in the Diocese of Atlanta, 1960) 92.

appreciated Jones's ability to combine conservative social values with Christian rhetoric.[82]

Nevertheless, the Presbyterian divine spoke unapologetically to Southern slaveholders, warning them that if they ignored the biblical injunction to provide the gospel to the slaves, then they could expect a harrowing experience before "the judgement [sic] seat of Christ!" Similarly, Jones predicted "disgrace and iniquity" would be the fate of derelict ministers. Jones softened his instructions when directly addressing the laity, urging them to work diligently and "be not weary in well doing." For Jones, religious instruction was the key to creating a harmonious biracial social order. He reminded *every lover of his country* that "the moral and religious improvement of two million eight hundred thousand" slaves was tied directly to "individual peace and happiness, and...national prosperity and honor."[83] Prior to the publication of *The Religious Instruction of the Negroes*, he tested his theories in Liberty County, Georgia. As a "well-educated, slave-owning clergyman," Jones captured the interest of area planters and "provided them with the leadership they required," according to one of his biographers.[84]

By virtue of his numerous publications and his unique plantation management style, Jones established himself as the foremost planter-prelate in the South. Although the Episcopal church had no proslavery theorist to match Jones in terms of public recognition and intellectual stature, Leonidas Polk emerged as one of the most significant proslavery clerics in the Gulf South region, and his efforts were virtually unmatched in his denomination. When Polk became bishop of Louisiana in 1842, he had already been recognized as a leading proponent of the plantation chapel system,[85] and the new jurisdiction provided him with a larger audience and a stronger position from which to integrate Episcopalian distinctives with slave missions. Polk's task, however, was formidable. Louisiana planters lived under a constant,

---

[82] "Negroes," *Spirit of Missions* 8/4, April 1843, 102–103.

[83] Charles Colcock Jones, *The Religious Instruction of the Negroes in the United States* (Savannah: Thomas Purse, 1842) 275–76.

[84] Donald Mathews, "Charles Colcock Jones and the Southern Evangelical Crusade to Form a Biracial Community," *Journal of Southern History* 41/3 (August 1975): 305.

[85] Trezevant P. Yeatman, Jr., "St. John's-A Plantation Church of the Old South," *Tennessee Historical Quarterly* 10/4 (December 1951): 334–37. Polk and his brothers were the founders of St. John's Church.

though not necessarily debilitating, fear of slave insurrection. For instance, the Deslondes revolt in 1811 left a permanent scar of distrust on the white inhabitants of New Orleans.[86] A decade later the Gulf South became aware of the slave preacher-insurrectionist Nat Turner and the rebellion that he had inspired in Southampton County, Virginia. Although historian Judith Kelleher Schafer discovered that "white apprehensiveness" grew significantly, she could find no direct evidence that Louisiana planters and legislators "suppressed" slave religion in the aftermath of the Nat Turner revolt, but they were extremely suspicious of anyone who was eager to evangelize the slaves.[87]

In 1835, Presbyterian slaveholder John McDonogh informed his good friend, Charles Colcock Jones, that "99 out of a hundred [Louisianians] are diametrically opposed to the introduction of religion among their slaves." To explain this defiant attitude, McDonogh simply concluded that the planters "having no religion themselves...are naturally opposed to the instruction of their slaves." The French Creoles, McDonogh continued, "generally...laugh at the idea of religion and the Americans who are settled amongst them forget if they ever had any" religion.[88] Disgusted but not discouraged, McDonogh forwarded to his friends and acquaintances a catechism that Jones had drafted for the slaves as well as a report on the progress that Jones had made in Liberty County, Georgia. McDonogh's efforts encountered stern opposition in the Louisiana legislature where one state senator rose to the floor, labeled the religious literature as "Highly Incendiary," and resolved that a $500 reward be established "to discover the person who had circulated them."[89]

While the McDonogh case was an extreme example, it illustrated a lingering animosity toward an overly aggressive religious campaign among

---

[86] Thomas Marshall Thompson, "National Newspaper and Legislative Reactions to Louisiana's Deslondes Slave Revolt," *Louisiana History* 33/1 (Winter 1992): 5–29.

[87] Judith Kelleher Schafer, "The Immediate Impact of Nat Turner's Insurrection on New Orleans," *Louisiana History* 21/4 (Fall 1980): 375–76.

[88] John McDonogh to Charles Colcock Jones, 26 January 1835, John McDonogh Papers, Joseph Merrick Jones Hall, Tulane University, New Orleans, Louisiana.

[89] John McDonogh to Charles Colcock Jones, 11 May 1835, McDonogh Papers. McDonogh repatriated approximately eighty of his own slaves to Liberia, favored gradual emancipation, and lobbied the United States Congress to fund the American Colonization Society. These positions alarmed Charles Colcock Jones, and the Presbyterian divine distanced himself from this zealous fellow-churchman.

the slaves, one that could not have dissipated fully in the seven years prior to Polk's election as bishop of Louisiana. Nevertheless, in 1843 Bishop Polk told the state Episcopal convention that "one of the chiefest [sic] charms of the Gospel of Christ, [is] that it seeks to equalize the human condition; and…compensate[s], by the richness of its spiritual provisions, for the disparities existing in…worldly circumstances." The gospel, Polk continued, was "eminently therefore the property of the poor," and "their claim…[is] greatly strengthened by their peculiar condition of dependence," a condition that "pre-disposes the mind to a teachable disposition, and a readiness to receive and obey the truth." Throughout his address, Polk referred to the slave population as "the poor," which could be interpreted as an attempt to convince Southern slaveholders that social solidarity could only be achieved in a biracial Christian community.[90] In fact, Polk envisioned the day when the Episcopal church would guard "less jealously…her intellectual reputation, and [demonstrate] more concern for the salvation of the perishing multitudes." Bishop Polk also believed that his church through "wise and temperate legislation" should create "a class of men suited to" the religious instruction of the slaves.[91] Accordingly, in 1845 Polk recommended to his diocese that a new church canon be adopted "for the ordination of an order of Deacons" who would minister to the slaves. Interestingly, this clerical order would possess "qualifications inferior to those, demanded by" the existing canons of the church. In sponsoring the amendment, Polk argued that in addition to the obvious "benefits…[for] the slave population" these changes would also address Episcopal concerns in urban centers and rural districts.[92] Bishop Polk's philosophy paralleled that of Presbyterian divine Charles Colcock Jones, and both men viewed Christianity as a means

[90] "Journal of the Fifth Annual Convention of the Protestant Episcopal Church of the Diocese of Louisiana, January 18–20, 1843," Historical Records of the Episcopal Church Collection, Joseph Merrick Jones Hall, Tulane University, New Orleans, Louisiana, 34–35.

[91] Ibid., 35.

[92] "Journal of the Seventh Annual Convention of the Protestant Episcopal Church of the Diocese of Louisiana, April 3–4, 1845," Historical Records of the Episcopal Church Collection, Joseph Merrick Jones Hall, Tulane University, New Orleans, Louisiana, 34–35.

for transforming individual behavior and for creating a biracial social order.[93]

For planters in the Gulf South to accept Polk's views on the religious education of slaves, the bishop would have to demonstrate successfully the spiritual and social merits of his case. Both Solon Robinson and his famed counterpart Frederick Law Olmsted observed that morality and discipline were well maintained at Leighton. These visitors were also quick to point out that slave marriages were an important part of the plantation's religious culture. Perhaps more than they realized.[94] "The greatest efforts," Polk's daughter recalled, "were made by the bishop to preserve among his servants the sanctity of family life." As a result, slave weddings were festive occasions and "were always celebrated" in Polk's home and every family member participated. Polk's wife added an element of grandeur and reverence to the event by presenting the bride and groom with specially tailored wedding garments. The bishop's children, "as the reward of good behavior," were given the privilege of holding the silver candlesticks while the bishop himself conducted the wedding ceremony. After the service, a "wedding-supper always followed," and the merriment continued into "the small hours of the night." There were, however, exceptions to this rule. For example, "if the couple had misbehaved, they were compelled to atone for it by marriage." In these instances, Polk's daughter remembered, "The guilty pair were summoned from the field" and escorted in their work clothes to the bishop's study where they were made man and wife, but without the formality and pomp of a traditional service. Hence slave marriages on Polk's plantation were more than a reward for good behavior; they were an attempt to integrate slaves into a socially conservative and paternalistic Episcopal culture.[95]

Moreover, in the narrowly defined sphere of sexual relations, Polk attempted to impose on his slaves a standard of behavior that comported with the highest expectations of Southern gentility. The slaves who agreed to these terms received the material benefits of a wedding holiday and the

---

[93] For an overview of Jones's proslavery thought, see Mathews, "Charles Colcock Jones and the Southern Evangelical Crusade to Form a Biracial Community," 299–320.

[94] Keller, *Solon Robinson, Pioneer and Agriculturalist*, 204; Olmsted, *The Cotton Kingdom*, 460.

[95] The daughter's account is quoted in Polk, *Leonidas Polk*, 1:198.

blessings of both the church and the master, which in this case were indistinguishable. More importantly, those slaves who accepted the terms of the paternalistic bargain extracted from Bishop Polk a measure of self-worth and dignity. However, not all slaves enjoyed these privileges. Some registered their protests by way of what Polk considered illicit behavior. Because of their resistance and disobedience, Polk forced them to participate in a perfunctory or even censorious wedding ceremony. There were other occasions when Polk used public humiliation as a deterrent to immoral behavior. For example, although he was adamant about suspending all work on the Sabbath even during the rolling season, he punished habitual chicken thieves on Sundays by forcing them to stand in a prominent place on the plantation with a live chicken tied around their neck.[96]

Aside from slave marriages, Sunday services were a central component of the religious culture at Leighton. As one visiting clergyman recounted, "sixty or eighty" slaves, Polk's family, and guests all assembled each Sunday in the largest room in Polk's home. The service began with the resident chaplain presenting an opening "devotion." Then the slaves dispersed into three groups. The male slaves remained with the chaplain and were examined "on the elementary principles of the Christian religion." They also sang hymns and anthems, which convinced the visiting clergyman of "their interest in the exercises." The female slaves, "numbering twenty or more," met with the family's governess, and the slave children gathered in yet another room where they attended the teaching of one of Polk's daughters. They too were quizzed or catechized and sang hymns and anthems. Following the Sunday school period, the slaves reassembled for more singing and the chaplain's prayers. As a final ritual Bishop Polk "rose from his knees, and with his hands extended over the company…pronounced the apostolic benediction," a sight one observer compared to an Old Testament "patriarch" blessing his household.[97]

Doctrinal instruction was often channeled through a church-approved catechism for slaves, which differed very little from the catechism for whites. When dealing with the fundamental issues of the fall of man and the way of salvation, the catechism itself outlined a universal human condition, one that did not differentiate based on color or condition of servitude:

---

[96] Ibid., 1:192
[97] The visiting clergyman's account is quoted in ibid., 1:197–98.

Q: You told me that when God first made man, he made him good; did he always stay good?

A: No; he became very bad.

Q: What was the first bad thing that he did?

A: He eat [*sic*] of the tree that God told him not to eat of?

Q: Have we got anything to do with that sin of Adam?

A: Yes; for we are his children.

Q: How are we his children?

A: He was the first man, and everybody came from him.

Q: When Adam did what God said he must not do, what did he then become?

A: A sinner.

Q: Are we all, then, coming from a sinful father, born in sin?

A: Yes.

The intention of the catechism was to shape for both blacks and whites an Episcopal theology based on such doctrines as the singular creation of man, the Adamic fall, and the Adamic transmission of sins. The notion that slavery was a function of the curse of Ham was not part of the Episcopal catechism. Acknowledgement by masters and slaves of these theological premises was designed to establish a common theological heritage. It is highly unlikely that many Southern slaveholders embraced such arguments, despite the clarity of the catechism.[98]

The catechism also supported the notion that salvation was not obtainable through good works but was only possible through faith in the atoning death of Jesus Christ. Furthermore, it linked Christian obedience with love for Jesus Christ, not the slave master:

Q: Ought we not to love Jesus Christ, who has done and suffered so much for us?

A: Yes.

Q: And how ought we to show that we love him?

A: By doing what he tells us.

---

[98] "A Catechism for the Religious Instruction of the Persons of Color," *Southern Churchman*, 3 January 1844[5], 200.

Q: In what book do we find what he tells us?
A: In the Bible.

Interestingly, the catechism identified Jesus Christ and the Bible as the arbiters of right and wrong. The message was the same for both blacks and whites: through prayer and the inspiration of the Holy Spirit, all believers could discern the path of Christian righteousness.[99] Episcopalians were hesitant, however, to place the Bible in the hands of a slave given the legal prohibitions against teaching slaves to read. One cleric, for example, reasoned that slaves could "find out what [was] in them [the Scriptures] by having them read, just as well as by reading them." There did exist, however, a few clerics who instructed slaves to call upon their masters and ask that the Scriptures be read to them. This small group also reminded Southern slaveholders on a regular basis of their moral obligation to present the gospel to their slaves.[100]

Unlike the Episcopal planters of North Carolina who were detached from the religion of their slaves, Polk's desire was to monitor closely and even participate in the religious world of his slaves.[101] Aside from the Sunday services, each morning the bishop called together his entire household, "white and black," for prayer, biblical instruction, and singing. Then, the family governess noted: "If there had been any dereliction of duty amongst children or servants, they were sure to hear of it at the morning readings, where the culprit perfectly well understood for whom the principal part of the lecture was intended though probably no one else did." Yet, Governess Beauchamp did not share the bishop's passion for creating a biracial Christian environment. Indeed, she found her role as Sunday school teacher to be "very difficult...no matter how edifying [she] fancied [her] instruction." Furthermore, the Polk family's "familiarity" with their slaves and their affection toward convalescing or dying servants "shocked" the governess's "European notions."[102]

---

[99] Ibid. "sermons for Servants–No. 1."

[100] "Search the Scriptures," *Southern Churchman*, 8 March 1844, 28. The sermon, "Search the Scriptures," was the first installment of a sermon series for slaves. The text for this sermon was John 5:39.

[101] Polk, *Leonidas Polk*, 1:198.

[102] Miss Beauchamp's recollections are quoted in ibid., 1:194. Miss Beauchamp was a native of Ireland.

It would be easy to overstate the extent to which Polk's slaves were part of an Episcopal religious tradition. Indeed the anecdotal evidence suggests that the majority of slaves on Leighton plantation refused to participate. Visitors to the plantation noted that sixty to eighty slaves attended Sunday services at Polk's residence. However, the bishop owned more than 215 slaves, which means nearly two-thirds of Leighton's slave population was disengaged from the religious experiment. Moreover, Polk's son remembered complaining to his mother "that the Negroes were permitted to fish and play" on Sunday, but he was not "accorded like privileges." Mrs. Polk explained to her son that he "had abundant opportunity for such amusements all week but that working people had no such privileges" except on Sunday. William Polk concluded that "the caste system had created different expectations or roles on the Lord's Day."[103] This evidence suggests that only a small percentage of the slaves at Leighton were even willing to consider the biracial Christian tradition as defined by Polk. Nevertheless, the bishop's efforts were distinctive in comparison to Episcopal programs outside of Louisiana, and members of Polk's diocese tacitly supported his initiatives.

For example, Reverend A. D. McCoy, who shepherded both a white congregation and a number of plantation chapels in Alexandria, Louisiana, admitted that "there is much to mourn over in the evident want of the spirit of true religion among the more favored class of our population." But the slaves' response to McCoy's preaching overwhelmed him. He rejoiced in "being permitted to scatter the good seed [of the gospel] in soil" that yielded so bountiful a harvest.[104] The numbers confirmed McCoy's enthusiasm. From 1847 to 1851, he baptized fourteen white adults and thirty-two white children, but during the same period he baptized 106 slave adults and 463 slave children. Alluding to the numerical evidence as a sign of God's blessings, McCoy boasted that among the 569 slave baptisms he discovered only one "unworthy" candidate. McCoy's success was due in part to the virtually unrestricted access he had to local plantations. In fact, within a seven-mile radius of Alexandria, McCoy ministered to approximately 1,050

---

[103] Quotes taken from an undated document in Miscellaneous Files, Leonidas Polk Family Papers, Historic New Orleans Collection, New Orleans, Louisiana. The document appears to be notes that William Polk, son of Leonidas, was compiling for a biography of his father.

[104] Report from Rev. A. D. McCoy, *Spirit of Missions* 17/6, June 1852, 178.

slaves from eleven different plantations, which suggests a high degree of cooperation from Louisiana planters.[105]

Generally speaking, Louisiana Episcopalians supported plantation missions more readily than their Gulf South counterparts in Alabama or Mississippi.[106] During an 1854 visit to Alabama, Frederick Law Olmsted encountered an Episcopal clergyman who had been struggling for seven years "to gain the confidence of the small number of Africans belonging to his congregation." The clergyman's efforts had produced meager results and he attributed his failure "to the negro's habitual distrust of the white race." Specifically, the Episcopal prelate believed that slaves perceived a direct contradiction between the minister's claim of the slave's spiritual equality to his master and the master's prohibition against allowing the slave to read the Bible and to "judge for himself...his duty" to his master. During this exchange between Olmsted and the clergyman, a planter was present who was also a member of the Episcopal church. The planter warned the clergyman that his views "were dangerous," and he insisted that the church must be counted on to enforce the laws that forbade teaching slaves to read. Courageously, the clergyman rejoined that "he had no design to break the laws, but...he considered that law which withheld the Bible from the negro [to be] unnecessary and papistical in character." Olmsted also asserted that while he visited at least fifty homes in Alabama where morning prayers were a daily occurrence "he never in a single instance saw a field-hand attend or join in the devotion of the family." In short, Olmsted observed that many Episcopalians in Alabama and Mississippi displayed an open distrust of both white Episcopal ministers and the disruptive potential in the gospel message that they carried to the slaves.[107]

It is difficult to determine whether the commitment of Louisiana Episcopalians to slave missions was the result of personal conviction or a response to the challenges set by Bishop Polk, Reverend McCoy, and other plantation chaplains. In all probability, Louisiana Episcopalians were

---

[105] Report from Rev. A. D. McCoy, *Spirit of Missions* 16/12, December 1851, 507.

[106] According to Blake Touchstone, Episcopalians in Alabama had only four plantation chapels, Mississippi had between six and ten, but Louisiana had twelve. See also Blake Touchstone, "Planters and Slave Religion in the Deep South," in *Masters and Slaves in the House of the Lord: Race and Religion in the American South, 1740–1870*, ed. John B. Boles (Lexington: University Press of Kentucky, 1988) 118.

[107] Olmsted, *The Cotton Kingdom*, 473, 461.

motivated by both factors. What is certain is that Leonidas Polk was willing to risk alienating Louisiana planters by stressing the need to Christianize slaves. Even the *Spirit of Missions*, despite its evangelistic fervor, cautioned Episcopalians against throwing the church "into a state of excitement" over the religious education of slaves.[108]

Given Polk's willingness to bring slaves into the orbit of Southern Episcopal churches, one must question his decision to sell Leighton in April 1854, which for all practical purposes ended his career as a planter-priest. Polk did purchase a 2,700–acre cotton plantation in Bolivar County, Mississippi, with his remaining resources, but he appointed his son Hamilton to manage the new estate and its 134 slaves, and he moved to New Orleans and disengaged himself from the planter lifestyle. Most historians oversimplify Polk's decision, contending that he sold Leighton to John Williams of New Orleans for $307,000 in order to escape the demands of his creditors. True, Polk had experienced financial difficulties beginning with the Harris debacle in the mid-1830s and continuing with the crop and equipment damage caused by the tornado in 1850. More trouble came in the spring of 1851 when Polk's recently hired financial broker embezzled from him a substantial sum of money. But, Polk always seemed able to stay one step ahead of his creditors; in the fall of 1847 he sold his Tennessee holdings to Rebecca Polk, the wife of his brother Andrew Jackson Polk, to relieve some debt, and his sugar production had reached record levels in 1852–1853 and 1853–1854. In addition, the Diocese of Louisiana increased the bishop's salary from $1,308 in 1853 to $4,000 in 1854.[109] Thus, if Polk had possessed the resolve he could have remained in the sugar business.

Without question, sugar planting in Louisiana was a lucrative business. Indeed, J. Carlyle Sitterson has argued that "despite heavy indebtedness, the fifties [1850s] was a profitable decade for sugar planters and foreclosures were infrequent. Planters were able to carry their heavy debts, build magnificent homes and maintain a high standard of living." Moreover, no significant degree of animosity existed between planters and their factors or commission agents. Hence, the fundamental question of success was whether or not a planter's income exceeded his expenses, which in the

---

[108] Report of C. C. Jones, *Spirit of Missions* 8/4, April 1843, 105.

[109] Parks, *General Leonidas Polk*, 113,107; Sarah E. Devereux to Thomas P. Devereux, 15 June 1854, Devereux Family Papers, Perkins Library, Duke University, Durham, North Carolina; Polk, *Leonidas Polk*, 1:208.

prosperous decade of the 1850s was a relatively easy task.[110] The yearly expenses on a typical Louisiana sugar plantation, one with 100 slaves of all ages and an annual sugar production of 400 to 500 hogsheads, fell within the general range of $11,000.[111] Although Leighton was a much larger operation than the one previously cited, Polk held annual operating expenses to $8,000, despite the atypical expenses of a chaplain ($500 per year) and a gardener ($500 per year). Using Polk's ten-year production average of 692 hogsheads or 761,200 pounds of sugar and 5.4¢ per pound as the average price of sugar during the same time, Polk had an estimated gross income of $41,000 per year or a net profit of nearly $33,000.[112] Polk, however, did have to pay the principle and interest on several mortgages out of his sugar profits. Still, the escalating value of his plantation should have enabled him to carry his debts and obtain more credit.[113] In short, the 1850s was an ideal time to be in the sugar business, income at Leighton exceeded operating expenses, and more credit could have been secured as a result of the increasing value of Polk's plantation. What then prompted Polk to leave the sugar business after his most productive seasons and at the height of Louisiana's decade of prosperity?

Apparently, Polk succumbed to the pressure of "financial embarrassments" caused by his accumulated debt.[114] He had long maintained that

---

[110] Sitterson, *Sugar Country*, 72, 164. See a concurring interpretation in Joe Gray Taylor, *Negro Slavery in Louisiana* (Baton Rouge: Louisiana State University Press, 1963) 93–94, 105.

[111] The example is based on the plantation records of E. J. Forstall whose actual expenses in 1844 were $10,685. This figure includes such expenses as the overseer's salary, insurance premiums, and corn, pork, and equipment purchases, but does not include purchases of land, slaves, or physical improvements. See, Sitterson, *Sugar Country*, 161.

[112] Expenses adapted from Keller, *Solon Robinson, Pioneer and Agriculturalist*, 203; Mrs. Issac H. Hilliard Diary, 7 February 1850, Louisiana and Lower Mississippi Valley Collections. Sugar production adapted from Champomier, *Statement of the Sugar Crop Made in Louisiana*, passim. Sugar prices adapted from Gray, *History of Agriculture in the Southern United States*, 2:1034.

[113] By way of comparison, William J. Minor's Waterloo plantation increased in value from $211,500 in 1837, to $370,000 in 1850, to $500,000 in 1860. Polk purchased Leighton for $100,000 in 1841, sold it for $307,000 in 1854, and could expect its value to reach $430,000 by 1860. The Minor figures are in J. Carlyle Sitterson, "The William J. Minor Plantations: A Study in Antebellum Absentee Ownership," *Journal of Southern History* 9/1 (February 1943): 73.

[114] Polk, *Leonidas Polk*, 1:183.

indebtedness was the worst affliction that could visit a minister of the gospel, and he frequently expressed a desire to keep his financial affairs private.[115] His family received the news of Leighton's sale with relief. Polk's sister-in-law, Sarah E. Devereux, espoused a prevailing sentiment when she remarked, "I am truly glad to hear that the Bishop has sold his plantation."[116] After Polk's death, his son William wrote that Polk could have "easily" recovered from all the "accidents and losses" relative to his sugar planting and indebtedness if he had not been so committed to "the full performance of [his] Episcopal duty." The bishop himself believed that if "world affairs" constituted his only allegiance, then he would "have experienced no difficulty" in recouping his losses.[117] Ultimately, Polk could no longer reconcile his role as a spiritual leader in the Episcopal church with the culture of materialism and debt that consumed many planters. The life of the absentee planter afforded Polk new opportunities for adapting Episcopalianism to the evangelical South. With this newfound freedom, he turned his attention to the creation of a distinctly Episcopal university in the South. Indeed, Polk's vision for the University of the South illustrated his dedication to denominational purity, but it also embodied the fundamental tenets of a religious and cultural-based Southern nationalism, which sought to preserve and defend the peculiar institution.

[115] Leonidas Polk to Charles P, McIlvaine, 10 August 1840, Leonidas Polk Papers; Leonidas Polk to Sarah Polk, 9 June 1843, Leonidas Polk Papers.
[116] Sarah E. Devereux to Thomas P. Devereux, 14 April 1854, Devereux Family Papers.
[117] Polk, *Leonidas Polk*, 1:183, 203.

CHAPTER 4

The Emergence of a Southern Nationalist

The decade of the 1820s marked the beginning of an increased sectional consciousness in the South, which, by the 1860s, ripened into a call for the creation of an independent nation. The national debate over slavery, more than any other issue, revealed the fundamental difference between the Northern and Southern societies. The defense of the peculiar institution was the foundation of Southern nationalism. Indeed, such proslavery theorists as James Henry Hammond, Josiah Nott, Henry Hughes, T. R. R. Cobb, and James Henley Thornwell defined the Southern slave society as a holistic or organic community and often used Christianity as a type of divine sanction for their worldview. In the end, many proponents of independence believed that the Confederacy could not succeed without the support of the region's religious leaders and institutions. Bishop Leonidas Polk's post-Leighton activities would take place in this highly-charged political and religious context.[1]

In his seminal study *Confederate Morale and Church Propaganda*, historian James Silver concluded that the amalgamation of the religious and

---

[1] John McCardell, *The Idea of a Southern Nation: Southern Nationalists and Southern Nationalism* (New York: W. W. Norton, 1979) 49–90; Drew Gilpin Faust, *The Creation of Confederate Nationalism: Ideology and Identity in the Civil War South* (Baton Rouge: Louisiana State University Press, 1988); Douglas Ambrose, *Henry Hughes and Proslavery Thought in the Old South* (Baton Rouge: Louisiana State University Press, 1996); Elizabeth Fox-Genovese and Eugene D. Genovese, "The Divine Sanction of Social Order: Religious Foundations of the Southern Slaveholders' World View," *Journal of the American Academy of Religion* 55/2 (Summer 1987): 211–33.

political spheres was the defining moment of the disunionist movement. He also maintained that Southern religious leaders contributed enormously to the creation of a distinctively Southern mindset. Subsequent studies have examined the impact that specific religious groups had on shaping public opinion during the sectional conflict. The focus has been primarily on the actions of the Presbyterian, Methodist, and Baptist denominations.[2]

For example, in *Broken Churches, Broken Nation*, C. C. Goen suggests that the denominational schisms of the late antebellum period—particularly the division of the Methodists and Baptists into regional organizations, which in both cases resulted from Northern opposition to missionary appointments to Southern slaveholders—transformed the slavery debate and functioned as "both portent and catalyst of the imminent national tragedy." Without national church alliances to promote cultural unity the American social fabric unraveled. Similarly, Mitchell Snay's *Gospel of Disunion* emphasizes a symbiotic relationship between religion and politics. Clerics representing both regions constructed a moral and spiritual discourse that defined their antagonists as defenders of an immoral or non-Christian society. In time, Snay argues, Southern political disunionists affirmed the viability of peaceable secession and in so doing followed the precedent set by the denominational secessionists. Although Goen and Snay have produced sophisticated analyses, they have ignored the connection between Southern Episcopalians and Southern nationalism. In fact, Goen and Snay agree that the relatively small number of Episcopalians in the South made the denomination inconsequential to their respective studies. It should be noted, however, that Episcopalians present a perplexing methodological problem for Goen and Snay because their denomination did not split over the slavery issue during the antebellum period. The Protestant Episcopal Church of the Confederate States of America emerged in the aftermath of the national political disunion. Then, the denomination reunited immediately after the war.[3]

---

[2] James W. Silver, *Confederate Morale and Church Propaganda* (New York: W. W Norton, 1957).

[3] C. C. Goen, *Broken Churches, Broken Nation: Denominational Schisms and the Coming of the American Civil War* (Macon GA: Mercer University Press, 1985) 6; Mitchell Snay, *The Gospel of Disunion: Religion and Separatism in the Antebellum South* (New York/Oxford: Oxford University Press, 1993).

Unfortunately, the historical marginalization of Episcopalians has prevented scholars from recognizing Leonidas Polk's role in the formulation and dissemination of Southern nationalism. Like most evangelical prelates, Polk abhorred partisan politics and avoided commingling the political and religious spheres. Nevertheless, as the sectional controversy intensified, he expressed views that complimented Confederate nationalism. His particular vision for the University of the South, for example, illustrated a commitment to both a Southern literary and cultural nationalism that vigorously defended the peculiar institution. Additional indicators of his support for the cause of Southern independence occurred when he presented an ecclesiastical justification for diocesan secession and when he accepted a combat assignment with the Confederate army. By leading the Louisiana diocese out of the General Convention of the Protestant Episcopal Church and by defining his military service in religious terms, Polk demonstrated that he was willing and capable of reconciling Episcopalianism and Confederate ideals.

Following the sale of Leighton plantation in April 1854, Polk turned his attention to educational reform. Since his days at West Point, he had expressed a deep interest in post-secondary education. He often corresponded with his father, who served on the board of trustees at the University of North Carolina from 1790 to 1834, about curriculum development, the teaching profession, the lack of preparedness exhibited by first-year college students, and the general inadequacies of the Southern educational system.[4] Polk, of course, was not the only one to recognize the inferiority of Southern colleges and universities. Most of the elite families of the South sent their children to the North for educational training. They displayed a strong preference for the three Ivy League schools of Harvard, Yale, and Princeton. For example, the sons of Thomas Butler, a communicant in Polk's Louisiana diocese, attended Yale University. Butler's brother-in-law, Stephen Duncan, the Natchez cotton baron who earned a medical degree from Dickinson College in Pennsylvania, also preferred the New England schools, and the swashbuckling filibusterer John A. Quitman

---

[4] Leonidas Polk to William Polk, 10 March 1823, Leonidas Polk Papers, Jesse Ball duPont Library, University of the South, Sewanee, Tennessee; Leonidas Polk to William Polk, 16 November 1825, Leonidas Polk Papers; Leonidas Polk to William Polk, 7 October 1828, Leonidas Polk Papers.

enrolled his son at Princeton.[5] Polk himself earned a degree from West Point; one brother, Alexander Hamilton Polk, attended Yale; and his brother-in-law Thomas P. Devereux, one of the wealthiest planters in North Carolina, graduated from Yale with honors. By selecting Northern over Southern schools, the Southern elite registered their dissatisfaction with their section's institutions of higher learning.[6]

However, as regional distinctiveness became more apparent and abolitionism emerged as the political and cultural antagonist of the slave society, Southerners resolved to improve their schools. Indeed, many members of the elite considered the liberal reform movements and contrasting economic system of the North to be a legitimate threat to their particular way of life. Even church-affiliated schools, Southerners believed, were not immune from these developments. While contemplating the decision to send his daughter to an Episcopalian preparatory school in New York, Virginian John A. Selden of Westover plantation discussed the biases in Northern schools with his neighbor Hill Carter of Shirley plantation and fellow Virginian Richard Baylor of Essex County. "I believe all these northern schools," Selden intoned, "are more or less tinctured with abolitionism." Despite some reassurances from Carter, whose daughter and niece attended the New York school, Selden remained suspicious of emancipationist sentiment and religious fanaticism in Northern locales. Similarly, John A. Quitman urged his son Frederick H. Quitman to inoculate himself against any political contagions circulating at Princeton, and he even considered transferring his son to the University of Mississippi. As the sectional crisis intensified, many Southerners came to embrace the views of Selden and Quitman, and they worked to elevate the quality of their colleges and universities.[7]

---

[5] William K. Scarborough, "Lords or Capitalists? The Natchez Nabobs in Comparative Perspective," *Journal of Mississippi History* 54/3 (Summer 1992): 256–58.

[6] Mrs. Frank B. Angellotti, *The Polks of North Carolina and Tennessee* (Easley SC: Southern Historical Press, 1984) 15; William S. Powell, *Dictionary of North Carolina Biography*, 6 vols. (Chapel Hill: University of North Carolina Press, 1979–1996) 2:59.

[7] John A Selden to Richard Baylor, 7 August 1852, Baylor Family Papers, Virginia Historical Society, Richmond, Virginia; Robert L. May, *John A. Quitman: Old South Crusader* (Baton Rouge: Louisiana State University Press, 1985) 211, 235, 270–98; Scarborough, "Lords or Capitalists? The Natchez Nabobs in Comparative Perspective," 260–61. I would like to thank Dr. Scarborough for the Selden letter and for sharing insights on the educational habits of Southern elites.

The University of Virginia, the University of North Carolina, and South Carolina College rated as the best of the Old South's institutions of higher education. The University of Virginia—the largest and most prestigious in the region—benefited immensely from its unmistakable identification with its founder Thomas Jefferson. At the University of North Carolina, enrollment nearly tripled from 1845 to 1860, and its stature increased under the capable leadership of President David Swain, who incidentally had been the roommate of Leonidas Polk during the latter's brief stay at Chapel Hill in the early 1820s. South Carolina College enjoyed a solid reputation due in large part to the influence of President James Henley Thornwell, the South's foremost theologian.

In order to compete with the premier universities in the North, these Southern universities recruited and employed a significant number of renowned scholars. Virginia's faculty included such eminent academicians as James P. Holcombe in law and George F. Holmes in history and literature, and North Carolina's J. De Bernière Hooper in Latin and French and William H. Battle in law were noteworthy educators in their respective fields. The one area in which Southern pedagogues clearly excelled over their Northern counterparts was in the area of the natural sciences. Here, mathematician Albert Taylor Bledsoe of Virginia, chemist and geologist Elisha Mitchell of North Carolina, scientists John and Joseph Leconte who bounced between Franklin College and South Carolina College, and Frederick A. P. Barnard of the University of Alabama and later chancellor of the University of Mississippi all were members of a distinguished Southern intellectual circle. Despite the improvement of state-sponsored schools in the late antebellum period, competing social and religious interests in the South limited the scope of educational reform. "The greatest handicap," as historian Avery Craven noted, "lay in the bitter rivalry between religious sects, which resulted in more denominational colleges than could be supported adequately and in a distrust and jealousy of the state universities."[8] Indeed, Southerners founded more than twenty-five denominational colleges and universities in the forty years preceding the Civil War, with each Southern state possessing at least one of these schools.

---

[8] Avery Craven, *The Growth of Southern Nationalism, 1848–1861* (Baton Rouge: Louisiana State University Press, 1953) 253–54, 271–73.

Thus, educational, religious, and regional identities fused together as Southern nationalism gained momentum.[9]

Against this backdrop of sectional strife, educational reform, and denominational assertiveness, Bishop Polk announced his plan for an Episcopal university in the South. In July 1856, Polk contacted the nine bishops of the Southern dioceses and outlined a strategy for educating the children of elite Southerners and for producing a highly-trained clergy. "A cardinal principle in the whole movement," Polk promised, "would of course be, that the institutions would be declaredly out and out Episcopal, founded by the Church for the especial benefit of her own children, for the advancement of learning generally, and for the propagation of the Gospel as she understands it." Hence, the mission entailed a broadly defined academic agenda and a narrowly construed denominational purpose. The Louisiana Bishop was troubled that "prejudice and ignorance" had cast a significant proportion of the region's population "under the control of other forms of religious opinions," a condition attributable in part to past failings of the Episcopal church, and he understood the reclamation of their souls as part of his spiritual calling. Also, the idea of cultivating a "native ministry," one sensitive to the "pursuits," "institutions," and "sympathies" of the Southern way of life represented a key feature of the university's cultural purpose. Polk argued that despite some occasions of "eminent and honorable success," the region's state-supported colleges and universities had failed to meet the needs of Southern people. Consequently, their children were "expatriated" to Northern schools. The unfortunate result, the bishop explained, was that these youngsters resided "beyond the reach of...supervision or parental influence [and were] exposed to the rigors of an unfriendly climate." Polk intended his appeal to resonate with those individuals who feared the taint of abolitionism in Northern schools and with those who recognized the compatibility of Episcopal traditions with the prevailing conventions of the Southern slave society.[10]

---

[9] Clement Eaton, *A History of the Old South: The Emergence of a Reluctant Nation*, (New York: Macmillan, 1975) 441–42; McCardell, *The Idea of a Southern Nation*, 177–83.

[10] Leonidas Polk, *A Letter to the Right Reverend Bishops of Tennessee, Georgia, Arkansas, Texas, Mississippi, Florida, South Carolina, and North Carolina from the Bishop of Louisiana* (New Orleans: B. M. Norman, 1856).

By no means was Leonidas Polk the only educational reformer among the Southern bishops. As early as 1832, Bishop James Hervey Otey of Tennessee attempted to establish a denominational college and seminary in his diocese. In fact, as Otey's understudy during the mid-1830s, Polk chaired several committees assigned the task of raising funds and soliciting support for an interdiocesan Literary and Theological Seminary. The plan, however, never received the necessary backing. After Polk became bishop of Louisiana, Otey proceeded with several smaller projects such as Ashwood School for Girls, Mercer Hall, Madison College, and Ravenscroft College, but they all failed. Otey's own poor health, inadequate financial resources, and a general lack of interest prevented the Episcopalians of Tennessee from creating a diocesan school. Conversely, the other major Protestant denominations in the Volunteer State were busier and more successful. The Baptists laid the groundwork for what became Carson-Newman College, the Presbyterians founded Tusculum College, and the Methodists assumed control of Lambuth College. The Episcopal dilemma in Tennessee was symptomatic of their record throughout the South. While the Presbyterians, Baptists, and Methodists produced a number of denominational colleges and universities, the Episcopalians made no substantial progress.[11]

When Polk unveiled his plan for an Episcopal university in the South, Otey responded enthusiastically, and as the senior bishop in the region he played an important role in promoting the venture. The two men, however, viewed the mission of the academic institution quite differently. "The prime end aimed at in our projected University," Otey contended, "is...to make the Bible the ultimate and sufficient rule and standard for the regulation of man's conduct as a rational and accountable being; to cultivate the moral affections of the young, while their intellectual powers are in the process of development, thus furnishing the community with an enlightened and virtuous class of citizens; and last of all, to supply convenient facilities for the acquisition of theological learning, that a native population may be served by a native ministry." Whereas Polk stressed the Episcopalian and regional nature of the school's identity, Otey accented its civic dimensions as a greater priority than the need for a "native ministry." The contrast

---

[11] David S. Armentrout, *James Hervey Otey: First Episcopal Bishop of Tennessee* (Knoxville: Episcopal Diocese in Tennessee, 1984) 69–78; Stanley J. Folmsbee, Robert E. Corlew, and Enoch L. Mitchell, *History of Tennessee*, 4 vols. (New York: Lewis Historical Publication Co., 1960) 1:447.

illustrated Otey's strong Whiggish political orientation that held that "the security of society, the supremacy of law, [and] the preservation of liberty" depended on a religiously educated and moral populace.[12] Otey recognized the wall of separation between church and state and concluded that churches along with Christian colleges and universities were responsible for shaping and cultivating public virtue.[13]

Otey also differed with Polk regarding the hazards or inconveniences of educating Southern children in Northern school systems. On the one hand, Polk did not want to expose the region's youngsters to what he perceived as a mounting hostility toward the South in most Northern intellectual circles. On the other hand, Otey simply regretted the "additional expense," the increased risk of physical injury, and the "weakening" of parental ties. In addition, the bishop of Tennessee repudiated any and all contentions that the Episcopal university advocated a sectional agenda. In fact, Otey celebrated an Episcopal identity that traced its heritage to the noble and victorious sons of the American Revolution. "And when we shall be found, under the color of religion, hatching treason against the peace and union of these [United] States," Otey proclaimed, "may desolation roll its wave over our habitations, and our names be swallowed up in infamy!" By inculcating his appeals with alarmist rhetoric and by issuing such an ominous prophecy, Otey demonstrated that he was not a Southern nationalist.[14]

As the elder statesman of the Southern wing of the Episcopal church, Otey was nominated by the Southern bishops to present the university proposal to the General Convention in the fall of 1857. With little fanfare, the resolution passed. Although, permission had been granted by the entire diocesan membership of the Protestant Episcopal Church in the United States, the Southern dioceses would actually own and operate the university through a board of trustees consisting of the bishop, one clergyman, and two

---

[12] James Hervey Otey, *Proceedings of a Convention of the Trustees of a Proposed University for the Southern States, Under the Auspices of the Protestant Episcopal Church* (Atlanta: C.R. Hanleiter, 1857).

[13] This was a standard theme of Otey's preaching. See also *The Duty of the Ministers of the Gospel, To Their People, Considered in their Civil Relations: Set Forth in a Primary Charge to the Clergy of the Diocese of Tennessee* (Nashville: S. Nye, 1837).

[14] Ibid.

laymen from each of its ten dioceses. By virtue of his seniority, Otey served as the school's first chancellor.[15]

Nevertheless, it was Leonidas Polk and his good friend Bishop Stephen Elliott of Georgia who became the driving forces behind the project. As chairman of the site selection committee, Polk oversaw the first important decision reached by the board of trustees. In his original communiqué of July 1856, Polk indicated that the foothills of the Allegheny Mountains in the southeast corner of Tennessee represented the best possible spot for the university. The most obvious advantage of this location was its accessibility to the major rail lines of the South. Polk estimated that from such points as Charleston, Savannah, Pensacola, Mobile, New Orleans, Shreveport, Vicksburg, Memphis, and Little Rock a student, faculty member, parent, or churchman could reach the site within a matter of thirty-six to forty-eight hours. Moreover, the mountain environment offered fresh air, "pure water," and protection from the epidemic-ridden cities of the Deep South. In addition, "the cost of living is cheap," Polk explained, and the location falls "within the pale of the plantation states." The final decision, however, required seventeen ballots from the board before they reached an agreement. Some had favored a more geographically-centered position such as Huntsville or Atlanta, but the trustees eventually selected a 5,000 acre tract just northwest of Chattanooga on the Cumberland Plateau known as Sewanee. Another important early decision involved the selection of a name for the newly-formed institution. Reverend J. Wood Dunn of Texas recommended The Church University, Bishop Thomas Atkinson of North Carolina submitted the University of Sewanee, but the board adopted the University of the South, which had been suggested by Bishop William Mercer Green of Mississippi.[16] The intention of some school supporters may have been to divest the entire enterprise of any sectional inferences, but by choosing the University of the South as the name, a measure of regional distinctiveness had been added to the institution's identity. Moreover, the

---

[15] Arthur Benjamin Chitty, Jr., *Reconstruction at Sewanee: The Founding of the University of the South and its First Administration, 1857–1872* (Sewanee TN: University of the South Press, 1954) 45–46.

[16] Quotes from Polk, *A Letter to the Right Reverend Bishops of Tennessee, Georgia, Arkansas, Texas, Mississippi, Florida, South Carolina, and North Carolina from the Bishop of Louisiana* [New Orleans: B. M. Norman, 1856]. See also Chitty, *Reconstruction at Sewanee*, 54–55.

appellation comported with the vision that Polk had devised and aimed to promote.

After the board of trustees selected the location and name of the university, Bishops Polk and Elliott concentrated their efforts on soliciting cash, checks, bonds, or pledges from interested benefactors. School organizers stipulated that a $500,000 endowment had to be raised before full academic operations could begin. Bishops Otey, Elliott, Polk, and others actually believed that $3,000,000 in gifts could be secured, which would provide an annual interest income of approximately $200,000. In comparison, South Carolina College and the University of Georgia received state appropriations of roughly $6,000 per year, and the University of Virginia received $15,000.[17] To meet the goal of the ambitious capital campaign, Polk intended to court the wealthy planters of the South, and his canvassing strategy reflected his awareness of the concerns and predilections of the region's elites. All along Polk understood that the University of the South had to establish itself as an institution of academic excellence and "rival" Harvard and Yale in terms of respectability and prominence. "I am perfectly and increasingly satisfied," Polk admitted to Elliott, "that nothing short of that will save us as a Church, and as a southern church in particular."[18]

Polk's juxtaposition of optimism and grave concern convinced Elliott and others that Southern Episcopalians could turn the idea of a church university into a "living and impressive reality." To expedite the process, the Louisiana bishop issued a virtual call to arms, announcing that the "signs of the times" demanded decisive action. "We shall have nothing left us but bitter and unavailing reproaches," Polk warned Elliott, "if we do not wake up to the necessity of providing amply for the emergency that is at the door." Specifically, Polk viewed the South as susceptible to the surge of abolitionist influence in Northern schools, churches, and political spheres. He also feared that he and Southern churchmen would no longer be able to sustain their denomination's neutral stance on the slavery issue. In light of

---

[17] Chitty, *Reconstruction at Sewanee*, 58–59. In his address before the General Convention, Otey estimated that real and personal estate values in the South for 1850 were $2,669,699,636 and that agricultural profits for that same year were $355,077,644. See Otey, *Proceedings of a Convention of the Trustees of a Proposed University for the Southern States*, 7.

[18] Leonidas Polk to Stephen Elliott, 23 July 1856, Leonidas Polk Papers.

Polk's own experiences as a planter, the bishop bristled with indignation at Northern criticisms of the Southern slaveholding society: "Talk of slavery! Those madcaps at the North don't understand the thing at all. We hold the negroes, and they hold us! They are at the head of the ladder! They furnish the yoke and we the neck! My own is getting sore, and it is the same with those of my neighbors in Church and State." Polk's frustration over the bitterly divisive nature of the slavery debate was clearly evident as was his desire to use the University of the South as a cultural safeguard against attacks on Southern values.[19]

Occasionally, Polk approved of Otey's nationalist representation of the university's identity but only on a conditional basis and usually to cater to the Whiggish-minded elements of Southern society. Interestingly, Polk adopted this approach when conversing with brother-in-law Kenneth Rayner, a prominent North Carolina politician and slaveholder. Rayner was something of a political oddity in the South. As described by his biographer, Gregg Cantrell, Rayner was at one time or another a Whig, Know-Nothing, secessionist, peace advocate, Redeemer, and Republican. At heart, Rayner embraced a Jeffersonian republicanism that extolled individual virtue and the role of constitutional law, and he was a determined foe of political corruption. The North Carolina politician, as a member of the 1855 Know-Nothing (American) party platform committee, supported the Kansas-Nebraska Act and the Fugitive Slave law but judged the repeal of the Missouri Compromise as unconstitutional. However, even as late as 1858, Rayner ranked such matters as voter fraud and machine politics as graver national issues than the slavery question.[20] Here, Polk and Rayner parted company because the bishop deemed abolitionist agitation as the greatest threat to the stability of the Union.

After a university-sponsored Independence Day celebration at Lookout Mountain, Tennessee, in 1857, Polk asked Rayner if he was satisfied with the patriotic flavor of Otey's keynote address and intimated that the "spirit of broad nationality" should appease the North Carolinian and those of his political persuasion. Yet, Polk was not afraid to hold these men accountable

---

[19] Leonidas Polk to Stephen Elliott, 30 August 1856, Leonidas Polk Papers.

[20] Gregg Cantrell, *Kenneth and John B. Rayner and the Limits of Southern Dissent* (Urbana: University of Illinois Press, 1993) 3–5, 100–101, 117–19. In additional to his unusual politics, Rayner fathered at least two mulatto children by his slaves, and he openly admitted this and showed the children special treatment.

and he welcomed the opportunity to test the pro-slavery resolve of the "Union-loving men" of the South. "We shall see what they mean when they cry, Down with the abolitionists and up with negrodom!" the bishop retorted. The University of the South, Polk argued, "will do more to compose and reconcile national feeling through the Church than anything, or all things together, that Episcopalians have attempted heretofore," and it will give "us as a section...an educational resource which will assure us a respectability and influence of more consequence than all sectional political combination." Once again Polk classified the university's mission as part of a joint Episcopalian and Southern agenda. Moreover, the bishop recognized that slavery was the hallmark of Southern distinctiveness.[21]

Throughout the South, the Episcopalian response to the proposed university was one of widespread support, and many agreed with the vision articulated by Bishop Polk. One of the staunchest advocates of the University of the South was Reverend Frederick Fitzgerald, editor of the *Church Intelligencer*, a weekly Episcopalian paper published in Raleigh, North Carolina. Fitzgerald hailed the University of the South as a noble endeavor designed for the glorification of God. He predicted that the "wise and conservative principles" of an Episcopalian educational program would produce generations of loyal churchmen endowed with the ability to fight "error, superstition, and fanaticism of any kind."[22] With a circulation of approximately 2,000 subscribers, the *Church Intelligencer* served as a regional forum that allowed Episcopalians to discuss a host of denominational issues including the University of the South. From Polk's adopted state of Louisiana, a New Orleanian applauded the school's mission as being ideally "suited to the wants and necessities of life in this age, and especially southern life." [23] Many were confident that the academic reputation of the University of the South would surpass those of the tradition-laden universities of France, England, and the rest of Europe. For example, an

---

[21] Leonidas Polk to Kenneth Rayner, 30 July 1857, Leonidas Polk Papers.

[22] Fitzgerald associated the university wholly with Polk and suggested that one day the bishop's ashes rest on the campus grounds as a tribute to the "monument" that he created. Also, the paper cited as one of its prime objectives the promotion of the University of the South. "University of the South," *Church Intelligencer*, 21 March 1860, 2.

[23] Henry S. Stroupe, *The Religious Press in the South Atlantic States, 1802–1865* (Durham: Duke University Press, 1956) 69–70; E, "University of the South," *Church Intelligencer*, 14 March 1860, 1.

Episcopalian from Mobile, Alabama, who had graduated from a German university, predicted that within thirty years "students from the Old World" would cross the Atlantic "to seek knowledge on the mountain plateau of Sewanee." The fulfillment of this dream, he promised, would place "the South in the front rank of civilized nations."[24] In accord with these grand expectations, some considered a $3,000,000 endowment an attainable goal. And one North Carolinian reminded Southern Episcopalians of the wealth they had gleaned from their divinely "favored" lands of cotton and sugar and urged fellow churchmen to contribute as part of their religious duty.[25]

As interest increased, several aspects of the university's program attracted special attention. First, the statutes regarding the boarding and lodging of students received praise from every observer. Specifically, school officials intended to abolish the so-called "barracks" or dormitory arrangement in favor of cabins or small houses that would accommodate no more than twelve pupils.[26] Critics of the old system claimed that it was a "source of constant and immense evil" and created a haven for pranksters and derelicts. Many, including Reverend Fitzgerald, lamented the lack of familial influence and supervision on most college campuses. They cited a decline in morals and genteel manners as evidence of their complaints.[27] Perhaps Fitzgerald, who possessed more than a passing knowledge of the Raleigh-Durham-Chapel Hill social scene, was aware of the kind of trouble that tempted college students like Bryan Grimes and Tippo Sahib Houghton. These young men attended the University of North Carolina in the mid-1840s, but they seemed much more interested in sexual exploits than academic pursuits. Houghton, who reconnoitered the area for potential liaisons, determined that "mulatto meat" was in good supply at nearby Edenton but that the "clapp" was so widespread in Raleigh that prostitutes should be avoided.[28] Concerned parents no doubt had grown tired of reports from campuses documenting the sexual escapades and corrupting influence of such fornicators as Grimes and Houghton. Fitzgerald believed that the

---

[24] "From the *Mobile Weekly Register*," *Church Intelligencer*, 25 April 1860, 3.

[25] S, *Church Intelligencer*, 30 May 1860, 5.

[26] E, "University of the South, *Church Intelligencer*, 14 March 1860, 1.

[27] Editorial, *Church Intelligencer*, 11 October 1860, 1.

[28] Bryan Grimes to Tippo Sahib Houghton, 18 November 1845, Bryan Grimes Papers, Southern Historical Collection, University of North Carolina, Chapel Hill, North Carolina. I would like to thank Michael Coffey for this letter.

close confines of the boardinghouses would curb such behavior. Ultimately, he hoped that the "home-influence" would lead to better study habits and provide a protective environment for students "during the trying days of college life."[29]

School officials also had other ideas about ensuring the basic tenets of Southern domesticity. For example, the University of the South intended to employ an academic calendar in which a winter vacation was substituted for the more traditional summer break observed by most colleges. A prime consideration in this adjustment was the desire to avoid the hot and stagnant summer weather on Southern plantations and to take advantage of the "wholesome" and refreshing climate of the Sewanee domain. By promoting this particular schedule, school supporters also dreamed of turning the University of the South into the new summer vacation destination of Southern elites, and as an enticement provisions were made to lease or license residences to wealthy patrons. The mountain retreat promised to preserve "the charm and blessing of a polished social circle." In fact, one Alabama Episcopalian believed that the accomplished men of the South would flock to the university to be near their children and to indulge themselves by listening to a distinguished lecturer of Practical Agriculture or be mesmerized by the economic commentary of "another Adam Smith." Without question, the University of the South expected not only to promote academic excellence but also to provide "the pleasures of a cultivated and refined society."[30]

In addition, significant attention was given to the academic training that students would receive at the University of the South. The university's statutes enumerated some thirty-two different "schools" or programs such as Greek Language and Literature, Mathematics, Civil Engineering, Theory and Practice of Agriculture, Commerce and Trade, Theology, and Fine Arts. The classics comprised a large part of the anticipated curriculum, and at least one interested party, who identified himself as "Amicus Curiae," hoped that a strong classics tradition would serve as a "*prophylactic* against

---

[29] Editorial, *Church Intelligencer*, 11 October 1860, 1. See also S, *Church Intelligencer*, 30 May 1860, 5. Here a Raleigh churchman echoes the sentiments of Fitzgerald.

[30] E, "University of the South," *Church Intelligencer*, 14 March, 1860, 1; S, *Church Intelligencer*, 30 May 1860; "From the *Mobile Weekly Register*," *Church Intelligencer*, 25 April 1860, 3; X, *Church Intelligencer*, 27 September, 1860, 7.

the narrowing and sharpening influence of professional studies." According to "Amicus," a number of colleges and universities had fallen victim to this trend by making classical studies optional. He lambasted the implementation of this policy at the University of Virginia and charged the Charlottesville institution with providing a "mere professional" rather than a liberal arts education. Furthermore, "Amicus" argued that unless Greek and Latin were recognized as "living and life-giving" languages and until students were trained "through the Comedies of Aristophanes, the Orations of Demosthenes, and the History of Thucydides and Tacitus" then colleges and universities would graduate "mere politicians" and not statesmen. He maintained that only through a systematic study of these texts could one come to understand the hallmarks of Athenian democracy.[31]

The scientific side of the University of the South's academic program also received the endorsement of some Southern Episcopalians. One German-trained scholar and churchman from Mobile, Alabama, expressed "gratification" over the announcement of a chair in Ethnology and Universal Geography. While acknowledging the importance of classical studies, this supporter recognized the shortcomings of a classics-only approach. He shrewdly cautioned that education must keep pace with an advancing and modernizing world. A chair of Ethnology and Universal Geography was one way in which to improve the curriculums of universities and colleges, the Alabamian concluded, and "the University of the South, in a spirit truly southern and with a far-seeing perception...has for the first time recognized the science which teaches the aptitude and comparative position of different human races" and has given the discipline a position of "equal rank with the older and traditional dimensions of profane learning."[32] This opinion complimented the racial inferiority or biological defense of slavery espoused by such Southern nationalists as Henry Hughes and Josiah Nott.[33] Although Bishop Polk personally upheld a proslavery defense rooted in biblical and sociological theories, the fact remains that most advocates of the University of the South, regardless of their respective proslavery doctrines, envisioned the school as an apologist of the Southern slave society.

---

[31] Amicus Curiae, "University of the South," *Church Intelligencer*, 21 March 1860, 12.

[32] "From the *Mobile Weekly Register*," *Church Intelligencer*, 25 April 1860, 3.

[33] McCardell, *The Idea of a Southern Nation*, 85, 90.

As momentum gathered for the University of the South, many supporters also expressed an appreciation for the Episcopalian nature of the school's identity. Strengthening the denomination and training a native ministry had been part of Polk's original pledge, but in light of a religious controversy at the University of North Carolina, the bishop's promises increased in importance. Specifically, Chapel Hill had a mandatory Sunday chapel attendance policy, and students were not allowed, even with parental permission, to leave the university and attend religious services of their own choosing. Concerned observers attacked the university from two positions. On the one hand, critics charged that by interfering with parental and individual prerogatives, the University of North Carolina was violating the spirit of the nation's commitment to religious liberty. On the other hand, complainants disapproved of the "eclectic system" of preaching offered by the various denominational representatives who alternately conducted the chapel services for the university. "We most decidedly object to any emasculated Christianity," opined the editor of the *Church Intelligencer*, who also contended that moral homilies could not be substituted for the "great doctrines of Christianity" if the young collegians were to be "prepared to meet the...infidelity of the age." Everyone realized that as a state-sponsored institution the University of North Carolina was obligated to observe the separation of church and state, and no one advocated that the university become a sponsor of the Episcopalian faith.

However, Episcopalians used the Chapel Hill incident to rally denominational loyalty. On a practical level, they demanded that students be released from the mandatory chapel attendance when a written parental request was submitted. Eventually, the University of North Carolina in response to the pressure exerted by Episcopalians as well as a significant number of Southern Methodists agreed to the recommendation.[34] But for some, the situation at Chapel Hill underscored the need for a denominational or diocesan college or university in the South; one proponent, Episcopalian R. B. C. of Cloverdale, North Carolina, of this view actually argued that the University of North Carolina had attained a distinctly "Presbyterian impress" and that university president Joseph Caldwell had cultivated a "quasi sectarian character" at the North Carolina

---

[34] Editorial, *Church Intelligencer*, 20 June 1860, 1.

institution.[35] Thus, as Episcopalians throughout the South considered the possible merits of the University of the South, such incentives as denominational purity and the school's commitment to Southern intellectual and social aims prompted widespread support.

For his part, Bishop Polk used these issues to garner the allegiance of Southern elites. In the fund-raising circular that he co-authored with Bishop Stephen Elliott, Polk pessimistically announced that "the world is trying hard to persuade us that a slaveholding people cannot be a people of high moral and intellectual culture." To combat the charges of cultural inferiority, Polk guaranteed that the university would "secure for the South a Literary center...[for] the wise, good, and the cultivated" elements of Southern society. "We, of all men," Polk reasoned, "should be the most highly cultivated" since we have a special "caste" to perform our labor, thereby granting us the "leisure" to devote ourselves to the "elegance of literature, and to such a culture as shall make" our civilization the "envy of all lands." Polk challenged potential donors to prove their "love for the South" and express their "indignation against those that were warring against her" by giving generously to the university cause. Indeed, Polk reminded Southern elites that their wealth was a blessing from God that should be used to "vindicate" their region and to provide for the welfare of their children.[36]

If financial donations are used to measure or judge the responses to Polk's entreaties, then the bishop certainly won the approval of Southern elites. From 1857 to 1860, he logged countless miles as he traveled throughout the slave states in search of benefactors. Not surprisingly, his greatest success occurred in his own Louisiana diocese where he raised $264,160.[37] In the early stages, Polk reported "many offers" of $1,000, several of $5,000, and one pledge of $25,000. He believed that no reasonable request for money would be turned down, and he even expected to secure at

---

[35] Viator, *Church Intelligencer*, 22 November 1860, 4. An accomplished mathematician and a Presbyterian minister, Caldwell was a member of a well-educated, Presbyterian, North Carolina family of lawyers, physicians, and educators. Powell, *Dictionary of North Carolina Biography*, I, 300–307.

[36] Leonidas Polk and Stephen Elliott, *Address of the Commissioners for Raising the Endowment of the University of the South* (New Orleans: B. M. Norman, 1860).

[37] Chitty, *Reconstruction at Sewanee*, 71.

least one contribution in the $75,000 to $100,000 range.[38] By mid-summer 1859, the university had collected roughly $320,000 from some fifty different patrons throughout the South.[39] Polk had a simple explanation for his success. "The Southern States," he informed Elliott, "are resolved to look out for themselves henceforth, and in nothing more than in the education of their children." On this point, Polk was totally convinced. He even advised Elliott's young son to work diligently at his studies so that one day he could become a professor or president at the University of the South because, as Polk phrased it, "we have concluded to be done with the Yankee boys altogether." This playful and charming demeanor no doubt appealed to adults as well. But, Polk also had a serious side. If the situation warranted, he was not averse to "agitation" and felt it was his duty "to arouse, and instruct and excite" when necessary. Moreover, he was not opposed to presenting his arguments in a religious context. Often, Polk remarked that only the Episcopal Church was capable of providing an educational facility on a scale comparable to the proposed University of the South. In Polk's mind, the Baptists and Methodists lacked "the bearing, or social position, or prestige, requisite to command the public confidence, [and] the Romanists in such a Protestant population [were] of course out of the question." Regarding the Presbyterians, Polk was more complimentary. He conceded that they possessed a certain degree of "bearing" and "organization," and feared that unless Episcopalians acted aggressively, the Presbyterians might gain control of the "public mind" of the South. Thus, the University of the South represented a way Southern Episcopalians could extend their influence in the region and at the same time limit the appeal of other denominations.[40]

By mid-1860 enough money had been raised to begin construction of the university. On 10 October a crowd estimated at 5,000 gathered for the laying of the cornerstone. There were a number of public rituals associated with this ceremony, and Bishops Elliott and Polk were visible participants. The bishop of Georgia deposited in the cornerstone a number of items, including a Bible, a Book of Common Prayer, the constitution of the United States, and various documents relating to the canons and history of the

[38] Leonidas Polk to Stephen Elliott, 31 January 1857, Leonidas Polk Papers.
[39] James H. Otey to Thomas Ruffin, 8 July 1859, in *The Papers of Thomas Ruffin*, ed. J. G. de Roulhac Hamilton, 4 vols. (Raleigh NC.: Edwards and Broughton, 1920) 3:37.
[40] Leonidas Polk to Stephen Elliott, 31 January 1857, Leonidas Polk Papers.

Episcopal church. Then, the bishop of Louisiana tapped the block three times and dedicated the university to "the cultivation of true religion, learning, and virtue, that thereby God may be glorified and the happiness of man may be advanced."[41]

Throughout the day the celebrants listened to speeches and choral performances. At noon, they enjoyed a catered luncheon banquet. Harmony reigned on the mountaintop that day, and, as one observer wryly noted, it may have been the first time that so many "representatives of differing opinion" had gotten "into the same bed!"[42] This insight may have been directed toward the contrasting theological positions of various individuals. Irrespective of the original intent, the comment in a metaphorical sense reflects the two prevailing viewpoints regarding the identity of the University of the South. There was the Unionist or nationalist tone that Otey sustained and the Southern and Episcopalian character that Polk championed.

Since Polk had served as the chief fund-raiser and because his Louisiana diocese had contributed nine-times as much money as Otey's Tennessee diocese, one might reasonably conclude that most of the serious financial contributors endorsed Polk's vision rather than Otey's.[43] If this conclusion is credible, then an examination of the types of individuals that Polk recruited for the educational project would be pertinent. One key supporter was John S. Preston of South Carolina. Preston was the embodiment of the aristocratic planter politician. He had married into the Wade Hampton family and operated within a circle of such prominent South Carolina politicos as Robert Barnwell, Wade Hampton, John L. Manning, and Christopher Memminger. In the early 1850s he operated one of the largest sugar plantations in Louisiana and owned 701 slaves. Although not a member of the radical Calhoun-nullifier tradition, Preston's work as chairman of the South Carolina Senate's Committee on Federal Relations confirmed his commitment to Southern nationalism. He was also part of a group that worked within the national Democratic Party to defend Southern institutions and rights.[44] Polk visited with Preston in early 1857, and the two

---

[41] Quoted in Chitty, *Reconstruction at Sewanee*, 63–65.

[42] Viator, *Church Intelligencer*, 22 November 1860, 4.

[43] Chitty, *Reconstruction at Sewanee*, 71.

[44] Lacy K. Ford, *The Origins of Southern Radicalism: The South Carolina Upcountry, 1800–1860* (New York/Oxford: Oxford University Press, 1988) 200; Harold S.

obviously connected on the issue of higher education in the South. Preston, who had recently enrolled his boys at Göttingen University in Germany, "fully endorsed" the bishop's plans and made several recommendations pertaining to building programs and faculty hiring procedures. Polk expected that Preston would provide a generous donation and was no doubt encouraged when the South Carolinian sold his Louisiana sugar plantation for $1,000,000 in 1858.[45] Ultimately, Preston became a very active supporter of the University of the South, and he received the honor of delivering the keynote address during the ceremonial laying of the cornerstone in October 1860.

For a time, the assembled guests may have forgotten the purpose of the occasion as Preston devoted the first three-fifths of his speech to a discussion of English History and the Protestant Reformation. The South Carolinian covered the reign of Alfred the Great and honored the monarch for freeing his surfs, instituting trial by jury, and championing "liberal" and "enlightened" education as a bulwark against the "dangerous superstitions of the Roman church." As the keynote speaker recited what he called the "Holy epic" that had inspired the founders of the University of the South, he continually pointed to the Reformation as an accelerant for the causes of religious and civil liberties. He defiantly proclaimed that "Protestantism was the refusal of men to live any longer in a general lie." Preston closed this lengthy segment of his speech by establishing a causal link between the "Protestant freedom of England" and "the universal freedom of America." He then recommended to his audience that they raise their "powerful voices" and cry out, "All hail, our mother!"[46]

Eventually, Preston reached the matter at hand, the purpose of the University of the South. Interestingly, he characterized the plan as the invention of the ten Southern dioceses and not that of the entire denomination. Their "oblation which, [presented] before God,...will come to be the chief element in His economy of redeeming, perpetuating, and

---

Schultz, *Nationalism and Sectionalism in South Carolina, 1852–1860* (Durham: Duke University Press, 1950) 22–23; John Barnwell, *Love of Order: South Carolina's First Secession Crisis* (Chapel Hill: University of North Carolina Press, 1982) 141–42.

[45] Leonidas Polk to Stephen Elliott, 31 January 1857, Leonidas Polk Papers.

[46] The Preston speech is in "Miscellaneous Documents on the History of the University of the South," Board of Trustees Collection, Jesse Ball duPont Library, University of the South, Sewanee, Tennessee.

exalting the people of these Southern states, with all their institutions, their liberties, and their hopes, for all time to come." This Southern way of life included slavery, and Preston lamented that the "Sovereign state[s]" of the North had begun to attack the South's peculiar institution. He was particularly critical of Massachusetts: "Another Sovereign state, made by your industry to rival the richest capitals of the old world, bids its chief Representative in our common council tell us, that we must yield our mission, or ourselves be made subjects to systems it chooses to impose." Likewise, Preston was dismayed that England had begun to castigate the South: "From beyond the seas in our own tongue, by those who read Bacon and Milton with us, and pray with our prayer-book, and who gave us this mission, [they now demand] that we must abandon it, or abandon our communion with the civilization of the age."[47]

In the South Carolinian's mind, the need for such an institution as the University of the South "had become obvious." He further explained, it is because of abolitionism's "hollow falsehood that we must be the better prepared to refute its scandal, and resist its aggressions, and give over its followers to the infamous notoriety that they have achieved, while we preserve that system which saves us from the sins and dangers growing naturally in the soil of Abolition." The "wealthy citizens" must fight to preserve order, the "Southern planter" must fight to preserve his way of life, and they cannot do so "without the very highest moral and intellectual culture...which this University proposes to furnish." Under the Episcopal banner and with the "Christian Bible" as the "corner-stone of the University of the South," the keynote speaker promised that "the heart [will be] made to comprehend, to regulate and to apply the vast duties which pertain to the citizen of the slaveholding states and the Christian." Having articulated the university's mission from a perspective that surely pleased Bishop Polk, Preston pronounced a benediction, "Be of good comfort; we shall this day light such a candle, by God's grace, as I trust, never shall be put out."[48]

Just four months later, John Preston was the South Carolina commissioner to Virginia's secession convention. The prominence of this secessionist at such an important event should not be overlooked, nor should the involvement of John Armfield, another of Polk's associates. Armfield and

---

[47] Ibid.
[48] Ibid.

his business partner Isaac Franklin had operated one of the South's most lucrative slave-trading businesses. After the two men sold their company in 1836, Armfield purchased a plantation in Louisiana and spent a great deal of time in New Orleans where he associated with bankers, cotton brokers, and local elites, and where he likely encountered Leonidas Polk for the first time. In 1854 Armfield acquired Beersheba Springs, a modest vacation hideaway that consisted of a tavern, dining hall, and guest cabins and rested on a 1,000-acre tract in Grundy County, Tennessee. The former slave trader intended to transform Beersheba Springs into a mountain resort. Between 1856 and 1858, he added some twenty cabins, which ranged in price from $1,500 to $3,500 each, and the other renovations included a new hotel building, ballroom, and a bowling alley, but no saloon, and professional gamblers were warned to stay away. Armfield became interested in the University of the South when school officials began debating possible locations, and he was pleased when they chose the Sewanee site, which was in close proximity to his own property. A local land developer remarked that Armfield's excitement was driven by his desire to make Beersheba Springs a profitable enterprise, and the general discussions about turning the university into a cultural retreat for Southern elites comported well with the entrepreneur's own business plans. But Armfield also appeared to support the academic and regional mission of the university. As confirmation of his support, Armfield made a generous endowment pledge of $25,000 per year for the rest of his life.[49] In addition, he constructed cabins for Bishops Otey and Polk at Beersheba Springs, and he typically extended invitations of hospitality to members of the university's board of trustees when they were in the area.[50] Polk's willingness to reach out to include such culturally and politically identifiable figures as John S. Preston and John Armfield in his plans for the University of the South was a poignant statement about the university's mission and purpose.[51]

---

[49] Isabel Howell, "John Armfield of Beersheba Springs," *Tennessee Historical Quarterly* 3/1 (1944): 46–64.

[50] James H. Otey to Thomas Ruffin, 8 July 1859, in *The Papers of Thomas Ruffin*, ed. J. G. de Roulhac Hamilton, 4 vols. (Raleigh NC: Edwards and Broughton, 1920) 3:37. Otey informed board member Ruffin of Armfield's offer.

[51] The Polk-Armfield connection extended to Lucius J. Polk and A. Hamilton Polk, the brother and eldest son of Leonidas Polk, who became shareholders of Beersheba Springs when Armfield sold it in 1858. See Howell, "John Armfield of Beersheba Springs," 59.

Accordingly, the curriculum of the University of the South was designed to advance what some have called "a Southern republic of letters." Advocates of a Southern literary nationalism constructed a Cavalier-Yankee antithesis, as historian John McCardell asserts, in an attempt "to restore order and purpose to an increasingly Yankee world" and to illustrate the "goodness and gentility" of the Southern way of life. Obviously, Polk was no William Gilmore Simms or Nathaniel Beverly Tucker. Yet, he understood their conceptualization of Southern society and he intended to make his university an integral part of their Southern republic of letters.[52] Polk conferred with a number of Southern ideologues including Albert Taylor Bledsoe of the University of Virginia, whom he approached about the possibility of filling the University of the South's chair in Moral Philosophy and the Evidences of Christianity. The two men also reached a gentleman's agreement whereby the University of the South would publish the pedagogue's forthcoming book on moral philosophy.[53] Bledsoe, a schoolmate of Polk's at West Point, taught mathematics at Virginia, but he was more widely known as a distinguished theologian and political theorist. His most important publications included *An Examination of President Edwards' Inquiry into the Freedom of the Will* (1845), *A Theodicy* (1853), and *An Essay on Liberty and Slavery* (1856). In these works, Bledsoe examined the concepts of spiritual freedom and human liberty, and he positioned himself as an antagonist to Jonathan Edwards and John Locke. As a theologian, Bledsoe plotted a middle course between Calvinism and Arminianism by proposing that because man was created in God's image he was "self active" and possessed a moral agency that was not subject to predispositions or external forces. In his political writings, Bledsoe represented a conservative tradition that refuted the Lockean claim that all men possessed an unalienable right to liberty. Although an ordained Episcopal priest, Bledsoe's views were controversial, which makes Polk's recruitment of the Southern ideologue rather intriguing.[54]

---

[52] McCardell, *The Idea of a Southern Nation*, 176, 166.

[53] Albert Taylor Bledsoe to Leonidas Polk, 8 October 1860, Leonidas Polk Papers.

[54] J. W. Cooke, "Albert Taylor Bledsoe: An American Philosopher and Theologian of Liberty," *Southern Humanities Review* 8 (Spring 1974): 215–28; Eugene D. Genovese, *The Slaveholders' Dilemma: Freedom and Progress in Southern*

Despite Polk's commitment to Southern literary nationalism and his consistent identification of slavery as the defining characteristic of Southern society, he, like most Southern evangelical clerics, avoided involvement in legislative policy debates and political party disputes. Hence, he was not part of a concerted political effort to promote secession. The issue of political secession was certainly not discussed in his sermons. For Southern evangelicals, preaching the "gospel" was their "preeminent duty," one that required them to expound on such basic doctrines as sin and salvation and to address such topics as pietistic living and denominational distinctiveness. Therefore, many Southern divines rejected so-called political preaching. However, as the abolitionist crusade developed a movement culture, one based on a political and sometimes religious identity, many Southern preachers were compelled to respond publicly to the attacks against their society, which meant they had to defend slavery.[55] Although Polk did not publish as extensively as such proslavery essayists as Thornton Stringfellow, James H. Thornwell, and Benjamin Morgan Palmer, he clearly, by means of example, established himself as an important and recognizable slavery apologist. Indeed, between 1840 and 1860, Polk never owned less than 100 slaves, and his efforts in the area of religious instruction of slaves placed him in the company of such slavery reformers-reactionists as Presbyterian divine Charles Colcock Jones.[56]

Polk became more aggressive in his defense of slavery when abolitionists assailed the South as an immoral society and denounced the region's prelates as puppets of a slaveocracy. In this regard, the bishop joined other Southern evangelicals who viewed abolitionists as demagogues and political extremists who ignored the basic doctrines of Christianity,

---

Conservative Thought, 1820–1860 (Columbia: University of South Carolina Press, 1990) 49–54.

[55] Anne C. Loveland, Southern Evangelicals and the Social Order, 1800–1860 (Baton Rouge: Louisiana State University Press, 1980) 38–42, 109–24; Lawrence Goodwyn, The Populist Moment: A Short History of the Agrarian Revolt in America (New York/Oxford: Oxford University Press, 1978) xviii. According to Goodwyn, the four stages of democratic-movement building are formation, recruitment, education, and politicalization.

[56] Larry Tise, Proslavery: A History of the Defense of Slavery in America, 1701–1840 (Athens: University of Georgia Press, 1987) 172. Only seventeen (6 percent) of Tise's 275 proslavery clergyman owned 100 or more slaves, and the office of bishop was one of the highest ecclesiastical positions in any denomination.

disregarded the biblical justification of slavery, and promoted dissension in churches and denominations by calling into question the Christian faithfulness of slaveholders.[57] One incident in April 1861 captures the depth of Polk's distrust and contempt for abolitionists in particular and the antislavery cause in general. During Polk's annual diocesan visitation, his wife and daughters, rather than accompanying the bishop or remaining in New Orleans, decided to leave Louisiana for a respite at Sewanee. On the night of 12 April an arsonist torched the Polks' cabin, and the women only escaped physical injury when their slave, Altimore, pulled them to safety. Polk's wife speculated that the fire was "the work of some abolitionist."[58] When the bishop learned of the ordeal, he immediately denounced the perpetrators and the "spirit of hell" that had inspired their actions. "How I should have liked to come upon the scoundrels," Polk fumed, "I am satisfied that it was the work of an incendiary, and that it was prompted by the spirit of Black Republican hate."[59] Although the convening secession conventions and the firing on Fort Sumter overlapped this personal episode, the bishop viewed abolitionist agitation as the root-cause of the national political crisis.

The clearest indication of Polk's Southern nationalism occurred in the aftermath of the election of Abraham Lincoln as president of the United States. The Republican's victory transformed the nature of the sectional controversy, especially in Polk's adopted home of Louisiana, and created a political and cultural environment that forced the bishop to state publicly and categorically his views on Southern nationhood. With South Carolina, Mississippi, Florida, Alabama, and Georgia having declared their independence by mid-January 1861, the immediate secessionists, who controlled Louisiana's convention, had little difficulty in passing an ordinance of secession. Although no minister was a member of the state's secession convention, many clerics did help align public opinion behind the independence movement.[60]

---

[57] Loveland, *Southern Evangelicals and the Social Order*, 188–97, 258–62.

[58] Mrs. Polk quoted in Joseph H. Parks, *General Leonidas Polk, C.S.A.: The Fighting Bishop* (Baton Rouge: Louisiana State University, 1962) 163.

[59] Leonidas Polk to Frances Devereux Polk, 27 April 1861, in William M. Polk, *Leonidas Polk: Bishop and General*, 2 vols. (New York: Longmans, Green, and Co., 1915) 1:326–27.

[60] Charles P. Roland, "Louisiana and Secession," *Louisiana History* 19/4 (Fall 1978): 389–99; Jefferson Davis Bragg, *Louisiana and the Confederacy* (Baton Rouge:

Perhaps the most influential religious explanation of the sectional crisis came from Benjamin Morgan Palmer, the minister of New Orleans' First Presbyterian Church. A native of Charleston, South Carolina, and a disciple of James Henley Thornwell, Palmer provided a scripturally-based rationale for disunion during a Thanksgiving Day address in 1860. Slavery, the prelate insisted, was ordained by God, and as such the South was predestined *"to conserve and to perpetuate the institution"* in any and all circumstances. In contrast to abolitionist critiques, the Presbyterian divine characterized Southern slaveholders as paternalistic masters dedicated to protecting an inferior and child-like race of workers. The cleric also ridiculed the North for hypocritically denouncing the South when the New England textile cities depended on cotton for their economic survival. Furthermore, Palmer asserted that Southerners were the defenders of God and true Christianity and were the political heirs of the nation's founding fathers. The North, Palmer argued, had given in to a godless "fanaticism" reminiscent of the Jacobin reign during the French Revolution. Consequently, the sectional controversy was a contest between two distinct civilizations, the "atheistic" North and the Christian South. Therefore, the South's desire to secede constituted a matter of self-defense. And if Southerners "arise" and speak in one voice, Palmer exclaimed, then God would protect them in battle and they could "roll back for all time, the curse" that was upon them. Southerners, the prelate concluded, could trust the Lord to help them achieve liberation from the Yankee peril.[61] The sermon, delivered in response to Louisiana Governor Thomas O. Moore's proclamation for a day of prayer and thanksgiving, became a type of "Holy Writ" for the separatist cause. At least 50,000 copies were printed in New Orleans alone, and, as historian Mitchell Snay has remarked, the exposition summarized the central tenets of the "religious logic of secession."[62]

Louisiana State University Press, 1941) 1–32; Ralph A. Wooster, *The Secession Conventions of the South* (Princeton: Princeton University Press, 1962) 101–20.

[61] Benjamin Morgan Palmer, *The South: Her Peril and Her Duty. A Discourse delivered in the First Presbyterian Church, New Orleans, on Thursday, November 29, 1860* (New Orleans: B. M. Norman, 1860) 3–10.

[62] For analysis of the sermon, see Haskell Monroe, "Bishop Palmer's Thanksgiving Day Address," *Louisiana History* 4/2 (Spring 1963): 105–18; Snay, *Gospel of Disunion*, 175–80.

Bishop Polk did not possess the oratorical skills of Benjamin Morgan Palmer, but his response to the national crisis was no less significant in terms of supplying a religious justification of secession. Beginning in late December 1860, Polk was convinced that Louisiana as well as Mississippi, Florida, Alabama, and Georgia would soon follow the example set by South Carolina. Anticipating the formation of a separate republic, he informed lame-duck president James Buchanan that an attempt to keep the South in the Union by force "would be madness" and would produce devastating consequences. "We believe that it is practicable," Polk contended, "for the two parties to separate peacefully; this we most earnestly desire." The bishop added that as long as slavery remained a profitable and socially advantageous labor system for Southern slaveholders, there would be no prospect for reunion.[63] At the same time, Polk issued a pastoral prayer to be used throughout the Louisiana diocese. In the jeremiadic tradition of Southern evangelicals, the bishop acknowledged the sinfulness of both the nation and mankind and petitioned God for forgiveness and mercy. He also prayed that peace, not war, would prevail in the absence of sectional reconciliation.[64] Despite the preference for peace over war, Polk's position was clear; slavery was the key issue and the South had the constitutional right to secede in order to protect its institutions. He waited, however, until Louisiana passed an ordinance of secession before making a bolder declaration in favor of independence.

On 30 January 1861, just four days after Louisiana adopted an ordinance of secession, Polk initiated a controversial process that would formally link Southern Episcopalians with the emerging Confederate nation. At that critical moment, Polk stated that Louisiana's recent political actions had created for the state's Episcopalians "an independent diocesan existence." He then announced to the clergy and laity of his diocese that "we must follow our nationality" and assert an ecclesiastical separation from the Protestant Episcopal Church in the United States. The bishop held no animosity toward Northern churchmen. Actually, he praised them for their loyalty to the constitution and for avoiding the slavery-induced schisms that plagued the other major denominations. Nevertheless, Polk favored a break

---

[63] Leonidas Polk to James Buchanan, 26 December 1860, in Polk, *Leonidas Polk*, 1:299–301.

[64] Prayer in Polk, *Leonidas Polk*, 1:303–304.

from the national church organization and consequently directed that certain changes be made to the Book of Common Prayer. Regarding the prayer for civil authorities, Polk substituted "the Governor of this state" for "the President of the United States." With respect to the prayer for the national congress, the bishop deleted "the people of these United States...[and] their senators and representatives" and inserted "the people of this State, and especially their legislature." More radical changes to the Book of Common Prayer came in late February 1861, when Polk entered "the President of the Confederate States" into the prayer for civil authorities and added "the Congress of the Confederate states."[65]

Polk's diocesan secession drew sharp criticism from Northern members of the Episcopal church. Southern reaction was divided. Several Southern bishops were unwilling to follow his example.[66] Southern prelates in general, according to historian Bertram Wyatt-Brown, "were...slow to join the political outcry for secession." There were three fundamental factors for clerical hesitancy: their moderate rather than "strident" defense of slavery, their "relationship to the national and regional polity," and their concern for maintaining a code of honor. However, the Thanksgiving Day address of Presbyterian Benjamin Morgan Palmer did serve as a type of watershed and thereafter more clergymen were willing to voice their support for secession.[67] Still, a number of prominent Southern divines, especially Episcopalians, deplored the prospect of disunion. For example, Bishop Nicholas Hamner Cobbs of Alabama proudly and defiantly proclaimed that he would rather die than witness the withdrawal of Alabama from the Union. As if part of some prophetic drama, Cobbs died on the morning of 11 January 1861; that afternoon Alabama passed an ordinance of secession.[68]

The most outspoken opponent of secession among Southern bishops was James H. Otey of Tennessee. In early February 1861, Otey informed James W. Patton of Greenville, Tennessee, that he considered himself a

---

[65] Pastoral letters in Polk, *Leonidas Polk*, 1:304–306, 308.

[66] For an interesting theological analysis of Polk's diocesan secession, see Robert L. Crewdson, "Bishop Polk and the Crisis in the Church: Separation or Unity?" *Historical Magazine of the Protestant Episcopal Church* 52 (March 1983): 43–51.

[67] Bertram Wyatt-Brown, "Church, Honor and Secession," *Religion and the American Civil War*, ed. Randall M. Miller, Harry S. Stout, and Charles Reagan Wilson (New York/Oxford: Oxford University Press, 1998) 89–109.

[68] Greenough White, *A Saint of the Southern Church: Memoir of the Right Reverend Nicholas Hamner Cobbs* (New York: J. Pott, 1897) 52.

"man of peace." In his judgment, secession was unnecessary so long as constitutional rights could be maintained. Moreover, Otey blamed Southern politicians for needlessly inciting and misleading the people.[69] Unlike Polk, Otey refused to aid the political separatists in his state by providing a religious endorsement of their cause. He opposed ecclesiastical separation and disapproved of any changes to the Book of Common Prayer. Relying on what he termed "common sense," the bishop of Tennessee argued that even if the government were "very inefficient and bad, and the President a very wicked man," the revision of the prayer book would not be appropriate. Otey demanded patience and optimistically declared that if Lincoln were "replenished with the grace of the Holy Spirit," then he might be inclined to "change his policy and restore peace to a distracted country!" In addition, Otey explained, by virtue of his ordination in the Protestant Episcopal Church in the United States, he was obligated to conform and obey its canons and doctrines or risk incurring the "wrath of God." The "scorn and contempt of man" was immaterial to him.[70]

There were, of course, other Southern Episcopalian bishops, aside from Polk, who vigorously defended slavery and supported disunion. For instance, Bishop Francis H. Rutledge of Florida openly advocated secession. Rutledge, a close personal friend of Florida fire-eater John Beard, encouraged secessionists by promising to donate $500 to the Florida state treasury if an ordinance of secession were adopted.[71] Rutledge even earned the praise of Virginia radical Edmund Ruffin when the latter visited Tallahassee during the state's secession convention. When they met, Rutledge bragged to Ruffin that "he had already seceded, with his native state" of South Carolina "in advance of Florida." The Virginia fire-eater noted in his diary that he "was very much pleased with the venerable old minister, & with his ardent & active patriotic sentiments." Considering Ruffin's ambivalence toward organized religion, this adoration was somewhat unusual but testifies to the power of Rutledge's pro-Confederate

---

[69] James H. Otey to James W. Patton, 2 February 1861, James Hervey Otey Papers, Southern Historical Collection. I would like to thank Dr. Bradley G. Bond for this letter.

[70] Otey quoted in "Bishop Otey's Views," *Church Intelligencer*, 16 May 1861, 1.

[71] Beard and Florida Governor Madison S. Perry were Episcopalians. Joseph D. Cushman, Jr., *A Goodly Heritage: The Episcopal Church in Florida, 1821–1892* (Gainesville: University of Florida Press, 1965) 42–45.

stance.[72] A less well-known bishop, Alexander Gregg of Texas, also agreed with Rutledge and Polk. Gregg, who graduated first in his class at South Carolina College in December 1838, embraced the John C. Calhoun "school of politics." As a small slaveholder, he deeply resented abolitionist criticism of slave masters, and he aggressively backed the cause of secession and the Confederacy.[73] In fact, the bishop clashed with one Northern-born cleric of his diocese over revisions to the prayer book, but he ultimately prevailed and implemented changes identical to those made by Bishop Polk.[74] Though he was confident of victory, Gregg did not underestimate the gravity of the times, and, in July 1861, he cautioned Texas Episcopalians about becoming vain and about ignoring the horrors of war. Expect to hear "the sounds of anguish, as the angel of death flies through our southern heavens," Gregg warned. Despite the admonition, the Texas bishop assured Southern patriots that a determined effort would produce a Confederate victory and eliminate "forever" the "spirit of wild and reckless infidelity and fanaticism, and of social anarchy and misrule" of the North.[75]

Although Rutledge, Gregg, Polk and others participated in the religious sanctioning of secession, the bishop of Louisiana took an unprecedented step when he accepted a combat assignment with the Confederate army. After the North and South exchanged blows at Fort Sumter in April 1861, Polk became particularly concerned with the safety of the Mississippi Valley. In early May he wrote Confederate President Jefferson Davis to express his fears about a possible invasion. Davis did not share his former West Point schoolmate's fears. Instead, the commander-in-chief trusted that the dreadful summer heat and the Confederate troops and

---

[72] William K. Scarborough, ed. *The Diary of Edmund Ruffin*, 3 vols. (Baton Rouge: Louisiana State University Press, 1972–1989) 1:524.

[73] Wilson Gregg and Arthur H. Noll, *Alexander Gregg: First Bishop of Texas* (Sewanee TN: University of the South Press, 1912) 8, 73, 86.

[74] Charles Gillette, *A Few Historic Records of the Church in the Diocese of Texas, During the Rebellion Together With a Correspondence between the Right Rev. Alexander Gregg and the Rev. Charles Gillette* (New York: J.A. Gray & Green, 1865).

[75] Alexander Gregg, *The Duties Growing out of It and the Benefits to be Expected, From the Present War* (Austin: Office of the State Gazette, 1861) 3–18. During the war, Gregg chastised Episcopalians for their self-centeredness, greed, and for not doing enough to support the Confederate war effort. See Alexander Gregg, *The Sin of Extortion, and its Peculiar Aggravations at a Time Like the Present* (Austin: Office of the State Gazette, 1863).

batteries positioned at Union City, Tennessee, and Corinth, Mississippi, would discourage an attack. Davis, however, did invite Polk to Richmond to consult with Confederate officials.[76] During his visit in June 1861, Polk conferred with the president, several cabinet members, and General Robert E. Lee. Based on information that he gathered, Polk believed that the Confederate military would be well served by such generals as Lee, John B. Magruder, P. G. T. Beauregard, Joseph E. Johnston, Robert Garnett, and Henry Wise. Also, Polk and Davis agreed over how "badly" they wanted Albert S. Johnston to assume command of the forces in the Western theater, but this mutual preference did not prevent the bishop from inquiring about field batteries for Tennessee and expressing opinions about other military matters.[77] The most important discussion occurred shortly after Polk arrived in Richmond when Davis offered Polk a command in the Confederate army, one that carried the rank of major general. Polk twice declined, but on Davis's third appeal he accepted, and in so doing he radically transformed the nature of his Southern nationalism.

Polk later explained that he had consulted with a number of individuals throughout his decision-making process. First, several "New Orleans people" who were in Richmond during [the] summer [of] 1861 had met with Polk and encouraged him to accept the offer. They knew that he shared their views on the importance of defending the Mississippi River and that as a general he would be in a better position to lobby on their behalf.[78] Second, Polk conferred with Bishop William Meade of Virginia. The distinguished cleric, whom Polk found "to be southern all through" and ready for a "down right good fight," evaluated the context of the times as well as Polk's background and current position. Meade concluded that "he could not sanction" Polk's acceptance of a military command, but he added that "all rules have exceptions" and that he would not "condemn" Polk if he decided to join the Confederate army. A third influence was Polk's aristocratic and martial heritage. As a descendent of a politically and socially well-connected North Carolinian and Revolutionary War hero, the West Point graduate and slaveholder determined under his "own judgment and conscience" that he owed an unconditional allegiance to the Southern way of life.[79]

---

[76] Jefferson Davis to Leonidas Polk, 22 May 1861, in Polk, *Leonidas Polk*, 1:355.

[77] Leonidas Polk to Frances Devereux Polk, 10 June 1861, Leonidas Polk Papers.

[78] Leonidas Polk to Frances Devereux Polk, 19 June 1861, Leonidas Polk Papers.

[79] Leonidas Polk to Stephen Elliott, 22 June 1861, Leonidas Polk Papers.

The decision surprised everyone including his family and close friends. The most interesting reaction came from his niece, Catherine Ann Devereux Edmondston, an ardent proponent of secession and the Confederacy who viewed emancipationist aims as "treason against liberty." The plantation mistress wondered who could have known that when "Rev Mr Polk married Aunt Fanny, first that he would ever be a Bishop, still less that he would return to his military life & yet be a Major General?" Throughout the war, the matter seemed to haunt Edmondston. During the battle of Shiloh, she noted in her diary "who could have predicted his career? When they saw him a young soldier of the cross donning the surplice for the first time, who could have foreseen that he would one day rise so high in the ranks of earthly warriors?" Following the battle of Perryville, she marveled at the transformation of the "peaceful young clergyman" into the battle-hardened military commander. Even after President Davis relieved Polk of his command amid the controversy surrounding Chickamauga, Edmondston caustically opined that the bishop "will now, I suppose, having sheathed the sword, resume the surplice—pity tis that he doffed it!"[80] Friend and confidant Bishop Stephen Elliott was equally frustrated with Polk's decision. The Georgian agreed in principle with Bishop Meade and warned that for those "who do unusual things—success or failure will be made the criterion of right or wrong. If you succeed, you will need no defenders; if you fail…you will have a pack of curs at your heels, especially all those you may have had occasion to kick during your previous life."[81]

The emergence of the bishop as general placed Southern Episcopalians in a tenuous position as they grappled to define the proper role of the clergy in the sectional conflict. Nominal Episcopalian fire-eater Edmund Ruffin may have been somewhat representative of those Episcopalians who found Polk's generalship difficult to accept. Ruffin "opposed making generals of civilians," except in "extraordinary cases" where the men had demonstrated "a natural genius of military command." He deemed the appointment of Polk as unfortunate.[82] Prior to Polk's announcement, Reverend Frederick

[80] Beth G. Crabtree and James W. Patton, eds., *"Journal of a Secesh Lady:" The Diary of Catherine Ann Devereux Edmondston, 1860–1866* (Raleigh NC: Division of Archives and History, 1979) 83, 146, 286, 478.

[81] Stephen Elliott to Leonidas Polk, 6 August 1861, Leonidas Polk Papers.

[82] Scarborough, *The Diary of Edmund Ruffin*, 2:113.

Fitzgerald, editor of the *Church Intelligencer*, discussed the responsibility of the clergy during the sectional controversy at great length. He decided that religious leaders "must not strive to lead in the Revolution." Instead, the editor instructed the clergy "to seek the honorable...office of chaplain" where they could minister to both the spiritual and material needs of the soldiers. Fitzgerald followed his own advice and accepted a chaplaincy in a North Carolina regiment.[83] In late June, the *Church Intelligencer* offered supplemental advice on the matter and stipulated that only in an "extreme case" should a clergyman "take up arms...and join in the ranks as a common soldier." An acceptable scenario required that the war turn so far against the South that "national existence" depended on one final or climactic battle. Then, any clergyman "capable of drawing a sword or touching a trigger" could march into battle under the "sanctification" of God. However, as the *Church Intelligencer* pointed out, the prescribed conditions had not yet materialized, and the paper believed militant acts by clergymen would be grossly "premature."[84] One churchwoman concurred with this basic interpretation and relied upon the lessons of history to validate her stance: "We turn away with unfeigned disgust from the description of the warrior bishops and priests of the middle ages, recognizing the monstrosity of a priest of God, with carnal weapons in his hands." This Episcopalian did allow as an exception the defense of "helpless women and children." Nevertheless, she refuted claims that the "aid of such soldiers will benefit the cause of the South," because, she argued, God would give victory to whomever he pleased.[85]

After Polk's decision became public knowledge, a number of Southern Episcopalians petitioned the *Church Intelligencer* for a review of the bishop's actions. The editor refused to elaborate on specific cases or personalities and referred the paper's readers to earlier positions and commentary. In addition, he expressed both "respect" for and "confidence" in Polk and speculated that unknown personal reasons may have driven the bishop to the act as he did. Furthermore, "if error it be," the editor opined, "it is a noble one, and it must, at least, seem venial in a class of men exempt by their profession from military service."[86] Similarly, a contributor to the *Church*

---

[83] "Duty of the Clergy for the Times," *Church Intelligencer*, 30 May 1861, 1.
[84] "The Clergy Non-Militant," *Church Intelligencer*, 27 June 1861, 1.
[85] Ibid.
[86] Editorial, *Church Intelligencer*, 18 July 1861, 2.

Intelligencer reasoned that "in this most righteous war of *Self-Defense*" Polk had responded much "like the shepherd guarding his fold against the wolves about to rush upon them." Despite these accolades, the feeling existed that Polk could be in error.[87]

Other Episcopalians, however, tendered a more vigorous defense of the bishop as general. A Virginian explained that Polk had not exchanged the crosier for the sword but had joined a cause that "above all" was fighting "for a race that had been, by Divine Providence, entrusted" to the Southern people. In addition, the churchman alluded to Polk's "birth, education, and talents" and the endorsements of Robert E. Lee, Jefferson Davis, Joseph E. Johnston, and John B. Magruder as sufficient justification for the bishop's military service.[88] Likewise, Dr. William A. Shaw composed an eight-stanza poem titled "Confederate Ode" and dedicated it to Polk.[89] Also, Sarah Dorsey, who had received her confirmation into the Episcopal church from Polk in 1857, prepared a military banner for the bishop-turned-general modeled on the Labarum of Constantine the Great. Although Dorsey was a latecomer to the separatist crusade, the election of Lincoln had transformed Dorsey into a true Confederate. "We are fighting the Battle of the Cross against the Modern Barbarians who would rob a Christian people of Country, Liberty, and Life," Dorsey told Polk.[90] Clearly, Dorsey interpreted the conflict between the North and South as a type of Holy War, and she discovered in Leonidas Polk "her Confederate ideal."[91]

After the initial shock of Polk's decision subsided and as support for the war intensified in the South, the bishop as general emerged as a symbol of the Christian warrior knight. When Polk arrived in Memphis in July 1861, a fervid spirit of Confederate nationalism engulfed the city. Businessmen and local elites urged the residents to pool their resources and invest in the war effort by constructing powder mills and percussion cap factories.[92] Civic leaders, who at one time held designs on converting the river city into the capital of the Confederacy, now touted Memphis as the headquarters of the

---

[87] "Surplice and Sword," *Church Intelligencer*, 2 August 1861, 1.

[88] Editorial, *Church Intelligencer*, 18 July 1861, 2.

[89] Dr. William A. Shaw to Leonidas Polk, 9 August 1861, Leonidas Polk Papers.

[90] Sarah A. Dorsey to Leonidas Polk, 20 February 1862, Leonidas Polk Papers.

[91] Bertram Wyatt-Brown, *The House of Percy: Honor, Melancholy, and Imagination in a Southern Family* (New York/Oxford: Oxford University Press, 1994) 119–36.

[92] "Sad Condition of Affairs in Kentucky," Memphis *Appeal*, 20 July 1861, 2.

Western army. Because Polk stressed the importance of defending the Mississippi River, most Memphians welcomed the bishop with open arms. V. E. Wilmine McCord of the city's *Appeal* applauded the appointment, which, he argued, demonstrated the "sagacity" and "fitness" of the Southern republic's leader, Jefferson Davis. According to McCord, Davis had selected Polk because of the latter's impeccable character and his ability to inspire the confidence of the people. Moreover, McCord viewed the war as a struggle between Northern infidelity and "the religion of Jesus Christ." He compared Polk to the bishop of Constantinople, who led the early Christians in their defense against the barbarian invaders, and he believed that the bishop as general would likewise drive "infidel usurpers" out of the South's "Christian dynasty." In a final acclamation, McCord proclaimed: "All hail our intrepid and wise chief, who has chosen to sanctify the western division of the Confederate army, by the mitre above the girdle and stars!"[93]

In the final analysis, Polk demonstrated little reluctance in making the controversial transition from bishop to general; he only hoped that the people of the South would understand his decision. Polk's transformation symbolized, on a regional and personal level, the complex and evolutionary development of Southern nationalism. What began as a recognition of slavery as the defining characteristic of Southern society evolved to a form of Southern literary nationalism and ripened into an enthusiastic and unwavering commitment to an independent Southern nation. To one questioner, Polk compared his course of action to a man whose house was on fire and who had left his "business" to extinguish the flames.[94] He never intended to leave the ministry permanently, and in fact he never officially relinquished control of his diocese. The urgency of the times, however, convinced the bishop to enter the war on behalf of the cause of "Constitutional liberty" and Southern "hearth-stones" and "altars." Moreover, Polk could not escape his family's martial heritage and the spirit of 1776 that had helped to define his forefathers. Ultimately, Polk defended himself against varying degrees of criticism by maintaining that he had been "unable" to refuse the invitation to serve because it appeared to him "to be a call of Providence." For Polk, his future and that of the South was "in God's

---

[93] V. E. Wilmine M'Cord, "Curiosities of History: The Appointment of Bishop Polk," Memphis *Appeal*, 7 July 1861, 1.

[94] Quoted in Polk, *Leonidas Polk*, 1:362

hands."[95] This reliance on God to determine the eventual outcome of the sectional controversy reflected the mindset of most Southern evangelicals as well as those social and political conservatives who were determined to build a slave society on religious ideals.[96] Thus, the bishop as general embodied the complimentary nature between Southern Episcopalianism and Confederate identity.

---

[95] Leonidas Polk to Stephen Elliott, 22 June 1861, Leonidas Polk Papers.

[96] Loveland, *Evangelicals and the Social Order*, 265; Eugene D. Genovese and Elizabeth Fox-Genovese, "The Religious Ideals of Southern Slave Society," *Georgia Historical Quarterly* 70/2 (Spring 1986): 1–16.

CHAPTER 5

The Bishop as General

The juxtaposition of the bishop as general makes Leonidas Polk one of the most fascinating characters of the American Civil War. Although he arrived in Memphis to a hero's welcome, controversy followed him throughout his four years of service in the western theater. For the Confederacy to realize independence, military success had to be achieved in the West. The Heartland of Dixie contained the Confederacy's largest concentration of raw materials and food items; housed key transportation hubs, railroads, waterways, and manufacturing centers; and offered an indispensable source of manpower.[1] Because of his extensive service and high-ranking position in the Army of Tennessee, Polk has received significant attention in the various studies on the war in the West. Therefore, it is not necessary to reconstruct a detailed narrative of the bishop's entire Civil War career. Instead, a review of such topics as his border state policy, which includes the case of Kentucky neutrality, his role in the failure of Confederate command in the West, and his participation in the religious life of the Army of Tennessee is the best and easiest way to assess the bishop's military career.

On 13 July 1861, Polk arrived in Memphis, Tennessee, where he established the headquarters for his Department No. 2. His command included portions of Tennessee, Mississippi, Louisiana, Arkansas, and Alabama, primarily the areas of these states that bordered on the Mississippi

---

[1] In this context, strategy refers to the objectives of individual campaigns as defined by national goals, and tactics refer to the execution of battlefield operations in the pursuit of the strategic objectives. Thomas Connelly, *Army of the Heartland: The Army of Tennessee, 1861–1862* (Baton Rouge: Louisiana State University Press, 1967); Thomas Connelly, *Autumn of Glory: The Army of Tennessee, 1862–1865* (Baton Rouge: Louisiana State University Press, 1971).

River. After the ceremonial introductions and speeches, Polk began to focus on his official duties. He had been instructed to integrate the 22,000 man provisional army of Tennessee into the Confederate military, a process that was already underway. Tennessee governor Isham G. Harris, who had helped organize the provisional force and appointed Gideon J. Pillow as the army's commander, received on 29 June 1861 the state's consent to make the transfer. Still, questions lingered despite the spirit of cooperation. A major concern in the transition was the preservation of rank for those provisional officers being transferred into the Confederate army, particularly the status of Major General Pillow, who happened to be one of the wealthiest and most politically powerful men in the state, and Brigadier General Benjamin F. Cheatham. To the dismay of both Harris and Pillow, the major general was demoted to brigadier general and lost command of the army to Polk. Meanwhile, Cheatham retained the rank of brigadier. Harris and Pillow's Democratic allies forwarded several letters of protest to Richmond, but their pleas fell on deaf ears. Pillow biographers, Nathaniel Hughes and Roy Stonesifer, contend that the demotion "humiliated" Pillow and the appointment of Polk baffled him.[2] According to Polk's biographer Joseph Parks, Polk agreed that Pillow should have maintained his previous rank, but despite the apparent vote of confidence, Pillow "never reconciled being subordinate to the inexperienced Polk." Only one week after arriving in Memphis, Polk made Pillow second in command and recommended a promotion to major general. These tokens of goodwill, however, did little to soothe Pillow's wounded pride, and he soon embarked on a crusade for personal redemption. Missouri became the stage on which Pillow hoped to display his martial genius. As commander, Polk would have to bridle Pillow's restless spirit. At the same time, the bishop faced more daunting tasks in developing a border state policy for both Missouri and Kentucky

---

[2] Peter Franklin Walker, "Building a Tennessee Army: Autumn 1861," *Tennessee Historical Quarterly* 16/3 (June 1957): 99–116; Nathaniel C. Hughes, Jr., and Roy P. Stonesifer, Jr., *The Life and Wars of Gideon J. Pillow* (Chapel Hill: University of North Carolina Press, 1993) 172–74. Christopher Losson suggests that Cheatham's good fortune was due in part to the "machinations" of Harris. See Christopher Losson, *Tennessee's Forgotten Warrior: General Frank Cheatham and His Confederate Division* (Knoxville: University of Tennessee Press, 1989) 30.

and in preparing the defenses of the Mississippi River, a responsibility that would have challenged the most seasoned soldier.[3]

As a border state, Missouri, like Kentucky, was extremely important to the Confederate war effort in the West. Aside from supplying manpower, manufacturing centers, and natural resources, a Confederate Missouri would strengthen the Southern hold on the Mississippi River. Missouri, of course, entered the Union originally under a cloud of national controversy, and forty years later the sectional hostilities continued to divide the state. Governor Claiborne F. Jackson favored secession, but a state convention blocked an attempt to leave the Union in February 1861. Then, in March, the Federals seized the state militia, and the state erupted into civil war. In late June, Pillow and Missouri cavalry officer M. Jeff Thompson devised a plan to liberate Missouri by means of a raid across the southern portion of the state, one that attacked St. Louis and the Federal arsenal and concluded with a climactic assault on Cairo, Illinois. At that time, Pillow lacked the necessary manpower for the operation, but when Polk reached Memphis in July, the Tennesseean renewed his interest in freeing Missouri. Immediately upon his arrival, Polk conferred with Pillow and received visits from Governor Jackson, General Thompson, and General William J. Hardee, who commanded troops stationed at Pocahontas, Arkansas. The combined influence of these three men convinced Polk to support the Missouri initiative.[4] On 23 July, Polk ordered Pillow to cross the Mississippi River into southern Missouri and occupy New Madrid. From there, Pillow would march northward and join with Hardee at Ironton, where an attack could be launched against St. Louis. If successful, Pillow had instructions "to proceed up the river, raising Missourians" as he went for a final assault on Cario.[5]

From the start, the Missouri campaign encountered a number of problems. First, Hardee was unable to unify his full complement of troops in a timely fashion. The delay allowed Union general John C. Fremont to

---

[3] Joseph Parks, *General Leonidas Polk, C.S.A.: The Fighting Bishop* (Baton Rouge: Louisiana State University Press, 1962): 173–74; Hughes and Stonesifer, *Gideon Pillow*, 177; Connelly, *Army of the Heartland*, 48.

[4] Stanley F. Horn, *Army of Tennessee* (Indianapolis: Bobbs-Merrill, 1941): 17–20; Hughes and Stonesifer, *Gideon Pillow*, 175–177.

[5] US War Department, *War of the Rebellion: A Compilation of the Official Records of the Union and Confederate Armies*, 128 vols. (Washington D. C.: US Government Printing Office, 1880–1901) ser. 1, vol. 3, pt. 1, p. 612–15. Hereafter cited as *OR*.

occupy Ironton, fortify rail points outside of St. Louis, and reinforce Cairo. When Polk learned that the Federals were in a position to threaten the Mississippi River, he ordered the fortification of Island No. 10, a strategic river fort just above Memphis. To the dismay of Pillow, Polk recalled one of Pillow's brigades and re-deployed them to Island No. 10. At the same time, Richmond instructed Polk to send two regiments to General Felix Zollicoffer in East Tennessee. Then, Polk received news that General Ben McCulloch had returned to Arkansas after defeating the Federals at Wilson's Creek on 10 August and was no longer interested in the Missouri campaign. Polk, therefore, decided against further action in Missouri. The Missouri campaign failed because the Confederates relied too heavily on faulty intelligence reports. In addition, the troops were ill-equipped and unprepared for such an undertaking. Ultimate success, however, demanded a unified command system and required cooperation between independent field commanders. In Polk's defense, he lacked the official authority to control the independent commanders since they received their orders directly from Richmond and not from him.[6] Yet, Polk had been appointed because of his familiarity with the people of the region and his skills as a natural leader. If the bishop possessed the potential for military leadership—and many including Davis believed he did—then Polk had failed in his first effort at delivering a Confederate victory. Kentucky would offer new chances for success.

Kentucky, the second of the slaveholding border states in the West, had a longstanding commitment to the doctrine of states' rights that dated back to the Kentucky Resolutions of 1798. Consequently, many Southerners expected the Bluegrass State to be loyal to their cause. Governor Beriah Magoffin was a staunch supporter of secession, but pro-Union elements controlled the legislature and overrode the governor's attempts to call a secession convention. The Confederate bombardment of Fort Sumter in April 1861 and Lincoln's subsequent call for 75,000 militia forced Kentucky to adopt a more concrete position. Magoffin quickly made his intentions

---

[6] Hughes and Stonesifer, *Gideon Pillow*, 174–92; *Official Records*, ser. 1, vol. 3, pt. 1, p. 650–655; Horn, *Army of Tennessee*, 25; Connelly, *Army of the Heartland*, 49. Some historians have charged that Polk bears the responsibility for failing to liberate Missouri. But the Confederates still had a number of chances in Missouri after Polk terminated his efforts. Their greatest opportunity came at the Battle of Pea Ridge (March 6–8, 1862) but Earl Van Dorn was routed by the Federals.

known. "I say emphatically," the governor declared, "Kentucky will furnish no troops for the wicked purpose of subduing her sister Southern States." On 24 April, Magoffin called the Kentucky legislature into special session to debate Kentucky's position in light of the new developments. In mid-May, the legislators adopted, by a vote of sixty-nine to twenty-four in the house and thirteen to nine in the senate, a position of "strict neutrality." The resolution stated that Kentucky would not participate in the war "except as mediators and friends to the belligerent parties." In addition, the house agreed, by a vote of eighty-nine to four, with Magoffin's refusal to supply the Union with troops from Kentucky.[7] Neutrality may have been declared but Unionist sentiment dominated the Bluegrass State. On 20 June, Kentucky held an election to select representatives for a special session of Congress called by President Lincoln, and Unionists scored an overwhelming victory with the State's Rights party carrying only one district in the extreme western part of the state. The voters also elected new members to their state legislature and the Unionists again won a decisive victory.[8]

Despite the pro-Union stance taken by most Kentuckians, many Southerners suffered under the illusion that the state would still join the Confederacy. For instance, Edmund Ruffin, the embodiment of radical Southern nationalism, believed that if an aggressor violated Kentucky's neutrality then the state would join the non-offending side. As of 17 June 1861, Ruffin felt that the Confederacy had held its own during the first months of the war and that the "rebellious movements" in Maryland and Missouri and the "declared neutrality" of Kentucky all worked to the South's advantage. He reasoned that the economic cost of maintaining military garrisons within these states limited the North's ability to wage war against the Confederacy. Ultimately, Ruffin expected that the border states would be "driven by oppression to join" the South.[9]

---

[7] James G. Randall, *The Civil War and Reconstruction* (Boston: D. C. Heath, 1937) 317–19; Magoffin quote in Horn, *Army of Tennessee*, 39–40; details on the Kentucky legislature in E. Merton Coulter, *The Civil War and Readjustment in Kentucky* (Chapel Hill: University of North Carolina Press, 1926) 37, 54–55.

[8] Horn, *Army of Tennessee*, 41; Coulter, *The Civil War and Readjustment in Kentucky*, 95–97.

[9] William K. Scarborough ed., *The Diary of Edmund Ruffin*, 3 vols. (Baton Rouge: Louisiana State University Press, 1972–1989) 2:45–46.

Conversely, some contemporaries in both sections viewed the neutrality policy with greater skepticism. Lincoln's private secretaries, John G. Nicolay and John Hay, considered Kentucky's neutrality a "preposterous assumption." They regarded armed neutrality as a "practical farce" and an "artful contrivance to kill secession." Moreover, Nicolay and Hay believed that strict neutrality "was not a true exponent of the public feeling" and that Unionist sentiment in the state was steadfast. Closer to the scene, Henry Villard, one of the North's most heralded war correspondents, drew similar conclusions. Reporting from Louisville, Villard described the state's neutrality policy as a "selfish" ploy designed to avoid the "horrors of war." Villard concluded that although Kentuckians "were doubtless for the maintenance of the Union" their "loyal feelings [were] not strong enough for immediate, hearty, unconditional support of the Federal government."[10]

In Memphis, attitudes of suspicion abounded. In mid-summer 1861, the editors of the *Appeal* railed against the "deceptive" nature of Kentucky neutrality and questioned the political and military viability of trusting the policy. Editorials often criticized the Lincoln government for "secretly" arming the Bluegrass State with "strangers, evidently in Kentucky for another purpose than that of protecting her soil" while publicly professing an observance of the "wall" of neutrality. These arguments revealed a deep concern regarding the vulnerability of Tennessee and the Mississippi River to Federal attacks. Consequently, the *Appeal* urged Jefferson Davis to fashion himself after the famed Napoleon Bonaparte and adopt a more aggressive approach to the Kentucky problem. As the battle lines formed in the East, the *Appeal* asked, did not conventional wisdom call for a "counter demonstration upon the North-west?" News of Unionist victories in Kentucky's June elections convinced many in the city of Memphis that Kentuckians no longer intended to remain faithful to their promise of neutrality. First-hand reports emanating from the Bluegrass State revealed an increasing "animosity" between pro-Union Kentuckians and the South. Moreover, rumors circulated that some of Kentucky's wealthiest slaveholders were "among the ranks of these aiders and abettors of the abolitionists," which shocked and angered the Memphis elite. With

---

[10] John G. Nicolay, and John Hay, *Abraham Lincoln: A History*, 10 vols. (New York: Century Co., 1886–1890) 4:229, 232–33; Henry Villard, *Memoirs of Henry Villard: Journalist and Financier, 1835–1862*, 2 vols. (Westminister, England: A. Constable 1904) 1:203–204;

emotions running high, the *Appeal* predicted that if the current situation did not change, then Kentucky could only "be redeemed from her thraldom by hard fighting with southern bayonets." This barrage of fiery rhetoric expressed an intensified distrust of Kentucky's neutrality policy.[11]

A host of capable historians have accepted the idea of Kentucky's fictional neutrality. Perhaps the most insightful analysis was drawn by E. Merton Coulter, who suggested that "mediatorial neutrality" had been jettisoned from the beginning and that an "armed neutrality" had emerged between the state's pro-Northern and pro-Southern factions. In the resulting race to secure arms, the Unionists of Kentucky, aided by the federal government, "forced the Southern rights men to act in self-defense."[12] Thus, given the reaction of the Memphis press and the city's elite as well as the impressions held by Lincoln's private secretaries, it was reasonable for Polk to question the validity and authenticity of Kentucky neutrality. Furthermore, Polk had to decide whether or not to address the Kentucky problem as a political or military problem; he would find it impossible to do both.

From the war's outset, President Lincoln understood the military importance of Kentucky. He approached the state of his nativity with "care and confidence" and a determination to hold it at all costs. To counter Governor Magoffin's refusal to provide a quota of troops, in early May 1861

---

[11] "Kentucky Neutrality," Memphis *Appeal*, 28 August 1861, 1, 4; "Curiosities of History: The Appointment of Bishop Polk," Memphis *Appeal*, 7 July 1861, 1; "The Necessity of a Vigorous Policy," Memphis *Appeal*, 13 July 1861, 1, 4; "Sad Condition of Affairs in Kentucky," Memphis *Appeal*, 20, July 1861, 2.

[12] E. Merton Coulter, *The Civil War and Readjustment in Kentucky*, 84–89. According to James G. Randall, Kentucky embraced the absurd notion that it could act as a type of isolated Switzerland, and its policy "revealed the slowness of the state to accept the fact of war." Christopher Losson called the approach "a hopeless but game strategy," while Stanley Horn opined that "Kentucky seemed hopelessly hypnotized by the fatuous dream of a miraculous, peaceful neutrality" in the midst of a bloody war. Horn also called Kentucky's neutrality a "sham" since most Southern sympathizers had already crossed the border and joined the Confederate forces at Clarksville, Tennessee, leaving the Bluegrass State in the hands of Union loyalists. See Randall, *The Civil War and Reconstruction*, 320–21; Losson, *Tennessee's Forgotten Warrior*, 32; Horn, *Army of Tennessee*, 40–46. Also supporting this interpretation is Frank Vandiver, who called Kentucky's neutrality a "charade." See Frank E. Vandiver, *Their Tattered Flags: The Epic of the Confederacy* (College Station: Texas A&M University Press, 1970) 48.

Lincoln recruited a "private" committee to serve as a "rallying point" in the state, act as a "medium of communication," and, most importantly, arm and train pro-Union Kentuckians. One member who served in this capacity was Joshua F. Speed, a prominent citizen of Louisville and a "most intimate friend" of Lincoln. The president also dispatched navy lieutenant William Nelson to work with Speed and others in organizing a Federal presence in Kentucky. Between the months of May and August, Lieutenant Nelson "quietly" moved 5,000 muskets to Louisville and "secretly appointed the officers and enrolled the recruits of four regiments from central Kentucky." After Kentucky's decisive June elections, Nelson "assembled" these men at Camp Dick Robinson, located just a few miles outside of the state capital. Major Robert Anderson, the martyr of Fort Sumter, received instructions in early May from Lincoln authorizing him to recruit as many three-year volunteers as possible from Kentucky and western Virginia. These men would be placed under Federal, not state, jurisdiction.[13]

Governor Magoffin objected to the troops being assembled at Camp Dick Robinson. He informed Lincoln of his desire to preserve the neutrality policy, which required that the "bodies of armed soldiers" from both sides be excluded from the state. Lincoln replied that he lacked "full and precisely accurate knowledge" of the Federal military forces in Kentucky and believed that any Federal action had been inspired by the "urgent solicitation" of the "Union-loving" citizens of Kentucky. Moreover, Lincoln suggested that the governor was the only prominent state politician requesting a withdrawal and that it was not the "popular wish" of Kentuckians to have the troops removed. Consequently, he refused to do so. The president's willingness to circumvent the declared neutrality indicated how committed he was to establishing a military foothold in Kentucky. The pro-Union position held by the majority of Kentuckians provided Lincoln with the political cover necessary to orchestrate a Federal buildup in the state. Conversely, Confederate authorities, particularly governors Magoffin and Harris as well

---

[13] Also included in the Speed-Nelson-Anderson circle were Kentuckians James Gutherie, Garrett Davis, and Charles A. Marshall. Nicolay and Hay, *Abraham Lincoln: A History*, 4:235–40; Abraham Lincoln to Robert Anderson, 7 May 1861, in Roy P. Basler, ed., *Collected Works of Abraham Lincoln*, 9 vols. (New Brunswick NJ: Rutgers University Press, 1953–1955) 4:359.

as President Davis, failed to counter Lincoln's clandestine operations and ignored the reality of a mounting Federal presence.[14]

In late August and early September 1861, a series of fast-paced events in Missouri and Kentucky convinced Polk that an invasion of the Mississippi Valley was imminent. First, Union General John C. Fremont unveiled a daring three-step plan designed to defeat the armies of Sterling Price and Ben McCulloch in the trans-Mississippi theater, strike Memphis and the armies guarding the city, and wrest control of the Mississippi River away from the Confederates. In the interim, on 30 August Fremont announced a state of martial law in Missouri. He declared that armed Confederate sympathizers would be executed and that their slaves would be freed.[15] Adding to the intensity of the moment, Major Robert Anderson left his headquarters in Cincinnati and relocated to Louisville on 1 September. Once in Kentucky, Anderson joined the 2,000 men that Lincoln had helped outfit and awaited further instructions. Next, General George H. Thomas assumed command of the forces at Camp Dick Robinson.[16]

Even prior to the Fremont proclamation, Pillow had advised Polk to move into Kentucky before the Federals acted first. The developments of late August and early September aroused Pillow's concern and aggressiveness even more. "Kentucky is now a boiling cauldron," he wrote, "neutrality is no longer regarded, if indeed it ever was." Pillow learned through newspaper reports that Major Anderson and others were actively involved in Kentucky, and he predicted that the "patriots" of Kentucky and Tennessee were in grave danger. In the same communication, the Tennesseean included a brief report that identified Columbus, Kentucky, "as the gateway to the interior of Tennessee." Thus, Pillow contended that the "possession" of Columbus was a "military necessity, involving the ultimate safety of Tennessee from devastating invasion." The Federal movements and the recommendations of his subordinates alarmed Polk and convinced him of the need for preemptive action. It seemed as if armed

---

[14] Beriah Magoffin to Abraham Lincoln, 19 August 1861, in Frank Moore, ed. *The Rebellion Record: A Diary of American Events*, 12 vols. (1861–1868; repr., New York: Arno Press, 1977) 3:29–30; Abraham Lincoln to Beriah Magoffin, 24 August 1861, in Basler, *Collected Works of Abraham Lincoln*, 4:497.

[15] Andrew Rolle, *John C. Fremont: Character as Destiny* (Norman: University of Oklahoma Press, 1991) 193–94, 205–207.

[16] *OR*, ser. 1, vol. 3, pt. 1, p. 612–18.

neutrality in Kentucky had advanced to the point where political solutions were no longer an option.[17]

On 3 September the Confederate invasion of Kentucky began, as Pillow, acting on Polk's orders, seized the town of Hickman. The next day Pillow captured Columbus. Federal forces under General Ulysses S. Grant responded by taking Paducah, a salient in the northwest corner of the Bluegrass State. In his memoirs, Grant recalled how quickly the events had unfolded. Grant did not assume command of the troops at Cario, Illinois, until 4 September, and thinking that "there was no time for delay," he informed Fremont that unless he "received further orders" he intended to make preparations "that night" for an invasion. Having received no countermanding orders, Grant arrived in Paducah shortly after sunrise on 6 September. For all practical purposes, the two armies simultaneously violated Kentucky's neutrality; strict neutrality would have required that Grant receive permission from the Kentucky legislature before responding to Polk's offensive.[18] When news reached Richmond that Polk's troops had entered Kentucky, Secretary of War Leroy P. Walker called for an immediate withdrawal. Tennessee governor Isham Harris supported Walker's position arguing that "as long as Kentucky remained neutral, Tennessee's exposed northern border would need no defense." Polk, however, explained that military "necessity justifies the action." Willing to trust Polk's judgment, Davis telegraphed Polk that "the necessity must justify the action," which Polk interpreted as an affirmation of his original decision.[19]

Meanwhile, Polk dispatched a letter to Magoffin informing the governor that he had made a military decision based on reliable information that suggested that "Federal forces intended and were preparing to seize Columbus." Polk acknowledged the likelihood of complaints from Kentucky legislators as well as the possibility that Unionist elements might use the

---

[17] *OR*, ser. 1, vol. 3, pt. 1, p. 686–87.

[18] *OR*, ser. 1, vol. 4, pt. 1, p. 179; Horn, *Army of Tennessee*, 44; Ulysses S. Grant, *Personal Memoirs of U. S. Grant*, 2 vols. (New York: Charles L. Webster, 1885) 1:264–65.

[19] Connelly, *Army of the Heartland*, 40; Leonidas Polk to Jefferson Davis, 4 September 1861, in Lynda L. Crist, ed. *The Papers of Jefferson Davis*, 11 vols. (Baton Rouge: Louisiana State University Press, 1971–2004) 7:325–26; Davis to Polk, 5 September 1861, in Crist, *The Papers of Jefferson Davis*, 7:327.

occupation as a "pretext" for taking other portions of the state. Therefore, Polk offered to withdraw his troops "provided" Grant agree to a bilateral retirement. In addition, the bishop requested a "guarantee" from state authorities "in which no troops from either side would be allowed to enter or occupy any point of Kentucky in the future." Shortly thereafter, Polk received a letter from John M. Johnson, chairman of a committee representing the Kentucky state senate, that expressed the senate's desire to maintain neutrality and demanded the withdrawal of Polk's forces. In his response, Polk complimented the original intent of strict neutrality but cited in detail how Kentucky, since the June elections, had allowed the Federals to violate its neutrality, particularly the buildup at Camp Dick Robinson. In the end, Polk used the same arguments that he had presented to Magoffin and made the same conditional offer of withdrawal.[20]

The Kentucky legislature flatly refused Polk's proposal. On 9 September debate commenced on a resolution requiring an unconditional withdrawal of Confederate but not Federal forces. The bill also contained provisions calling for Federal aid. After two days of deliberation, the resolution passed and the legislators instructed the governor to carry out their handiwork. Magoffin protested by vetoing the legislation and attempted unsuccessfully to substitute an amendment requiring both sides to withdraw, one that actually represented the position of strict neutrality.[21] Polk informed Davis of these developments. The Confederate president expressed his "desire to treat Kentucky with all possible respect" and cautioned Polk that military necessity must be unmistakable. Polk learned from John L. Helm and E. M. Covington that a few pro-Confederate Kentuckians objected to his occupation of Columbus, but the general explained to Davis that they exaggerated "the importance of the seizure on the public mind of Kentucky." Helm, Covington, and Polk did agree, however, that the legislature's consistent coddling of the Lincoln government had deprived the state of the right to defend itself. "It would have been better to have seized the place some months ago," Polk offered in

<hr>

[20] Leonidas Polk to Beriah Magoffin, 8 September 1861, in Polk, *Leonidas Polk*, 2:21; John M. Johnson to Leonidas Polk, 8 September 1861, in Polk, *Leonidas Polk*, 2:23; Leonidas Polk to John M. Johnson, 9 September 1861, in Polk, *Leonidas Polk*, 2:26.
[21] Coulter, *The Civil War in Kentucky*, 114.

retrospect, but now was the time to make a "vigorous" stand.[22] Davis admitted that political risks existed but maintained that "we cannot permit the indeterminate qualities, the political elements, to control our actions in cases of military necessity." In addition, he concurred that further "respect" for Kentucky neutrality required Federal and not just Confederate withdrawals from the state.[23]

Polk also found sympathizers in the western sections of Kentucky and Tennessee. One civilian from Hickman, Kentucky, identified only as J. W. Y., claimed that the Confederates had entered Kentucky at its moment of "trial and danger" in order to defend the state from "Lincoln's troops." The idea that Lincoln had provoked Polk's response also resonated with the citizens of Memphis. The *Appeal* rebuked the Kentucky legislature for not renouncing its ties to Lincoln and challenged the authenticity of the neutrality stance. In early September 1861, the paper described Kentucky's maneuverings as the "red-tape theory of diplomacy" and admonished the state to resist "abolitionist domination." The hard-liners of Memphis viewed the situation with pessimism and declared that Kentucky must "never be allowed to cast [its] destiny with the North...if Southern bayonets can rescue her." If the *Appeal* spoke for the people of Memphis on the Kentucky question, then the message was clear: "We need her and must have her." In many ways, these statements represent the interpretation of Kentucky's neutrality held by Polk and his advisers, namely that Southerners would acquiesce to neutrality as long as Lincoln observed it but not simply because Kentucky declared it.[24]

On 18 September, Kentucky officially ended its neutrality policy and sided with the Union. In some respects, a *de facto* allegiance had existed since the June elections. Davis and the Confederates certainly regretted Kentucky's decision, but they believed they had acted properly. In November 1861, the president informed the Confederate Congress that the invasion of Kentucky "was justified not only by the necessities of self-defense...but also by a desire to aid the people of Kentucky."[25] Despite what

---

[22] *OR*, ser. 1, vol. 4, pt. 1, p. 191–92.

[23] Ibid., ser. 1, vol. 4, pt. 1, p. 188.

[24] "The Crisis in Kentucky," Memphis *Appeal*, 6 September 1861, 1, 4; J. W. Y., "From Kentucky," Memphis *Appeal*, 11 September 1861, 1; "Occupation of Columbus Statement of the Citizens," Memphis *Appeal*, 13 September 1861, 2.

[25] Davis quoted in Horn, *Army of Tennessee*, 45.

Polk and many residents of the Mississippi Valley understood as proof of
Federal infractions against Kentucky's neutrality and substantive evidence
that Grant was poised to strike, some historians have reasoned that Polk
acted prematurely and made one of the most serious mistakes of the war.
Such arguments are predicated on the notion that Kentucky could have
maintained its splendid isolation indefinitely even as war was waged in the
West and that the state actually preferred and adhered to a policy of strict
neutrality.[26]

In the final analysis, Polk allowed military concerns to prevail over
political considerations. The elections of June 1861 that placed the
legislature in the hands of Unionist sympathizers, the tacit consent given to
Lincoln's military buildup within Kentucky's borders, and the legislature's
refusal to accept a bilateral withdrawal after Polk seized Columbus and
Grant occupied Paducah prove that Kentucky was not politically
redeemable. Thus, Polk's role in the Kentucky quagmire should only be
evaluated in terms of its military significance, and specifically as it related to
the defense of western Tennessee and the Mississippi River.

It should be noted that conflicting strategic interests existed in
Tennessee. On the one hand, the defense of West Tennessee and Memphis
depended on a well-protected Mississippi River. On the other hand, Middle
Tennessee and Nashville were more vulnerable to attacks originating from
the Tennessee and Cumberland rivers. Encouraged by a large contingent of
citizens, the Memphis military board, and Generals Gideon Pillow and
Benjamin Cheatham, Polk determined that Memphis and the Mississippi
River were in the most immediate danger and chose to occupy Columbus,
leaving the defense of Nashville to the capital city's elite.[27] Within this
strategic framework, the bishop erred, however, by overlooking the military
importance of Paducah and by failing to include the city as one of his
principal objectives. Together, Paducah and Columbus would have
strengthened the Confederates' hold on the Mississippi River. The
occupation of the former would have prevented inland invasions of Middle
and West Tennessee via the Tennessee and Cumberland Rivers. The failure

---

[26] Steven E. Woodworth, "Indeterminate Quantities: Jefferson Davis and the
End of Kentucky Neutrality" *Civil War History* 38/3 (December 1992): 289–97.

[27] The support of Cheatham surprised biographer Christopher Losson because
the policy endangered the Tennessee general's land holdings and native region. See
Losson, *Tennessee's Forgotten Warrior*, 85.

to secure Paducah before Grant moved or to dislodge the Federals afterward demonstrated that Polk lacked the aggressiveness and the strategic vision that the Western army so desperately needed at that time. Still, the misstep was correctable and was not the reason for the subsequent loss of Fort Henry and Fort Donelson or the surrender of Nashville. As a number of historians have shown, Albert Sidney Johnston bore the primary responsibility for these reversals when he dispatched only part of his army to meet Grant at the critical moment of the campaign. Such factors as manpower shortages, the defective location of Fort Henry, overconfidence in the durability of Kentucky neutrality, and the unbelievable lack of concern that the Nashville elite displayed for the safety of their city also contributed to the collapse of the Heartland's northwest defensive front.[28]

The initial breaches in the defense of the western theater certainly alarmed Southerners, and rightfully so. Yet, the Confederacy still maintained the ability to wage an effective war against the Federals if military and political representatives of the West could convince President Davis that their region represented a strategic priority. At a minimum, they needed to persuade the commander-in-chief and his military advisers to allocate more attention to the western theater.[29]

Although Polk had made critical military decisions during his handling of the border state crises, he had yet to be truly tested on the battlefield. His opportunity came in November 1861 when Union and Confederate forces clashed at Belmont, Missouri. Belmont has been described as "a name rather than [a] place" and as "a steamboat landing rather than a town." Its importance rested in the fact that it lay some 800 yards directly across the Mississippi River from Columbus, Kentucky, the northern terminus of the Mobile and Ohio Railroad and one of the Confederacy's most fortified positions on the Mississippi River.[30] Indeed, Camp Johnson, the Confederate camp at Belmont, "was of no military importance," serving

---

[28] Charles P. Roland, *Albert Sidney Johnston: Soldier of Three Republics* (Austin: University of Texas Press, 1964) 284–91; Horn, *Army of Tennessee*, 83–98; Benjamin Franklin Cooling, *Forts Henry and Donelson: The Key to the Confederate Heartland* (Knoxville: University of Tennessee Press, 1987).

[29] Thomas Connelly and Archer Jones, *The Politics of Command: Factions and Ideas in Confederate Strategy* (Baton Rouge: Louisiana State University Press, 1973) 55–63, 82–86.

[30] Nathaniel Cheairs Hughes, *The Battle of Belmont: Grant Strikes South* (Chapel Hill: University of North Carolina Press, 1991) 82–83.

primarily as an "outpost" of the Confederate position at Columbus. The camp consisted of one infantry regiment, a battery of artillery, and a small cavalry force. There were no breastworks to protect the camp.[31] This vulnerable target attracted the attention of Union General Ulysses S. Grant.

Grant's interest in Belmont was twofold. He claimed that his fundamental intention was to prevent a buildup of Confederate forces in Missouri. Yet, biographer William McFeely acknowledges that Grant was simply eager for a fight. Although Grant was a seasoned soldier, he was "for the first time" assuming "the sole responsibility for an attack."[32] From his position in Cairo, Illinois, Grant and some 3,000 men boarded six steamboat transports on 6 November and headed down the river with two gunboat escorts. In concert with Grant's move, General C. F. Smith left Paducah, Kentucky, with roughly 2,000 men and marched toward Columbus. Grant's men disembarked some three miles north of Camp Johnson on the morning of 8 November and the gunboat escort proceeded to attack the Confederate batteries at Columbus. The two-pronged movement forced Polk to consider several options. Should he engage Grant at Belmont with his full compliment of men before the Federals advanced on Columbus or should he proceed cautiously against Grant in order to guarantee the security of Columbus? His decision more closely resembled the later option.[33]

Polk ordered General Gideon Pillow and some 3,000 troops to cross from Columbus to Belmont in an effort to hold Camp Johnson. The ensuing battle has been characterized as "a military engagement in its simplest and most elementary form—two approximately equal bodies of infantry fighting in parallel facing lines."[34] Simplicity aside, "the two armies engaged in two hours of close, bitter fighting."[35] Pillow made one of the first tactical mistakes when he positioned his men poorly and failed to conduct adequate reconnaissance. As a result, Grant's men overwhelmed the Confederate forces at Camp Johnson. Having "pinned down" Pillow's men, the Federals, who were low on ammunition, no longer viewed the Rebels as a threat and turned to looting the Confederate camp. Polk observed this

---

[31] Horn, *Army of Tennessee*, 64.
[32] William S. McFeely, *Grant: Biography* (New York: Norton, 1981) 94.
[33] Hughes, *The Battle of Belmont*, 67–77.
[34] Horn, *Army of Tennessee*, 64.
[35] McFeely, *Grant*, 92.

scene from the safety of the other side of the river, and from that location he decided to reinforce Belmont once again.[36]

Polk personally accompanied the reinforcements, although General Benjamin Cheatham would actually direct the troops. After Polk assessed the situation, Cheatham's reassembled Confederate force exchanged volleys with Grant's men. Then, Cheatham ordered a bayonet charge, which broke the Federal line forcing Grant's men in a hasty and confused retreat. Although Polk ordered Cheatham to pursue the fleeing Yankees, the Confederates were not able to capture the main body of Grant's army. The Federals narrowly escaped, boarded the transports, and headed back up river to safety. The battle of Belmont was over.[37]

William McFeely has concluded: "If the action at Belmont was a battle, Grant lost; if a raid, he won." In considering Belmont as a raid, the significance of the encounter was that Grant's untested men came away with a markedly increased level of confidence. He also learned that war was more like a marathon, not a sprint, and that victory would be a function of sustained persistence and endurance. Confederate casualties at Belmont were noteworthy and exceeded those incurred by the Federals: 105 killed, 419 wounded, and 117 missing. In addition, Camp Johnson had been torched and supplies and Confederate artillery had been destroyed. Without question, Grant's forces inflicted considerable damage on Polk's army. Nevertheless, the Confederates controlled the battlefield at the end of the day, and the bishop general proudly proclaimed that his army had won the battle.[38]

"My first acknowledgments for this signal triumph or our arms and the defeat of the machinations or our enemies are due to the favoring providence of Almighty God," Polk recorded in his official report, "We have felt we could put our trust in His protection and defense, and He has given us victory."[39] Polk received a congratulatory telegram from General Albert S. Johnston, who remarked that "the 7th of November will fill a bright page in our military annals, and be remembered with gratitude by the sons and daughters of the South."[40] President Jefferson Davis offered his "sincere

---

[36] Hughes, *The Battle of Belmont*, 77–119.
[37] Ibid., 143–70.
[38] McFeely, *Grant*, 93, Hughes; *Battle of Belmont*, 184–85
[39] *OR*, ser. 1, vol. 3, pt. 1, p. 308–09.
[40] *OR*, ser. 1, vol. 3, pt. 1, p. 311

thanks for the glorious contribution you have just made to our common cause. Our countrymen must long remember gratefully to reward the activity, the skill, the courage, and devotion of the army at Belmont."[41] This collective euphoria surrounding the self-proclaimed victory at Belmont masked the reality of the situation. Indeed, the Confederates suffered more casualties winning the battle, 641, than the Union did losing the battle, 590. Moreover, Camp Johnson was in such disrepair that Polk abandoned the outpost.

Perhaps, the most important aspect of the battle of Belmont was Polk's performance during his first true test as a field commander. His West Point education provided him a proficient understanding of military science. In fact, when he arrived at Belmont he devised a somewhat complex plan to trap Grant, with Colonel Preston Smith's 154th Tennessee Infantry playing a key role. As Smith recalled, Polk ordered him "to move the head of my command forward to the river, above the boats of the enemy, and, facing by the rear rank, throw my left below them, thus encircling and preventing them returning into the woods." Unfortunately for the Confederates, Polk did not have a clear understanding of the area's typography or know the exact location of all the troops under his command. As a result, Smith's response was a bit clumsy. The colonel explained that "while executing this order it became necessary to change the movement on account of obstacles, and believing them [the enemy] about to move off, I caused Lieutenant Colonel Wright to move the right wing of the One hundred and fifty-fourth Senior Regiment to the right and below the enemy." The time necessary to complete these moves contributed to the conditions that allowed Grant's men to board the transports and avoid capture.[42]

There is no evidence that Polk properly used his ten companies of cavalry at Belmont nor is there any evidence that his field artillery was effectively used against Grant. Additional failures of command included what one historian of the battle calls a "careless, almost criminal, neglect of Belmont's defenses." In the final analysis, Polk's performance as a field commander indicated that he "lacked boldness" and the driving compulsion to seek out and destroy the enemy."[43] These tendencies—overly deliberate

---

[41] Ibid.

[42] *OR*, ser. 1, vol. 3, pt. 1, p. 345.

[43] Hughes, *Battle of Belmont*, 199–200.

or plodding planning and a lack of aggressiveness—would define Polk's generalship as a corps commander in the future campaigns of the Army of Tennessee.

Following Shiloh, the Army of Tennessee, which was the principal Confederate presence in the West, underwent a number of changes and none was more important than the appointment of Braxton Bragg as the new commander. When Bragg assumed command of the Confederate force that would later be called the Army of Tennessee, some officers had already formed a negative opinion of the new commander based on their observations and experiences. In time, the opposition to Bragg grew into a larger movement to have the general removed from command. The politics of command, Bragg's inability to control his subordinates, and his inability to fashion effective command relationships were major factors in the defeat of the Confederacy in the West. Among the disappointed was Patrick Cleburne, one of the West's most respected and effective generals.[44] Leonidas Polk would also become part of the anti-Bragg faction. He viewed Bragg as an inept field commander and constantly urged Davis to replace him. Bragg held a similar opinion of Polk and on more than one occasion tried to have him reassigned. The origins of their feuding can be traced to the failed Kentucky campaign of 1862.

By mid-1862, the immediate strategic concern in the West was the need to reverse the Federal advances into the Mississippi Valley and the

---

[44] At Shiloh, Cleburne served as brigade commander under General William Hardee, but as the battle unfolded he received orders from the then corps commander Bragg, who had the responsibility of directing the majority of Confederate forces on the field during the two-day battle. Although not part of the wretched assaults on the Hornet's Nest, Cleburne encountered on the Confederate left flank an equally resilient foe in General William T. Sherman and his three Ohio regiments. On the first day, Cleburne's six regiments sustained heavy casualties. On the second day only 800 of 2,700 of Cleburne's men answered the roll call. When the battle resumed, Bragg directed Cleburne to make another attack with his remaining troops. The junior officer questioned the order to storm Sherman's well-fortified breastworks, but he followed it dutifully. Outflanked and without support, Cleburne's brigade virtually disintegrated. Distressed by the carnage, Cleburne called the assault on the second day an "unfortunate attack." The Shiloh experience, according to Cleburne biographer Craig Symonds, left the Irishman with "bitterness toward Bragg" for ordering the attacks that decimated his brigade. Craig L. Symonds, *Stonewall of the West: Patrick Cleburne and the Civil War* (Lawrence: University Press of Kansas, 1997) 72–79.

Tennessee heartland. In July of that year, Davis offered Bragg the choice of trapping General Don Carlos Buell and the Army of the Ohio in Middle Tennessee or he could draw the Federals into battle by invading Kentucky. With these options, Bragg and the Army of Tennessee commenced their first campaign together under his leadership. The new commander headed to Chattanooga at the end of July and met with General Edmund Kirby Smith, whose 18,000 men defended East Tennessee. They agreed that a unified strike against the Federals in Middle Tennessee was the more prudent course of action. But Bragg needed more time to prepare his men and therefore in the interim permitted Kirby Smith to concentrate his efforts on the Federal forces holding the Cumberland Gap. This decision, however, produced unintended consequences, and over the course of the next month, the original plan changed dramatically. First, Kirby Smith informed Bragg that he could not remove the Federals from the Cumberland Gap and would instead drive straight for Lexington, Kentucky. Bragg then decided to follow Kirby Smith into Kentucky on a parallel route. By jettisoning the plan established at Chattanooga and rushing into Union territory, Bragg and Kirby Smith fell victim to what some have termed "Kentucky fever," a mesmerizing faith in both the Confederacy's ability to liberate Kentucky and the Kentuckians' willingness to join the Southern states. The fever spread wildly throughout Dixie in the late summer of 1862, especially in the wake of Kirby Smith's victory at the battle of Richmond, Kentucky. When Bragg reached Glasgow on 13 September, he perceived himself as the head of an army of liberation.[45]

The Army of Tennessee "offer[s] you an opportunity to free yourselves from the tyranny of a despotic ruler," Bragg informed the citizens of Glasgow upon his arrival. The Confederate army had entered Kentucky not to subdue it, Bragg proclaimed, but "to restore" its civil liberties, to protect its "homes and alters, to punish with a rod of iron the despoilers of...[its] peace, and to avenge the cowardly insults" directed against its women. Bragg expected a great deal from Kentuckians. He originally believed that by appealing to their sense of duty, honor, and manhood he could enlist their fervent support.[46] Yet, two weeks after his arrival, Bragg began to doubt

---

[45] James Lee McDonough, *War in Kentucky: From Shiloh to Perryville* (Knoxville: University of Tennessee Press, 1994) 76–85; Grady McWhiney, *Braxton Bragg and Confederate Defeat* (New York: Columbia University Press, 1969) 260–75.

[46] *OR*, ser. 1, vol. 16, pt. 2, p. 822.

whether Kentucky would ever be redeemed. From Bardstown on 25 September he informed Confederate Adjutant General Samuel Cooper that few recruits had turned out and unless the situation improved shortly his only alternative would be to "abandon Kentucky...to its cupidity."[47] Bragg placed most of the blame for the apathetic response in Kentucky on General John C. Breckinridge, who was a former vice president of the United States and Kentucky politician. "The failure of Gen Breckinridge" to recruit and enlist volunteers, Bragg complained to President Davis, "has seriously embarrassed me" and threatens the success of the "whole campaign." What Bragg failed to realize, as Breckinridge biographer William C. Davis asserts, was that the Kentuckian had failed to carry his own state during his bid for the presidency in 1860, and as such there was little chance that "those who would not vote for him...[would] come out and fight for him."[48]

Still, Bragg pushed on, assuming that General William Preston, a native of Louisville and a former United States congressman from Kentucky, could compensate for Breckinridge's failures and improve recruiting efforts.[49] In addition, Bragg turned his attention to installing Richard Hawes as the provisional or secessionist governor of Kentucky. Although the duly elected representatives of Kentucky had cast their lot with the Federals after the neutrality controversy, diehard secessionists had managed to elect a shadow government, which consisted of a governor, lieutenant governor, and a congressional delegation. All were officially recognized by the Confederate government. Distracted by the forlorn hope of a Confederate Kentucky, Bragg ignored military realities in order to pursue an impractical political goal. "We shall put our Governor in power soon," Bragg wrote Polk on 4 October, "and then I propose to seek the enemy...wherever [he] may be."[50] On inauguration day in Frankfort, Bragg learned the location of a portion of Buell's army when the salvos of Federal artillery interrupted the installation ceremony. Actually, the action against Frankfort was only a feint and the majority of Buell's army was converging on the town of Perryville. On 8 October, Polk attacked the main body of Buell's army inflicting heavy damage on the Federal left flank before being

[47] Ibid., ser. 1, vol. 16, pt. 2, p. 876.

[48] William C. Davis, *Breckinridge: Statesman, Soldier, Symbol* (Baton Rouge, 1974) 327–28.

[49] *OR*, ser. 1, vol. 16, pt. 2, 892.

[50] Ibid., ser. 1, vol. 16, pt. 2, p. 905.

repulsed in a counterattack. For several days the two armies maneuvered but did not clash. Finally, Bragg decided to retreat and led his army out of Kentucky and back to Chattanooga, having failed to accomplish his objective.

From the outset, the Confederates encountered a number of difficulties in the Kentucky campaign. The most serious problem was a flaw in the Confederate command system, which permitted Kirby Smith to operate independently of Bragg until their respective forces united. Only then, by virtue of his superior rank, would Bragg command both armies. This undisciplined approach allowed Kirby Smith to alter the original plan established at Chattanooga—that of attacking Buell in Middle Tennessee—leaving Bragg without a clear-cut military strategy or objective when he entered Kentucky. Once in Kentucky, Bragg wasted valuable time attempting to install Hawes, and the delays let Buell dictate the terms of engagement. Outnumbered at Perryville, saddled with supply shortages, and alarmed by the news of Earl Van Dorn's defeat at Corinth, Mississippi, Bragg made the decision to withdraw from Kentucky. In the aftermath of Perryville, Davis summoned Bragg to Richmond to explain the failure of the Kentucky campaign; he apparently satisfied the president because he retained his command.[51] Although there was plenty of blame to assign for the mistakes of the Kentucky campaign, Bragg directed his wrath toward the spiritless civilian population of the Bluegrass State and the Confederate leaders from that state. Bragg opined that the success of the campaign "was predicated on a belief" that Kentuckians "would rise in mass to assert their independence." Despite every opportunity to come forward, they had, Bragg lamented, refused "to risk their lives or their property" in pursuit of Southern independence.[52] To his wife Elise, Bragg revealed with true candor his impressions of the Kentuckians he had attempted to inspire. He swore that he would no longer sacrifice "brave Southern men" for the "cowards" of the Bluegrass State.[53]

Alone, these caustic remarks were enough to drive a wedge between Bragg and the Kentuckians. Breckinridge and Simon Bolivar Buckner felt personally insulted by the charges, and the bitterness grew into outright

---

[51] McDonough, *War in Kentucky*, 200–308; Horn, *Army of Tennessee*, 162–89.
[52] *OR*, ser. 1, vol. 16, pt. 1, p. 1088.
[53] Quoted in McWhiney, *Braxton Bragg and Confederate Defeat*, 322.

hatred by December 1862. One incident in particular, the execution of Corporal Asa Lewis of the 6th Kentucky, symbolized the depth of contempt between Bragg and the Kentuckians. Lewis, whose enlistment status was not clearly defined, left the army after Perryville to help his family on the promise that he would return to duty after fulfilling his familial obligations. Despite the evidence of Lewis's good service record and the strenuous appeals of Breckinridge, Buckner, and others, Bragg considered desertion an unpardonable offense and ordered the death sentence to be carried out in the presence of the corporal's Kentucky brigade. The execution of Asa Lewis, William C. Davis writes, "destroyed...forever" any reasonable possibility of reconciliation between Bragg and Breckinridge.[54] By condemning Kentuckians for his failed campaign and by holding Asa Lewis accountable to a severely legalistic interpretation of military conduct, Bragg had alienated a significant portion of his officer corps. The battle of Stone's River would only make matters worse.

Meanwhile, trouble was brewing in the Federal army. Prior to the battle of Perryville, several of Buell's officers met secretly and signed a petition stating that they had lost confidence in him and that he should be relieved of command. Although President Lincoln never received the document, the commander-in-chief reached a similar conclusion after Buell failed to pursue Bragg when the latter retreated to East Tennessee after Perryville. Accordingly, Lincoln replaced Buell by naming General William S. Rosecrans, the victorious general at Iuka and Corinth, Mississippi, as the new commander of the Army of the Cumberland in October 1862. Thus, Bragg faced a new opponent in the Tennessee heartland.[55]

In late December, Rosecrans marched from Nashville to do battle with Bragg, and their armies faced off at Stone's River, a tepid little tributary of the Cumberland River just a few miles northwest of Murfreesboro, Tennessee. Stone's River, the Nashville Turnpike, and the Nashville and Chattanooga railway all bisected the battlefield, and, ironically, both

---

[54] Davis, *Breckinridge: Statesman, Soldier, Symbol*, 331–32.

[55] When Rosecrans assumed command, the Army of the Ohio changed its name to the Army of the Cumberland. It was also between Perryville and Stone's River that the Army of Tennessee adopted its name in place of the former appellation the Army of Mississippi. McDonough, *War in Kentucky*, 224; Peter Cozzens, *No Better Place to Die: The Battle of Stone's River* (Urbana: University of Illinois Press, 1990) 12–23.

commanders straddled their armies in relatively balanced proportions across the thoroughfares with the intention of using their left wings to attack their opponent's right flank. The Confederates attacked first on the morning of 31 December, inflicting heavy damage and turning the Federal flank, but by mid-day Rosecrans had established a new line of defense and was able to stall the Confederate thrust. As the fighting continued, the Federal stronghold centered on a point known as the "Round Forest" or "Hell's Half-Acre." In scenes eerily reminiscent of the Confederate charges against the "Hornet's Nest" at Shiloh, Bragg ordered several attacks against the Federal salient but they met with little success. Then Bragg called on Breckinridge to lead yet another frontal assault. But the outcome was the same.[56]

The two armies recouped on 1 January. Bragg believed that Rosecrans would retreat, but the Federals remained in their positions. On 2 January, Bragg resumed the offensive and again selected Breckinridge's division to spearhead the attack. Based on his own reconnaissance, Breckinridge explained to Bragg that the Federals held the high ground opposite the proposed line of attack and that Rosecrans's artillery would cut his men to pieces. Bragg dismissed Breckinridge's concerns and over the Kentuckian's adamant protest demanded that his orders be followed. Breckinridge's brigade commanders also denounced the decision. Kentuckian Robert W. Hanson, who commanded four Kentucky regiments in Breckinridge's division, called Bragg's plan "absolutely murderous." Although incensed, Breckinridge could conceive of no other option than to obey the order. Late in the afternoon of 2 January, Breckinridge led 4,500 men into battle, and after just forty-five minutes of fighting his worst fears were realized. Federal artillery rained down on the charging Confederates and Breckinridge's division sustained over 1,500 casualties, 500 of them from Kentucky units. Among the fallen was Robert Hanson. He had been unable to escape his own prediction regarding Bragg's plan; the Kentuckian was mortally wounded in the fight. The losses nearly destroyed Breckinridge's spirit, and one of his officers remembered that "tears broke" from the general's "eyes when he beheld the remnant of his own brigade." Breckinridge never

---

[56] Horn, *Army of Tennessee*, 198–205; Cozzens, *No Better Place to Die*, 101–66.

forgave Bragg for ordering the fatal attack, nor for that matter had he forgotten the Kentucky campaign or Corporal Asa Lewis.[57]

After conferring with several of his top generals, Bragg retreated from Murfreesboro, and the army spent the next six months in Tullahoma, Tennessee. Since his appointment as commander following the battle of Shiloh, Bragg had led two campaigns. Each time the opposing forces fought to a bloody stalemate. Yet, it was the Confederate army that had the distinction of retreating from the battlefield on both occasions. Consequently, Bragg became the target of criticism.[58] Some newspapers, for example, erroneously reported that "while the enemy was in full retreat" the commander of the Army of Tennessee ordered the withdrawal from Murfreesboro against the "opinion and advice" of his senior officers. To counter such charges, Bragg appealed to his officer corps for vindication. Specifically, he posed two questions (in the form of a circular) to his corps and division commanders. He hoped their responses would silence his detractors. First, he asked whether or not they had approved the retreat from Murfreesboro. Bragg then inquired about the army's confidence in him as a leader and offered to resign if the men doubted his ability to lead.[59]

If Bragg's circular had presented only the first question, he might have avoided further condemnation. Breckinridge, William J. Hardee, Benjamin Cheatham, Patrick Cleburne, and Leonidas Polk all acknowledged that they either participated in the council of war that produced the decision to retreat from Murfreesboro or consented after-the-fact to the council's determination. The second question proved more problematic. Although expressing "the highest respect for [Bragg's] patriotism," Breckinridge and his camp informed the embattled commander that he did "not possess the confidence of the army to an extent" that would enable him "to be a useful commander." Hardee concurred, feeling that a change in command was "necessary," and he suggested that Bragg place "the peril of the country" above "all personal considerations." Cleburne praised Bragg for his "patriotism and gallantry and...great capacity for organization," but he

---

[57] Quotes from Davis, *Breckinridge: Statesman, Soldier, Symbol*, 339–48; Horn, *Army of Tennessee*, 205–10; James Lee McDonough, *Stones River-Bloody Winter in Tennessee* (Knoxville: University of Tennessee Press, 1980) 182–201.

[58] James M. McPherson, *Battle Cry of Freedom: The Civil War Era* (New York/Oxford: Oxford University Press, 1988) 582.

[59] *OR*, ser. 1, vol. 20, pt. 1, p. 699.

observed that the general lacked "the confidence of the army" that was absolutely necessary "to secure success." Polk, who left Tullahoma on furlough before Bragg issued the circular, only answered, at Bragg's insistence, the first question, in which he acknowledged his support for the retreat. Later, however, Polk informed President Davis of his misgivings regarding Bragg's leadership.[60]

The vote of no confidence convinced Bragg that a few malcontents in his own army were trying to damage his reputation because they resented "the sting of his discipline."[61] Moreover, the referendum on Bragg's tenure as commander led to a series of bitter personal conflicts. In his official report on the battle of Stone's River, Bragg blamed Breckinridge for the failure of the 2 January assault. He even tried, through clerical procedures, to distort the casualty figures of the Kentuckian's division to insinuate that only a half-hearted effort had been made. Based on correspondence with his supporters in Washington and the fact that one of Breckinridge's staff officers had leaked damaging information to the press, Bragg concluded that Breckinridge had orchestrated the conspiracy within his army and had fanned the flames of public disapproval. Although rumors circulated that Breckinridge would challenge Bragg to a duel, the Kentuckian reacted to Bragg's accusation rather calmly. Perhaps he believed that a military court of inquiry would find him innocent, but the opportunity never materialized and Breckinridge accepted a transfer to Mississippi.[62] With Breckinridge out of the way, Bragg prepared to eliminate another nemesis, Leonidas Polk.

Caught in the vortex of blame and denial after Stone's River, in April 1863 Bragg decided to revisit the mistakes of the failed Kentucky campaign of 1862 and he issued another circular to several officers. Specifically, Bragg accused Polk of disobedience and misconduct at Bardstown on 2 October and at Perryville on 8 October. Bragg omitted the complaints from his preliminary reports after the battle of Perryville in October 1862, which suggests that the accusations were a function of the commander's face-saving ploys. Ironically, he had commended Polk, Hardee, Cheatham, Buckner, and General Patton Anderson for their gallant efforts in Kentucky

---

[60] Breckinridge also spoke for Generals Gideon Pillow and William Preston and Colonels R. P. Trapue and Randall Gibson. Bragg's circular and the respective responses are in ibid., ser. 1, vol. 20, pt. 1, pp. 682–84, 699–702.

[61] Ibid., ser. 1, vol. 20, pt. 1, p. 699.

[62] Davis, *Breckinridge: Statesman, Soldier, Symbol*, 350–62.

and had declared that "the country owed them a debt of gratitude."[63] Now, the politics of command forced Bragg to recant his earlier statements. With respect to the 2 October engagement, when Bragg learned that the Federals were on the move—a movement that was subsequently identified as a feint—he directed Polk to leave Bardstown and attack the enemy at Frankfort with his "whole available force." Realizing that if he followed this course of action the main body of Buell's army would envelope his corps, Polk assembled a council of war and in agreement with his consultants disregarded Bragg's order. In the estimation of most Civil War historians, Polk made the correct decision.[64] Regarding the incident on 8 October, Bragg told Polk to march against the Federals at Versailles before Buell could link up with the forces at Perryville. But Polk repeated the approach he had followed at Bardstown by calling a council of war. He then chose to take matters into his own hands and confront the enemy at Perryville first. This time Polk appears to have made several tactical errors, principally he failed to advise Bragg of the exact location of the main force of Buell's army, which left the Confederates unprepared and limited their potential for tactical success in the battle.[65]

By resurrecting these issues, Bragg intended to prove that Polk bore the primary responsibility for the failure of the Army of Tennessee during the Kentucky Campaign and at the battle of Stone's River. If successful with his plan, Bragg believed that President Davis would be forced to relieve Polk of his command. Bragg thought that by pressuring Generals William T. Hardee and Simon Bolivar Buckner, who had participated in both councils

---

[63] Bragg's April circular and October report are in *OR*, ser. 1, vol. 16, pt. 1, p. 1088, 1097–98.

[64] Stanley Horn is extremely critical of Bragg for misjudging Buell's movements, and even Polk critic Thomas Connelly argues that Polk's disobedience was "necessary" and excusable," although he faults the bishop for not providing his commander with a better explanation of the developments in the field. See Horn, *Army of Tennessee*, 178–80; Connelly, *Army of the Heartland*, 247–52. It should be noted that a handful of historians, including Grady McWhiney, fault Polk for the debacle at Bardstown. McWhiney contends that a concerted effort by Polk and Kirby Smith would have defeated the Federals at Frankfort, thereby depriving Buell of part of his army, and at the very least would have provided a pretext for unifying Bragg's widely scattered army. See McWhiney, *Braxton Bragg and Confederate Defeat*, 300–307.

[65] Connelly, *Army of the Heartland*, 257–61.

of war, he could turn several high-ranking officers against Polk and gather evidence for a court-martial proceeding. The public disclosure of the councils of war, Bragg intimated to Hardee, would compromise his reputation and implied that he disobeyed orders. Bragg presented Hardee with a way of escaping possible censure if the corps commander admitted that he supported Polk's decision without the knowledge of the original order. But the independent-minded Hardee declined to answer the specific allegations in Bragg's circular because he did not deem it a "proper" inquiry. In a letter to Polk, Hardee explained that he feared Bragg's investigation would lead to a court-martial proceeding and would open the Kentucky campaign to further scrutiny "which at this time ought to be avoided." Simon Bolivar Buckner also refused to address Bragg's questions for the same reasons. Yet the Kentuckian assured Bragg "that while there were essential differences of opinion in regard to the conduct of the campaign" the subordinate commanders zealously performed their assignments. Then, Buckner offered Bragg some very frank advice: "Every officer...must expect the legitimate criticism of the public and of military men." Buckner also reminded Bragg, "It is true that these criticisms may sometimes be urged with intemperance, but that should not the less prevent us from awaiting the matured verdict of public opinion and of history." Apparently, Hardee and Buckner wished to end the bitter feuding within the high command of the Army of Tennessee, and Buckner in particular urged Bragg to sacrifice a "little personal pride" for the greater cause of the Confederacy.[66]

Hardee, however, confided to Polk that if the bishop chose "to rip up the Kentucky campaign," then he could "tear Bragg into tatters." Polk appreciated Hardee's support and began preparing his defense, believing that "an arrest and trial" were imminent. In short, he planned to argue that Bragg's orders were open to various interpretations. At Bardstown, Bragg instructed Polk "to move with all...available force" for a flank and rear strike on the enemy. Here, Polk placed the emphasis on "available force," contending that with Buell's main body directly in front of him a move from Bardstown would expose his corps and therefore he "had no troops...available for the execution" of Bragg's order. With respect to the Perryville incident, Bragg's order read: "In view of the news from Hardee

---

[66] The respective correspondence is in *OR*, ser. 1, vol. 16, pt. 1, p. 1097–98, 1101, 1105–107.

you [Polk] had better move with Cheatham's division…and give the enemy battle immediately &c. No time should be lost in these movements." Polk claimed that Bragg's communiqué did not specify whether "immediate" meant a night attack or "early the next morning." Moreover, the bishop reasoned that "the language [you had better move] was clearly not peremptory, but suggestive and advisory, and left me the use of my discretion as to the details of the attack." In any event, Polk declared that the councils of war validated his decisions. Throughout the exchange, Polk refused to acknowledge any "disobedience of orders." He further maintained that while he lacked "a talent for quarrelling" he felt confident in his ability to redeem his reputation. The anticipated court-martial trial never convened.[67]

Polk's responses were eerily reminiscent of the argumentative strategy he employed as a cadet at West Point when he was disciplined for soliciting and receiving money from his father and when he was a culprit in the drawing scandal. The self-serving, legalistic parsing of Bragg's orders more closely resembled the handiwork of a bishop enthralled in a theological debate than a corps commander seeking to destroy the enemy. An unfortunate commonality between both incidents was Polk's hypersensitivity to criticism and his unwillingness to cast aside controversy or confrontation when he perceived that his personal honor was at stake. Indeed, Polk contacted President Davis and sought the removal of Bragg as commander of the Army of Tennessee.

In early February 1863, during the discussions of the withdrawal from Murfreesboro, Polk informed Davis that the poor condition of the army warranted "immediate attention" and that Bragg "had better be transferred." As a replacement, Polk recommended General Joseph E. Johnston because he could "cure all discontent and inspire the army with new life and confidence."[68] The turmoil in the Western theater convinced Davis to send Colonel William Preston Johnston, son of General Albert Sidney Johnston, on an inspection tour of Bragg's army. Johnston visited with Hardee, Buckner, Polk, and others who expressed a lack of confidence in their commander, but the president's emissary reported that the army was in good

---

[67] Ibid., ser. 1, vol. 16, pt. 1, pp. 1098, 1101–103.
[68] Leonidas Polk to Jefferson Davis, 4 February 1863, in Polk, *Leonidas Polk*, 2:206.

spirits and well supplied. After Johnston's visit, Polk repeated to Davis his unfavorable opinion of Bragg and suggested that the latter be transferred to the Inspector General's office in Richmond where his talents for organization and discipline would better serve the Confederacy. Polk also repeated his support for Joseph Johnston. "Whether General Johnston is the best man for the place…is not the question," Polk argued, "the army and the West believe it is so, and both would be satisfied with the appointment."[69] Ultimately, the president reached the same conclusion, but before the change could be made Johnston became ill and was unable to assume command. For nearly four months, an internecine war raged within the high command of the Army of Tennessee. Despite Davis's intervention and intentions no effective solutions were reached, and Bragg's officers still expressed serious doubts about his ability to lead. Furthermore, the discontent lingered as Bragg prepared to meet Rosecrans again, this time at the battle of Chickamauga.

Confederate defeats at Vicksburg and Gettysburg during the summer of 1863 caused a heightened sense of urgency in the Western theater. As a result, the authorities in Richmond transferred General James Longstreet and 12,000 men from the Army of Northern Virginia to Tennessee, thereby assuring Bragg of numerical superiority in his rematch with Rosecrans. The battle commenced on the morning of 19 September at Chickamauga Creek, some 12 miles south of Chattanooga. Unfortunately for the Confederates, Longstreet himself had not arrived and only half of the reinforcements from Virginia completed the 900-mile trip in time to engage the enemy on the first day. Dense woods and thick underbrush made the fighting difficult, but did not lessen its severity, and neither side emerged from the field on that day with a distinct advantage. Longstreet reached the Confederate headquarters just before midnight, at which time Bragg opted to reorganize the command structure of his army. Basically, there would be two wings, one commanded by Longstreet and the other by Polk, but the restructuring was more complicated than it appeared because both men would have to locate their newly assigned division commanders and be prepared to attack early the next morning. From the beginning, Bragg's plan had been to trap Rosecrans in McLemore's Cove, and even after the maneuvering of the first day he could still accomplish his objective if he could turn the Federal left

---

[69] Leonidas Polk to Jefferson Davis, 30 March 1863, 2:209–11.

flank. For this critical assignment, Bragg chose Polk and instructed him to strike Rosecrans's left at sunrise on 20 September.

The attack, however, did not begin until mid-morning. An incensed Bragg then ordered Longstreet to hit the right side of the Federal line before Polk could complete the turning movement. In what has since been described as sheer luck, Longstreet charged directly into a gap in the Federal line created by Rosecrans when he withdrew several divisions to reinforce his left flank. The Confederates poured through the opening sending nearly one third of Rosecrans's army into a full retreat. Only the heroic efforts of Generals George Thomas and Gordon Granger saved the Federal army from further defeat. Longstreet requested reinforcements from Polk's wing to pursue the fragments of Rosecrans's army before it reached Chattanooga, but Bragg refused, claiming that the army had suffered too many casualties. Moreover, Bragg decided against renewing the offensive on 21 September because the possibility of trapping Rosecrans in McLemore's Cove no longer existed. The Confederates had won a tactical victory on the battlefield at Chickamauga, but Rosecrans's escape and subsequent occupation of Chattanooga rendered Longstreet's success meaningless in terms of strategic consequences. When the dust settled, the disparate elements of the western concentration bloc agreed that Bragg had failed them, and they emerged more unified than ever before.[70]

Based on past experiences, Bragg knew what to expect from his critics. On previous occasions, he had responded by accusing subordinates of incompetence or insubordination. He once again returned to his old tactics. Most historians agree that there were at least three instances prior to Chickamauga when Bragg ordered strikes against portions of Rosecrans's army that if successful would have created a tremendous advantage for the Confederates. Only one of the missed opportunities involved Polk.[71] But Bragg considered Polk's conduct at Chickamauga on the morning of 20 September to be the most flagrant. In fact, Bragg suspended Polk from his command immediately after Chickamauga, formally charging him with

---

[70] McPherson, *Battle Cry of Freedom*, 671–74; Horn, *Army of Tennessee*, 257–73; Connelly, *Autumn of Glory*, 201–20.

[71] McPherson, *Battle Cry of Freedom*, 671; Steven E. Woodworth, *Six Armies in Tennessee: The Cickamauga and Chattanooga Campaigns* (Lincoln: University of Nebraska Press, 1998): 67–78. Woodworth sees these missed opportunities as extremely significant and as evidence of Polk's premeditated insubordination.

"disobedience of the lawful command of his superior officer" and with "neglect of duty to the prejudice of good order and military discipline." The former complaint stemmed from Polk's failure to attack at sunrise on 20 September, while the latter maintained that the general on the morning in question remained at his headquarters and made no effort to see that the battle orders were carried out or to report any non-compliance.[72] By dismissing Polk and several of his senior officers and by sending them to Atlanta to await trial, Bragg intended to preempt any criticism. However, his actions only intensified the feelings of personal animosity within the upper echelons of the Army of Tennessee.

To counter the indictment, Polk conferred with generals D. H. Hill, Benjamin Cheatham, and W. H. T. Walker. Before an actual trial began the bishop general presented his case directly to President Davis. He explained that he had issued orders by courier from his headquarters at 11:30 PM on 19 September, and that Cheatham and Walker had received their instructions but that Hill could not be found. The confusion after the first day of fighting at Chickamauga and Bragg's ill-advised reorganization of his army just a few hours before a major offensive contributed to the poor communication between Polk and Hill. In addition, Polk downplayed the significance of his delayed attack. Polk asked, "Did we occasion any failure in our success of the battle?" He continued, "For the enemy were clearly beaten at all points along my line and fairly driven off the field." Polk's primary concern was that Bragg refused to pursue and defeat the enemy before it reached Chattanooga, which he felt demonstrated irrefutably the general's inability to lead the army to victory. Indeed, he asserted that the commander "did not know what had happened" on the battlefield at Chickamauga and "allowed the whole of the fruits of this great victory to pass from him by the most criminal negligence, or rather, incapacity, for there are positions in which weakness is wickedness." Moreover, Polk welcomed the opportunity to vindicate his reputation and expose Bragg's incompetence before a court of inquiry.[73]

Perhaps in what amounted to a moment of desperation, one not necessarily designed to save his own command but rather to have Bragg

---

[72] Bragg also suspended Polk's division commanders D. H. Hill and Thomas Hindman for similar reasons. Also, Hindman had been responsible for one of the three missed opportunities prior to Chickamauga. *OR*, ser. 1, vol. 30, pt. 2, p. 55.

[73] *OR*, ser. 1, vol. 30, pt. 2, p. 67–68.

relieved of his, Polk petitioned General Robert E. Lee to assume control of the Army of Tennessee. Virginia's favorite son replied that Federal threats in the form of General George Meade as well as rheumatism in his back prevented the fulfillment of the proposition. Instead, Lee submitted an intercessory prayer for the safety of Polk's "brave men" and hoped that the bishop would regain his command. Lee's casual rejoinder minimized the urgency of the situation and illustrated his unwillingness to become involved in the controversy.[74]

Realizing that the Federals still occupied Chattanooga and that the morale of the Army of Tennessee's officer corps had deteriorated to an alarming level, Davis went to Georgia to meet with Bragg and his generals in early October. Although Longstreet—who appeared interested in taking charge of the army in the Western theater—Hill, Buckner, Cheatham, and Cleburne all recommended that Bragg should be replaced, the president backed his beleaguered commander. Privately, Davis reminded Bragg that the "public calamity" and crisis of morale was in some way linked to the "former estrangements" caused by the general's regrettable "interrogatives."[75] To avoid the controversy that a court-martial of Polk was guaranteed to ignite, Davis encouraged Bragg to accept a compromise solution, and when he agreed, the president transferred Polk to Mississippi. Additional changes included Buckner's demotion from corps to division commander and General Nathan Bedford Forrest's reassignment to the Department of Mississippi. For the moment, Bragg had withstood the challenges of the internal rebellion, but he could not recover from the Confederate disaster at Missionary Ridge in late November and subsequently resigned his post.[76]

In summary, the lack of *esprit de corps* among high-ranking officers certainly limited the effectiveness of the Army of Tennessee. Polk's personal feud with Bragg accented the malaise that plagued the entire army, and his ridiculous parsing of his commander's orders demonstrated his amateurish approach to military matters. The bishop, however, cannot be held

---

[74] Ibid, ser. 1, vol. 30, pt. 2, p. 69.

[75] Ibid, ser. 1, vol. 30, pt. 2, p. 535.

[76] Thomas Connelly and Archer Jones, *The Politics of Command: Factions and Ideas in Confederate Strategy* (Baton Rouge: Louisiana State University Press, 1973) 70–73; Woodworth, *Jefferson Davis and His Generals*, 119–126; Hallock, *Braxton Bragg and Confederate Defeat*, 109–26.

responsible for inciting and sustaining the discord between Bragg and his other officers such as Patrick Cleburne, John C. Breckinridge, Simon Bolivar Buckner, William J. Hardee, and James Longstreet, especially in the case of the Kentuckians who felt that Bragg not only defamed their individual character but sullied the character of their state. Finally, if the politics of command played a decisive role in the failure of the Western command then Bragg contributed mightily to the breakdown by compounding tactical and strategic loses on the battlefield with vindictive campaigns against the public images of the men whose respect he so desperately needed in order to succeed.

Throughout his colorful military career, Polk remained extremely popular among both his fellow officers and the enlisted ranks. In fact, President Davis warned Bragg after Chickamauga that the arrest and conviction of Polk would undoubtedly provoke additional "controversy…[and] entail further evil." Recognizing that Polk "possessed the confidence and affection of his corps," Davis advised Bragg to pursue a "lenient course" and utilize the bishop's "influence" to his own benefit and to avoid turning the dispute into a popularity contest, which Bragg could not win. Perhaps Private Sam Watkins, who often spoke contemptuously of officers, understood this appeal when he recalled that "Bishop Polk was ever a favorite with the army, and when any position was to be held, and it was known that Bishop Polk was there, we knew and felt that 'all was well.'" Watkins's remarks give some indication of the bishop's importance as a cultural figure. For many, Polk personified the concept of God and honor in the Old South. This cultural paradigm gained wider acceptance as the rhetorical framing of the Civil War was cast in terms of religious imagery and evangelical ethics. Such characters as Stonewall Jackson and Leonidas Polk became the embodiment of the militant Christian knight, the standard bearer of the Christian faith and the symbol of "nobility in war." Polk's identity within this Christian ethos was complicated by the fact that he was both a bishop and a general.[77]

Although historian Ezra Warner has demonstrated that over 70 percent of the Confederacy's 425 generals were citizen soldiers, only

---

[77] *OR*, ser. 1, vol. 30, pt. 2, p. 535; Sam Watkins, *"Co. Aytch," Maury Grays First Tennessee Regiment* (1882; repr., Jackson TN: McCowat-Mercer Press, 1952) 154; Bertram Wyatt-Brown, "God and Honor in the Old South," *The Southern Review* 25/2 (April 1989): 293–96.

Leonidas Polk and two others shed their clerical robes to become generals in gray.[78] However, in the early years of the war, Polk adhered to a strict interpretation of Episcopalian conventions that precluded him from performing his clerical duties. Whereas Mark Perrin Lowrey, Southern Baptist minister turned Confederate general, often preached to his troops before and after battles, Polk and many Episcopalians believed that clergymen were members of a "particular class" whose "vocation [was] purely a spiritual one" that should not be confused with military and political affairs.[79] In a certain way of thinking, Polk had secularized himself by becoming a combat officer. Consequently, he attempted to dispel any misperception regarding his role in the conflict by assuming and fulfilling only military responsibilities. Early in the war an incident occurred that demonstrated Polk's reluctance to function as both bishop and general. The incident involved the death of Major Eddy Butler, a member of a prominent Louisiana family. Interestingly, postwar reminiscences and memoirs imply that Polk met with the fallen soldier on his death bed and administered a form of last rites. However, Polk's letter of condolence to the senior Butler was void of religious language:

> I return to you the dead body of your gallant son. He fell, as he chose to say…as a Butler ought to fall, in the discharge of his duty. His manly bearing and soldierly conduct had endeared him to his command, & to those who had the opportunity to know him. He loved his country & has died in its defense. You have reason to be proud of such a son & to be consoled by such a death. After he fell, he was taken to my quarters; where every attention was shown him.

As an added measure of "tender sympathy" toward the major's mother, Polk returned a number of Butler's personal items. Clearly, Polk relied on the societal definitions of bravery, honor, and courage, while avoiding the more problematic theological dimensions of the soldier's death when consoling the Butler family. As a young convert and seminarian, Polk had

---

[78] Ezra J. Warner, *Generals in Gray: Livers of Confederate Commanders* (Baton Rouge: Louisiana State University Press, 1959) xxi-xxii. An additional study of the prewar occupations of 137 found one Methodist clergyman. See, Bruce Allardice, *More Generals in Gray* (Baton Rouge: Louisiana State University Press) 13. Sixty-seven percent of the Union's generals were citizen soldiers with only one general coming from the ministry. See, Warner, *Generals in Blue*, xix.

[79] "The Clergy Non-Militant," *Church Intelligencer*, 27 June 1861, 1.

used death as a means to initiate discussions about salvation, eternal damnation, and the omnipotence of God. Yet, such discussions were conspicuously absent from the Butler condolence letter. It seems that Polk had not discovered how to reconcile his military duties with his ministerial calling.[80]

Polk's dilemma was not limited to the Butler incident. It was also evident at the wedding of cavalryman John Hunt Morgan. Here, Polk formally presided over the occasion in a religious capacity, but he officiated "in [a] full Lieutenant General's uniform." George St. Leger Grenville, a Morgan confidant, worried that marriage "would render" the flamboyant military hero "less enterprising." But Grenville eventually reasoned that a wedding conducted by "an Episcopalian bishop-militant, clad in [a] general's uniform...certainly ought not to soften a soldier's temper." With respect to the ceremony, Polk appreciated not the sacredness of holy matrimony but the military distinctiveness of the occasion. Afterward, he confessed to his wife that Morgan at least had the privilege of being married by a "lieutenant-general."[81]

Although Polk struggled with public expressions of his religious identity, on a personal level he continued to draw strength from his faith in God. Following the carnage at Shiloh, Polk proclaimed: "All glory and honor be unto His holy Name for my protection and defense" in the recent hostilities. "It was He," Polk remarked to his wife, "who covered my head in the day of battle."[82] The reference to divine protection, part of which was a quotation from Psalm 140:7, illustrated that Polk's providential worldview and belief in the sovereignty and omnipotence of God remained unaffected by what at that time was the bloodiest military encounter in American history. Likewise, there appeared to be little change after the Battle of Stone's River as he offered "thanks and praise...to Almighty God, the Lord of Hosts, for the success of our arms and the preservation of our lives." But,

---

[80] Leonidas Polk to Eddy Butler, 9 November 1861 (handwritten copy of the original), Butler Family Papers, Historic New Orleans Collection, New Orleans, Louisiana.

[81] Grenville account in Basil Duke, *A History of Morgan's Cavalry* (1867; repr., Bloomington: University of Indiana Press, 1960) 322; Leonidas Polk to Frances D. Polk, 17 December 1862, Leonidas Polk Papers, Jesse Ball duPont Library, University of the South, Sewanee, Tennessee.

[82] Leonidas Polk to Frances D. Polk, 10 April 1862, in Polk, *Leonidas Polk*, 2:114.

Polk was not so blinded by a teleological view of history that he overlooked the "spirit of dauntless courage" that sustained his men in their attacks against the well-fortified positions of the enemy.[83] Even after the trials and tribulations of Chickamauga, Polk expressed no regrets about the paths he had traveled. His parting words to his men reverberated with a steadfast hope in God for a Confederate victory: "Whoever commands you, my earnest exhortation and request to you is, to fight on and fight ever, with true hearts, until your independence is achieved. Thousands of hearts may fall crushed and bleeding under the weapons of the foe, or the passions and mistakes of friends but the great cause must never be sacrificed, or our flag abandoned. Our cause is just, and your duty to your country and God is as clear as the sun in the heavens." Polk signed his farewell message, "Your friend." His unwavering commitment to the dream of a Southern nation no doubt brought comfort to the men under his charge.[84]

Aside from inspirational oratory, Polk helped in tangible ways to set the religious tone for the Army of Tennessee. His personal behavior and genteel standards of conduct earned him a reputation for possessing "the manners and affability" of a Christian gentleman. British military observer Arthur Fremantle humorously noted in his diary that Polk's most trusted division commander, Benjamin F. Cheatham, did "all the necessary swearing in the 1st *corps d'armie*, which General Polk's clerical character incapacitates him from performing."[85]

In fact, the men of Polk's 1st Corps often referred to an amusing incident that transpired on the eve of the Battle of Chickamauga as evidence of the bishop's high ethical standards. In an effort to inflame the passions of war, Cheatham rode his mount up and down the gray line bellowing incentives, punctuated by, "forward boys, and give them hell." Following in the wake of the hard-drinking and coarse-talking division commander, Polk could only add: "Do what General Cheatham says, boys." Polk's participation in the pep rally seems comical but many soldiers admired the bishop general's piety, and his willingness to draw his sword on the field of battle created a point of mutual identification. On a more substantive level, Polk arranged for Episcopalian cleric Charles T. Quintard to serve as

---

[83] *OR*, ser. 1, vol. 20, pt. 1, pp. 691, 693.

[84] *OR*, ser. 1, vol. 30, pt. 2, p. 65.

[85] Arthur Lyons Fremantle, *Three Months in the Southern States: April-June, 1863* (New York: John Bradborn, 1864) 139, 146.

chaplain-in-chief for his corps. As a trained physician, Quintard ministered to the soldiers' physical and spiritual needs. Private Sam Watkins of the 1st Tennessee Regiment called Quintard "one of the purest and best men I ever knew." The chaplain's reputation for procuring obscure but much-needed supplies and amenities was legendary. Yet, Quintard's ministry involved more than the providing of earthly comforts. For example, after the disappointment of the Battle of Chattanooga, Watkins recalled that because of Quintard's "divine services...the private soldier once more regarded himself as a gentleman and a man of honor." Thus, religion not only emboldened and reassured the soldiers as they faced death on the battlefield, but it possessed the ability to restore manhood and individual dignity.[86]

Quintard's success as an evangelist also prompted a change in the nature of Polk's participation in the religious life of the Army of Tennessee. During the encampment of Polk's corp at Shelbyville, Tennessee, in May and June 1863 when the high-command was embroiled in the throes of controversy, Quintard confronted the Army of Tennessee's commander, Braxton Bragg, and prevailed upon him the importance of personal salvation. The general accepted the invitation with discernible thanksgiving and informed Quintard that he would become a communicant of the Episcopal church if the cleric provided "the necessary instruction." Bishop Stephen Elliott of Georgia, Polk's close personal friend, officiated at the baptism and confirmation that took place in a private ceremony. Afterward, Bragg "shook hands" with Polk, and both men exchanged heartfelt words of encouragement with the respective members of their staffs. This solemn occasion, which apparently transcended any personal animosity between the two men, forced Polk to reassess his role as a spiritual leader.[87]

Only twelve days after Bragg's conversion, Polk confided to his wife that the increased religious activity excited him and he hoped to use his position and influence to "foster in every way" its continued existence. In most cases, the rank-and-file soldier claimed membership in or preference for the Baptist or Methodist denominations. Aware of the religious diversity within the army, Polk wanted the best teachers from each religious tradition to appeal to their respective "classes," which meant that Episcopalian

---

[86] Watkins, "Co. Aytch," 118, 136, 21, 132.

[87] Arthur L. Noll, ed., *Doctor Quintard: Chaplain C. S. A. and Second Bishop of Tennessee, Being His Story of the War, 1861–1865* (Sewanee TN: University of the South Press, 1905) 78–80; Fremantle, *Three Months in the Southern States*, 162.

representatives would proselytize the social elites in the army. Thus, Polk envisioned some degree of denominational distinctiveness within the army's religious culture. But there were additional purposes for revivalism and Christianity in the Confederate camps. Polk feared that without a Christian influence the "pressure of this scourging war" might incite "our troops to give vent" to a host of "feeling[s] and passions...totally" at odds with a "well-disciplined and chastened civilization." The bishop concluded that "since literally now the country is the army...its moral condition should be well watched, and its spiritual condition cared for and elevated."[88] In this context, Polk supported an army evangelicalism that addressed the societal needs of a changing South. He anticipated that revivals could lay the foundation for a value system that would pilot the demobilized Confederate soldier as he adjusted to the social order of the New South. The bishop's attitude seems to confirm historian Drew Faust's contentions that "army evangelicalism had its greatest impact among the common soldiers" and that officers supported revivalism for its potential benefits regarding "the thorny problem" of army discipline.[89] However, Faust's study of Christianity in the Confederate armies fails to consider why so many officers—so many high-ranking officers—stepped forward not as religious propagandizers but simply as Christian converts. Aside from Braxton Bragg, Generals John Bell Hood and Joseph E. Johnston, all of whom at some point commanded the Army of Tennessee, converted to Episcopalianism during the war. Their conversions were very private affairs, and none of the three men became known as messengers for religious revivals. Interestingly, Polk played a prominent role in the spiritual awakening of both Hood and Johnston.

Prior to the Civil War, John Bell Hood had expressed only a marginal interest in organized religion. Hood, however, did consider himself a Christian, and in the early years of the war he maintained a close friendship with his regimental chaplain, Nicholas Davis. Hood seemed to derive spiritual comfort from his conversations with Davis, but he also experimented with Bible roulette—the age-old practice of randomly opening the Bible, blindly selecting a verse, and accepting the result as a message from God. In January 1862 Hood and some officers played a game

---

[88] Leonidas Polk to Frances D. Polk, 14 June 1863, Leonidas Polk Papers.

[89] Drew Gilpin Faust, "Christian Soldiers: The Meaning of Revivalism in the Confederate Army," *Journal of Southern History* 53/1 (February 1987): 88, 90, 63.

of Bible roulette, "and his eyes fell upon Psalm 118:17 and he read aloud: I shall not die but live." Hood regarded the experience as providentially inspired and as a divine guarantee for safe passage through the horrors of war.[90] By mid-1864, after multiple brushes with death and having sustained injuries that resulted in the amputation of a limb, Hood began to question the scope of his survival promise. Consequently, he visited with Polk, who had rejoined the Army of Tennessee after General Johnston replaced Bragg as commander, and concluded that he should be baptized. Hood preferred to have the ceremony performed immediately but with the start of the Atlanta campaign only a few days away and the more incidental concern of the absence of a baptismal font, he doubted whether an opportunity for baptism would present itself. During a rain shower on the night of 12 May 1864, Polk met with Hood and discussed a course of action that would potentially satisfy the young general's dilemma regarding the sacrament of baptism. Hood accepted the solution and Polk proceeded with his plan. First, the bishop stepped outside of the house that served as Hood's headquarters and collected rainwater in a "tin cup of ordinary army variety." Next, Hood, hampered by a mangled arm and a prosthetic leg, knelt and the officers in attendance "arranged themselves around" the candidate. Then, Polk "in the garb of a ranking officer of the Confederate army" poured the water over the head of Hood, and finally the appropriate catechism questions were asked and answered. Colonel Walter H. Rogers, who witnessed the baptism, remarked that Polk "was probably never so proud as on that simple occasion…when he had won his friend over to the Kingdom of God." As for Hood, he "looked happy and as though a burden had been lifted." Rogers later recalled that the ceremony "was one of the most unique experiences of the war."[91]

General Johnston also allowed Polk to function as a spiritual mediator. Strangely, the impetus for Johnston's inquiries was not a yearning for personal safety or divine comfort, but the concerns of a loving wife. Mrs. Johnston wrote Polk and asked the bishop to "lead [her] soldier nearer to God." When Polk approached the general concerning baptism, Johnston obliged in a ceremony remarkably similar to Hood's in terms of reverence

---

[90] Richard M. McMurry, *John Bell Hood and the War for Southern Independence* (Lexington: University Press of Kentucky, 1982) 32–33.

[91] Newspaper clipping, "Scrapbook of Louisiana History," Howard Tilton Library, Tulane University, New Orleans, Louisiana, 2:9.

and privacy. Johnson biographers have minimized this event; in fact, Craig Symonds describes the baptism as "one more piece of business" at a staff meeting. Conversely, contemporaries ascribed a greater significance. S. A. Cunningham believed that at no time since the armies of Oliver Cromwell or Gustavus Adolphus had an army cultivated a religious character like Joseph Johnston's Army of Tennessee. With the coronation of Johnston as the head of a crusader army, Cunningham implied that the general and his army shared a common religious identity.[92] In the absence of personal conversion narratives, one can only speculate as to why Braxton Bragg, John Bell Hood, and Joseph E. Johnston converted not just to Christianity but to Episcopalianism during the war. Possibly, these men, like most soldiers who undergo a religious conversion in wartime, were searching for peace of mind and assurances about life, death, and the afterlife. As for their denominational affiliation, Bragg, Hood, and Johnston most likely embraced Episcopalianism because in their minds the denomination was the most effective conductor and transmitter of Southern honor and because they hoped the denomination's cultural heritage would allow them to project publicly the image of the Christian warrior. In that vein, Polk helped mold the religious culture of the Army of Tennessee by serving in that capacity himself. Indeed, Polk's persona as a Christian gentleman and gallant soldier justified the Confederate cause, and his moral authority was an important component in the maintenance of morale of his corps.

By examining Polk's violation of Kentucky's neutrality, his adversarial relationship with Braxton Bragg, and his contributions to the religious culture of the Army of Tennessee, a picture emerges of a complex individual who struggled to reconcile his identity as a bishop with that of a general. Despite compiling a suspect military record, Polk remained extremely well-liked by his fellow soldiers. Perhaps, the private thoughts of his niece, Catherine Ann Devereux Edmondston, shed some light on his perplexing military career. The ardent secessionist and keen observer of Southern culture noted in her diary that "tho the clerical Gen has not a great military reputation in the Army himself...each subaltern has his favorite" and since

[92] L. McLane Johnston to Leonidas Polk, 16 May 1864, Polk Papers; Craig L. Symonds, *Joseph E. Johnston: A Civil War Biography* (New York: Norton, 1992) 290; S. A. Cunningham, "Religion in the Southern Army," *Confederate Veteran* 1/1 (January 1893):15; *OR*, ser. 1, vol. 38, pt 4, p. 776.

Bragg is one of the "incapables" then Polk becomes popular by default.[93] But then, the answer may not be quite this simple. For Southerners who ordered their world around a value system based on God and honor, the juxtaposition of the bishop as general served as a reminder of the sacredness of the Confederate cause. Also, Polk's symbolic portrayal of the militant Christian knight, which celebrated specific notions of Southern as well as Episcopalian distinctiveness, was important to his native region as it sought to understand and assign meaning to the Civil War experience.

---

[93] Beth G. Crabtree and James W. Patton, eds., *"Journal of a Secesh Lady:" The Diary of Catherine Ann Devereux Edmonston, 1860–1866* (Raleigh: North Carolina Division of Archives and History, 1979) 508.

CHAPTER 6

Soldier of Stone

After the Confederate debacle at Chattanooga, President Jefferson Davis relieved Braxton Bragg of his command and replaced him with Joseph E. Johnston. The change in command allowed Polk to return from his exile in Mississippi and rejoin the Army of Tennessee. The reunion took place on 11 May 1864, in Resaca, Georgia, but there was little time for celebration. Union General William T. Sherman and nearly 100,000 men were marching toward Atlanta, and the Confederates could marshal no more than 70,000 to stop the advance. Known as a defensive-minded general, Johnston refused to engage Sherman's superior force in an open battle and instead coordinated a series of limited strikes against the enemy. The most serious of the early confrontations occurred at Resaca (13–16 May) and New Hope Church (25–28 May). Although the Confederates fought well, especially at New Hope Church, Sherman's numerical advantage allowed him to employ three quarters of his army against Johnston's entire force and still maintain a sizeable unit for flanking movements against the Confederate army, which, under its new commander, adopted a pattern of hit, retreat, and entrench. During the early weeks of June, the two armies appeared on a collision course for another battle at Kennesaw Mountain. But Polk would not be a part of the Confederate resistance.[1]

As a prelude to the 27 June battle at Kennesaw Mountain, skirmishing and maneuvering centered around a point northwest of Kennesaw, Georgia, known as Pine Mountain. On the morning of 14 June, Johnston, William J. Hardee, and Polk rode to the crest of Pine Mountain to assess the enemy's

---

[1] Albert Castel, *Decision in the West: The Atlanta Campaign of 1864* (Lawrence: University Press of Kansas, 1992) 121–326; Craig L. Symonds, *General Joseph E. Johnston: A Civil War Biography* (New York: Norton, 1992) 280–305.

position and decide on a course of action. As Johnston peered through his field glasses, a Federal artillery shell flew over the group. Sensing the imminent danger, Johnston advised a withdrawal. As the generals and some of their staff scampered to safety, a second shot passed over their heads, but Polk followed "walking thoughtfully along, with his hands folded" behind his back. The Yankees then fired a third shot, which struck Polk in his left side, tearing through his heart and lungs before striking a tree and exploding.[2] The three-inch artillery shell killed Polk instantly. Johnston and Hardee, who rushed back to their fallen comrade, found a mangled torso covered with blood. The two battle-hardened veterans were stricken with grief, and with tears in his eyes Johnston said, "I would rather anything than this."[3] The random shots were actually the beginning of a sustained artillery exchange between the two forces, and Polk was not the only casualty.

During the Civil War, improbable and gothic-like circumstances sometimes accompanied tragedy. Such was the case when Private John S. Jackman, a member of Kentucky's famed Orphan Brigade, sustained an injury the same day that Polk was killed. Three months after that fateful day, he recorded the events in his notebook.

> For two days not a shell had been thrown at our position—and when a shell came shrieking over the mountain to our left, I remarked to the captain [John W. Gillum, Co. A 9th Kentucky Mounted Infantry], that some General and his staff, no doubt, had ridden up to the crest of the hill, and Federal batteries were throwing shells at them. "Yes," said the captain, "and I hope some of them will get shot. A general cant ride around the lines without a regiment of staff at his heels." About this time we heard a second shell strike—I thought it struck into the side of [the] hill; but it had struck Lt. Gen'l Polk. Where he was killed, was not a hundred yards from us, but the trees were so thick, we couldn't see…what was going on, and we did not learn what had happened for some minutes.

Shortly thereafter, the Kentuckian sat down to write a report, and as he was affixing his colonel's name to the report, a shell fragment struck him in the

---

[2] Nathaniel Cheairs Hughes Jr., ed., *The Civil War Memoir of Philip Daingerfield Stephenson, D.D.: Private, Company K, 13th Arkansas Volunteer Infantry, Leader, Piece No. 4, 5th Company, Washington Artillery, Army of Tennessee, CSA* (Baton Rouge: Louisiana State University Press, 1995) 189.

[3] Quoted in Symonds, *General Joseph E. Johnston*, 306.

head, leaving him dazed and momentarily unconscious. His wound was not life threatening but he did require extended convalescence and was transported to a Confederate hospital in Atlanta. As a fitting end to this bizarre story, Jackman traveled to Atlanta on the same train that transferred the remains of Bishop Polk.[4]

In the midst of the firefight, stretcher-bearers had retrieved Polk's body and carried him "to a curious little depression" on the other side of Pine Mountain. There, Private Philip D. Stephenson of the elite Washington Artillery unit observed the slain bishop: "His eyes were wide open and bright, the film of death not yet drawn over them. His lips close shut with an expression natural to him in life. Life's coloring indeed had hardly receded from his face, and as I gazed down into his eyes, they met mine with not the stare of death, but with a questioning gaze. It was as though the last thought registered by that busy intellect was a startled inquiry raised by that deadly interruption of the shell." The Army of Tennessee had lost its talisman—its symbol of Christian righteousness—and the men paused briefly to consider the tragedy.[5]

Sadness filled the Gray ranks that day, Private Sam Watkins of the First Tennessee regiment recalled, and the men felt that a "friend" had been taken from them.[6] Some expressed a sense of outrage and condemned the Yankee "sons of bitches" for killing the Confederate general.[7] Most, however, were simply shocked, but they managed to interpret Polk's death within the context of a providential worldview. Confederate nurse Kate Cumming noted in her diary, "Another of our brightest and best has left us; a star has gone from earth to shine in the bright galaxy around God's throne."[8] Joseph Johnston, who one month earlier had been baptized by Polk, expressed a similar sentiment. In an official tribute, the commander of the Army of Tennessee hoped to transform the tragedy into a lesson of inspiration for his men by proclaiming, "In this distinguished leader we have

---

[4] William C. Davis, ed. *Diary of a Confederate Soldier: John S. Jackman of the Orphan Brigade* (Columbia: University of South Carolina Press, 1990) 141–43.

[5] Hughes, *The Civil War Memoir of Philip Daingerfield Stephenson*, 190–91.

[6] Sam Watkins, *"Co. Aytch," Maury Grays First Tennessee Regiment* (1882; repr., Jackson TN: McCowat-Mercer Press, 1952) 155.

[7] Quoted in Stephen Davis, "The Death of Bishop Polk," *Blue and Gray Magazine* 6/3 (June 1989): 14.

[8] Richard Barksdale Harwell, ed., *Kate, The Journal of a Confederate Nurse* (Baton Rouge: Louisiana State University Press, 1959) 205.

lost the most courteous of gentleman, the most gallant of soldiers. The Christian patriot soldier has neither lived nor died in vain. His example is before you; his mantle rests with you."[9] Johnston's requiem captured the essence of the bishop as general. For the Army of Tennessee, Polk's persona as a Christian gentleman and gallant soldier justified the Confederate cause, and his moral authority was an important element for those who ordered their world around a value system based on God and honor. But the daunting presence of William Sherman and his war machine convinced the Confederates that they had little time to mourn, so they quickly made arrangements to have the body transported to Atlanta.

The city of Atlanta willingly accepted the first opportunity to honor the Confederate general. A committee representing the mayor, a contingent of Episcopal clergymen and laity headed by Reverend Dr. Charles Quintard, and a military escort accompanied Polk's remains from the train depot to St. Luke's Church where the body was placed in state. Atlanta resident Sallie Clayton remembered the occasion as "one of the saddest" in the city's history, and she added that "the good old Bishop's death seemed a personal loss to everyone who looked upon his bloodless face that day." Thousands assembled to pay their respects, and many who stopped at the open casket shed a tear or deposited a "leaf, or flower, or twig" on the "flag that draped his remains." With astonishment, Clayton recalled that "it was the first and only time in some years to come that flowers were used in Atlanta" during a funeral. Quintard delivered a short eulogy, and then the funeral attendants removed the body from St. Luke's. As the hearse and pallbearers returned to the train station, the mourners followed with "bowed heads," and Clayton observed that "the beauty of the morning seemed a mockery to the gloom and sorrow of Atlanta that day." The final service and burial would take place in Augusta at St. Paul's Church.[10]

Polk's family requested that Bishop Stephen Elliott of Georgia deliver the funeral oration. Through their efforts on behalf of the Episcopal church and the University of the South, Elliott and Polk had developed a deep and unwavering admiration for one another. The circumstances of Polk's death

---

[9] US War Departement, *War of the Rebellion: A Compilation of the Official Records of the Union and Confederate Armies*, 128 vols. (Washington DC: U.S. Government Printing Office 1880–1901) ser. 1, vol. 38, pt 4, p. 776. (Hereafter cited as *OR*.)

[10] "Sallie Clayton Reminiscences," in unprocessed folder, Clayton Torrence Papers, Virginia Historical Society, Richmond, Virginia.

provided the bishop of Georgia with an opportunity not simply to honor his friend and fellow churchman but also to defend the Confederate cause. The prelate chose as his text John 11:28, "The master is come and calleth for thee," a reference to Jesus' summoning of Mary, the sister of Martha and Lazarus. Strangely, this scriptural reference was only a corollary exchange in the more dramatic story of Lazarus' resurrection. Indeed, Jesus, standing before the entrance of Lazarus' tomb, commanded his deceased friend to vacate the sepulcher. Then, according to John 11:44, "He that was dead came forth, bound hand and foot with grave-clothes: and...Jesus saith unto them, Loose him, and let him go." Elliott, however, would not duplicate the Nazarene's miracle.

For the Christian, Elliott began, "Nothing is more beautiful than Death when it comes to one who has faithfully fulfilled all the duties of life, and is ready for its summons." He believed that Polk had met those conditions and had followed in the tradition of such Christian martyrs as Stephen and James, all of who had died at the hands of a dastardly "fanaticism." As he pondered Polk's personal sacrifice and the cause for which he died, the bishop rhetorically asked: "Does the fire which is lighted from hell ever cease its fury against the children of the Most High?" By casting the Civil War as a contest between the righteous and the ungodly, the bishop of Georgia established the perfect pretext for addressing the religious justifications of Polk's military service. Elliott, who originally questioned the necessity of Polk's decision to accept a combat assignment, now argued that in becoming a general, Polk had copied the "bold" and "impetuous" nature of St. Peter, the most zealous apostle who drew his sword in defense of the Son of Man when the Pharisees and temple captains made their clandestine arrest. The Georgia cleric also suggested that his friend had imitated the righteous indignation displayed by the Savior when he cleansed the temple of the wicked money-changing infidels. By virtue of these examples the eulogist reasoned that Polk had not violated any spiritual laws in his military service. Curiously, Elliott misrepresented Bishop William Meade's original response to Polk's acceptance of a military commission, claiming that the Virginia prelate had "blessed" the move when he had only promised not to "condemn" the decision. Moreover, the bishop of Georgia conveniently forgot that his reaction to Polk's announcement had been identical to Meade's.[11]

After justifying the bishop of Louisiana's martial exploits, Elliott discussed how Polk's ministry had supported and advanced the Christian foundation and ideals of the Southern slave society. The Episcopal Church in the South, the Georgian maintained, "needed a large slaveholder, who might speak boldly and fearlessly to his peers" about their general "duty" as well as their religious obligation to the slaves. In addition, the Episcopal church required a leader who possessed "manners as well as energy—cultivation as well as Christian courage," one who could teach the "ignorant," enlighten the "blind," and comfort "the suffering slave." Thus, Polk was imminently qualified to represent the Episcopal church in the South. Ultimately, Polk had been called upon by God to fix his bayonet in defense of the peculiar institution, and his participation in the bloody conflict invested the Confederacy with an unparalleled degree of "moral grandeur."[12]

Then, in what was unquestionably the most dramatic moment of the service, Elliott turned symbolically to the North and ascribed to the Northern bishops and churchmen their complicity in Polk's death. "In the presence of the body of this my murdered brother," Elliott declared, I "summon you to meet us at the judgment seat of Christ." The bishop of Georgia believed that the Northern churches had contributed to abolitionist fanaticism and had supported the persecution of Southern slaveholders. He also accused them of desecrating the Christian religion and defiling Southern women. The result of their actions was an "unjust and cruel war." Elliott predicted that the South would be vindicated when the Yankees faced the day of judgment, and he had little hope for Northern redemption. "I leave justice and vengeance to God," Elliott proclaimed, and "may He have mercy upon you on that day of solemn justice and fearful retribution!" On one level, this indictment matched the verdict God had rendered against

---

[11] Stephen Elliott, *Funeral Services at the Burial of the Right Rev. Leonidas Polk, D. D.: Together with the Sermon Delivered in St. Paul's Church, Augusta, Georgia, on June 29, 1864* (Columbia SC: Evans & Cogswell, 1864). For the initial reaction of Meade and Elliott, see Leonidas Polk to Stephen Elliott, 22 June 1861, Leonidas Polk Papers, Jesse Ball duPont Library, University of the South, Sewanee, Tennessee; Stephen Elliott to Leonidas Polk August 6, 1861, Leonidas Polk Papers.

[12] Elliott, *Funeral Services at the Burial of the Right Rev. Leonidas Polk*, 16–23.

Cain for the murder of his brother Abel and captured the deep-seated animosity between the two regions as well as the Southern belief in the righteousness of their cause. On another level, Elliott had taken upon himself the responsibility of vindicating his friend and in the process provided the thematic core of Polk's Lost Cause narrative. When Elliott died in December 1866, the burden of completing Polk's Lost Cause identity fell elsewhere.[13]

Despite historian Charles Reagan Wilson's assertion that "Sewanee Episcopalianism...fostered the growth of the Lost Cause and gave it a peculiar shape," the University of the South did very little to cultivate a regional appreciation of Leonidas Polk in the immediate aftermath of the Civil War.[14] Moreover, the University of the South did not promote the Lost Cause as a type of civil religion, as a form of corporate therapy, or as a literary movement, at least not in ways that promoted white social cohesion throughout the South. Although the school employed former Confederates as faculty and staff, the postwar organizers based their academic and cultural mission on the Episcopalian and Oxonian traditions. Without a slave labor system upon which a Herrenvolk democracy could be constructed, school officials were forced to abandon their master class ideology and they no longer aspired to mold the public mind of the South as Polk once did. They chose instead to isolate themselves from the social and political flux of the New South. At times, this attitude had an abrasive edge as demonstrated by local businessman and university patron William M. Harlow, who also served as the editor of the *University News*.

Prior to the end of the Reconstruction era, Harlow editorialized that a "false charity" had infected the Sewanee environs and had created a class of dependents. The dependents "only want to have a little money now and then to buy whiskey," the editor complained, and they contribute nothing to society. Harlow's solution was to drive the miscreants off the mountaintop and into the valleys. "Let them die or starve," he asserted, "we have no room for them here."[15] Other residents of the academic community also encouraged a separation between Sewanee and the rest of the South. In a

---

[13] Ibid, 26.

[14] Charles Reagan Wilson, *Baptized in Blood: The Religion of the Lost Cause, 1865–1920* (Athens: University of Georgia Press, 1980) 160.

[15] *University News*, 12 January 1876, 1. This was an independent publication but Harlow donated a portion of the paper's profits to the University of the South.

letter to the *University Record*, a writer known only as "Amicus" described Sewanee as "a refuge and asylum for...the better classes of the Southern people." By turning to Sewanee, the dispossessed elite could "escape" tyrannical carpetbaggers and political demagogues as well as the social turmoil that raged in the "Africanized" Southern states. "Amicus" boasted that Sewanee's so-called government consisted not of a mayor and elected council but of "that religious and moral self-restraint which is the essence of all good governments." For "Amicus," Sewanee was the only remaining vestige of "liberty and protection" in the South. This atmosphere of self-determination and independence precluded the postwar founders of Sewanee from implementing a value system that would shape and influence the development of the so-called New South.[16]

In 1874, an Episcopal clergyman from Mississippi cited "three particular excellencies" as indicative of the postwar identity of the University of the South. First, the university maintained the basic tenets of Southern domesticity by requiring that all students reside in private homes rather than dormitories where they were apt to "lose...the restraints and refining influences of society." Second, a program of regular church attendance, chapel obligations, and religious instruction in both the academic and family settings fostered a decidedly Episcopalian tradition. The third characteristic was Sewanee's Oxonian or classical approach to higher education.[17] Some years later, theology professor William S. Bishop expressed agreement with these observations and felt confident in announcing that Sewanee had provided "American boys" with an academic center of excellence comparable to Oxford and Cambridge. Bishop also contended that the "pedagogic value" of the Anglo-Episcopal tradition vested students with a virtuous character and served as a bulwark against the "weak-backed, boneless, substanceless, liberalism" of American higher education.[18] In practice, many people contributed to the postwar Sewanee identity. However, Charles Quintard, William Porcher DuBose, and Josiah

---

[16] *University Record*, March 1874, 1. This was a University of the South publication.

[17] *University Record*, August 1874, 2.

[18] William S. Bishop, "Impressions of Sewanee," n.d., vertical file: Sewanee Description, 1900–1940, Jesse duPont Library, University of the South, Sewanee, Tennessee.

Gorgas—three former Confederates—symbolized the struggle to establish the Episcopalian and Oxonian traditions at the University of the South.

Charles Quintard, a one-time Confederate chaplain, served as Sewanee's first vice-chancellor, and historian Arthur Chitty believed that in all likelihood Quintard was "the most influential Episcopalian in the South during Reconstruction."[19] Quintard's strategy was simple; he wanted to reestablish ties with Northern Episcopalians. Shortly after the war he made his intentions known by urging a congregation of "Federals and Confederates" to do their "utmost to heal the wounds and to hide the seams and scars of the fratricidal war" that had nearly destroyed the nation. A few months later, the Episcopal General Convention of 1865, named him as Tennessee's second bishop, replacing James Hervey Otey who had died during the early years of the war. When Bishop John Henry Hopkins of Vermont consecrated Quintard as the duly elected bishop of Tennessee, the former Confederate recalled: "I felt the war between the states was over."[20] Quintard traveled extensively on behalf of the university, serving as its chief fundraiser, and he earned a reputation for being a highly skilled and inspiring orator. Eventually, the general public derived their impressions of Sewanee from the persona of Quintard. Their encounters with Quintard led them to believe that the Sewanee vice chancellor was a sincere reconciliationist rather than an unreconstructed Rebel.

Interestingly, William Porcher DuBose and Josiah Gorgas traveled similar paths in their respective journeys to Sewanee. Both DuBose, a former Confederate combat officer and chaplain, and Gorgas, the chief of the Confederate Ordnance Bureau, failed on a variety of fronts to make the transition from the Old South to the New South. Consequently, both men found in Sewanee an opportunity for success and redemption. According to historian Moultrie Guerry, William Porcher DuBose "did much to set the tone and outline the principles of [Sewanee's] religion and worship."[21] DuBose, as university chaplain and professor of ethics, endorsed an

---

[19] Arthur Benjamin Chitty, Jr., *Reconstruction at Sewanee: The Founding of the University of the South and its First Administration, 1857–1872* (Sewanee TN: University of the South Press, 1954) 91.

[20] Arthur H. Noll, ed., *Doctor Quintard: Chaplain C.S.A. and Second Bishop of Tennessee* (Sewanee TN: University of the South Press, 1905) 144, 148.

[21] Moultrie Guerry, *Men Who Made Sewanee* (Sewanee TN: University of the South Press, 1932) 82.

Episcopal tradition that promised to balance the "reality" of human experience with "dignified" exhibitions of worship. At a time when certain factions within the Episcopal church contemplated the formation of a separate denomination, DuBose insisted that church unity was a greater necessity and a more noble purpose. Through DuBose, Sewanee determined that its *raison d'être* involved "the accumulation and organization of that which is common" to the Episcopal church and not the mythmaking and ritual observances of the Lost Cause.[22]

Based on the recommendations of such former Confederates as Robert E. Lee and Jefferson Davis, the University of the South elected Josiah Gorgas to the positions of Headmaster of the Grammar School and vice-chancellor. Gorgas accepted the offer because his Brierfield Iron Works had been a financial disaster, and he desired to remove his daughters from the "objectionable society" created by Alabama's Reconstruction government.[23] Gorgas, who began his duties in July 1869, had been assigned the monumental tasks of increasing student enrollment and placing the university on a solid financial foundation. As a West Point graduate, Gorgas brought to Sewanee the same disciplined and scientific approach to education that he had learned at the nation's top military academy. His pragmatic inclinations soon convinced him that Sewanee had over-committed to "Latin and Greek authors" at the expense of a "practical" education.[24] To compensate, Gorgas wanted to build dormitories and institute a West Point-style disciplinary system. For a brief time, the Gorgas's influence was apparent as the "grammar school boys and college students all wore uniforms and drilled."[25]

The Gorgas approach, however, clashed with the vision of Quintard, DuBose, and other classicists. In July 1871, the board of trustees voted to implement the cap and gown system for university students and professors, and only the grammar school continued the military tradition. The change in fashion actually signaled a determined effort by the adherents of the

---

[22] William Porcher DuBose, *Turning Points in My Life* (New York: Longmans & Greens, 1912) 66, 126, 135.

[23] Sarah Woolfolk Wiggins, ed., *The Journals of Josiah Gorgas, 1857–1878* (Tuscaloosa: University of Alabama Press, 1995) 236.

[24] Quoted in Frank Vandiver, *Ploughshares into Swords: Josiah Gorgas and Confederate Ordnance* (Austin: University of Texas Press, 1952) 289.

[25] Guerry, *Men Who Made Sewanee*, 88.

Oxonian tradition to pull the university in their direction. Gorgas found himself in a veritable crossfire and became a casualty of the classicist-militarist debate. In 1878, the board of trustees decided that the vice-chancellor's position must be held by an Episcopal clergyman, and despite his success as an administrator, Gorgas resigned his post in light of the new policy. Historian Arthur Chitty concluded that not long after the Gorgas saga the battle was over and "the classicists had routed the militarists."[26]

Indeed, Sewanee had come "to represent...culture for culture's sake." William Porcher DuBose made this claim in 1905 and declared resolutely that "utilitarianism or professionalism or specialism of any sort" had no chance of survival at Sewanee. DuBose appreciated Sewanee's ability to provide "sufficient leisure from labor" where individuals could pursue such questions as the meaning of life. Assuredly, the arts were a vital part of the cultural life at the university. Literary societies for both students and faculty members flourished on campus.[27] For Dubose, the production of Greek plays signaled "the persistent efforts" of the university "to provide in every way intimacy" with the fine arts and illustrated its desire to forge a classical outlook.[28] Notwithstanding the emergence and triumph of the Episcopalian and Oxonian traditions, the relevant point is that the University of the South, through its self-imposed isolation and its narrowly-constructed cultural mission, failed to become the guardian of the South's moral conscience. In addition, Leonidas Polk had intended for the university to train a "native" ministry and equip Southern prelates for an aggressive, and if necessary, protracted defense of the distinctively Southern way of life. Without the slave labor system as the foundation of Southern society, the Lost Cause represented the greatest opportunity for Sewanee Episcopalians to influence regional discourse and culture, but they did not seize the opportunity. Furthermore, the Sewanee community failed, or simply refused, to consider how Episcopalians would compete and function effectively in the postwar evangelical South.

Although the Sewanee identity centered around the Episcopalian and Oxonian traditions, the university did make conscious efforts to remember

[26] Chitty, *Reconstruction at Sewanee*, 125.

[27] William Porcher DuBose, "The Romance and Genius of a University," *Sewanee Review* 13/4 (October 1905): 500–501.

[28] *Sewanee Daily Purple*, 26 July 1884, 3. This was a University of the South publication.

the Confederate dead. On the occasion of Robert E. Lee's death, Joseph P. B. Wilmer, who had replaced Leonidas Polk as bishop of Louisiana, addressed the student body and reiterated the standard Southern interpretations of the war. Wilmer, a native Virginian, assured the student body that General Lee would not have supported a cause whose sole objective was the perpetuation of slavery. Likewise, Wilmer argued that the Confederacy had not lost the will to fight but had only succumbed to superior numbers in terms of manpower and resources. However, Wilmer was most emphatic about Lee's commitment to Christianity, not his service to the Confederacy. Wilmer suggested that at Washington and Lee the former general had "above all things endeavored to raise them [the students] to a new and higher life with God." Moreover, Lee had not been a proponent of a "creedless religion" but a faithful communicant of the Episcopal church. Therefore, Lee could be looked upon as a man of "heroic virtue." Wilmer also proposed that if a man sought "true honor" then he should look no farther than the "religion of Christ."[29] This linking of Episcopalianism with Christian honor became the cornerstone of Sewanee's remembrance of the Confederate dead. In fact, one could infer that Wilmer had a sectarian agenda when he honored Lee as the quintessential gentleman-Episcopalian. Yet, Polk possessed the same social and educational background as Lee and also epitomized the ideals of the Christian knight, but neither Wilmer nor the university promoted the bishop general as the model of Southern Episcopalianism.

Similarly, one could argue that William Porcher DuBose's eulogy of Ellison Capers illustrated how the university distanced itself from an outright association or endorsement of the rhetoric and philosophy of the Lost Cause. Ellison Capers, a former Confederate general who entered the Episcopal ministry after the war, had been a conspicuous participant in the Lost Cause movement. He served as chaplain general of the United Confederate Veterans and earned the unofficial title of "Orator Laureate of the Lost Cause." Because of Capers's extensive involvement in the Lost Cause, historian Charles Reagan Wilson called him "an expression of the Confederate myth and at the same time a mythmaker himself." In addition,

---

[29] Joseph P. B. Wilmer, *General Robert E. Lee: An Address Delivered Before the Students of the University of the South, October 15, 1870* (Nashville: Paul & Tavel, 1872) 5–12.

Wilson asserted that the Christianity admired and celebrated in Capers "was not that of a gentle Christ, but that of a Jesus vigorously driving the unrighteous from the temple." Thus, Wilson viewed Capers as the epitome of the militant Christian knight.[30] Yet, William Porcher DuBose declined to accept this characterization of Capers. While acknowledging that as a soldier Capers was both an "idol and inspiration to his men," DuBose admired Capers more for sacrificing a certain and successful postwar political career in order to enter the ministry and serve the Episcopal Church. Also, DuBose revered the collegial demeanor in which Capers tackled "the moral emergencies" and ecclesiastical dilemmas that confronted the Episcopal Church in the postwar period. Although Dubose recognized Capers's celebrity status as the "*Orator Laureate* of the Confederacy," he regarded the prelate's Christian sympathy as "his distinctive and characteristic trait." In fact, DuBose saw in Capers the Jesus who turned the other cheek, not the temple evictor. In short, the tributes paid to Confederate icon Robert E. Lee and Lost Cause standard-bearer Ellison Capers suggest that the Sewanee community was not actively engaged in the dissemination of Lost Cause mythologies in the same manner as die-hard enthusiasts.[31]

Not only did the university refrain from participating in typical Lost Cause celebrations, Sewanee leaders struggled to interpret the Civil War career of Leonidas Polk. At the August 1879, board of trustees meeting, Chancellor William Mercer Green revisited the issue of Polk's military service. As Green explained, many Episcopalians had questioned the "necessity" of Polk's participation in the Confederate army, although few questioned the "the purity of his motives." Indeed, Green remarked that Polk "thought that he saw a political party of great power, determined to write *Iliumfuit* in the ashes of our Southern rights and institutions." Moreover, those who held reservations about Polk's generalship also maintained that there was no greater honor than to fight for one's country. Still, the matter haunted and perplexed Green. He speculated that "an All-wise Providence saw fit that [Polk] should atone for the error—if error it was—with his own noble blood." The chancellor seemed reluctant to

[30] Wilson, *Baptized in Blood*, 55–56.
[31] William Porcher DuBose, "Ellison Capers," *Sewanee Review* 16/2 (April 1908): 370, 373, 368.

condemn Polk's actions. But in the dualism of his reasoning, Green posited, "we are sure that the Recording Angel must have sympathized with the deed...and we trust that the blood of a Redeeming God has blotted it out forever."[32] Green never questioned the legitimacy of the Confederate cause, but nearly fifteen years passed until a university spokesman emphatically exonerated Polk.

Although the University of the South refrained from using Leonidas Polk as a symbol of its postwar identity, various groups and individuals worked diligently to make the bishop an enduring character in the Lost Cause narrative. In the early 1880s, Sam Watkins, a former Confederate private, wrote that "second to Stonewall Jackson" the loss of Leonidas Polk "was the greatest the South ever sustained." On the surface this analogy appears ridiculous, but within the context of certain Lost Cause themes, startling similarities existed between the two generals. Among these were their West Point education, their defense of slavery and secession, and—most importantly—their identity as Christian soldiers. But Watkins also spoke as a member of the Army of Tennessee. Indeed, Watkins explained such issues as the origins of the war, combat motivation, officer competence, and the reasons for Confederate defeat in the Western theater. Perhaps, the former soldier exaggerated the importance of Leonidas Polk in an effort to establish a favorable perception of the Army of Tennessee. Clearly, his portrayal of the bishop countered the negative image the army had acquired through its lack of military success and by its identification with the maligned and detested Braxton Bragg. In addition, Watkins's literary contributions illustrated a fundamental aspect of the Lost Cause: the Lost Cause identities rose in direct proportion to their usefulness in explaining the Old South, the Civil War, and the standards of Christian gentility and were not solely dependent on military reputations. Thus, a comparison of the respective Lost Cause identities of Jackson and Polk will reveal how mythmakers developed and utilized the public memory of the two generals and how each man became a significant cultural symbol within the Lost Cause movement.[33]

---

[32] William Mercer Green, *Address Delivered before the Board of Trustees, University of the South, Sewanee, Tennessee, August 4, 1879* (Charleston, SC: Walker, Evans & Cogswell, 1879) 18.

[33] Watkins, "*Co. Aytch,*" 154.

Without question, Thomas J. Jackson was one of the preeminent military figures of the Civil War and one of the South's first war heroes, but his posthumous fame would surpass even his impressive military record. In the years prior to the Civil War, Stonewall Jackson had been an anonymous figure except to the citizenry of Virginia's Shenandoah Valley. The region of Jackson's nativity admired his fortitude in overcoming a tragic childhood, one in which he essentially "never knew his father" and lost his mother at the tender age of seven. They also applauded Jackson's academic achievements at the United States Military Academy and acknowledged his heroic exploits in the Mexican War. Yet, there was no large-scale public appreciation of Jackson outside of the valley. In fact, when Jackson resigned from the army in 1851 to take a faculty position at the Virginia Military Institute (VMI), the Lexington community soon discovered that he was a peculiar introvert and a dull academician. In recognition of these deficiencies, students at VMI referred to Jackson as "Tom Fool," and one cadet who studied under the professor remarked that his optics course was taught by a *"hell of a fool."* Historian James Robertson has argued that Jackson's academic reputation suffered as a result of his inexperience as a teacher and the difficulty "of both the content and the learning process" in the courses he taught. Moreover, Robertson has suggested that the majority of complaints came from the "young cadets" (third and fourth classmen), and by the 1860s students generally exhibited a genuine "admiration" for their enigmatic pedagogue.[34]

Notwithstanding Robertson's apologetics, the cult of Jackson actually began on 13 April 1861, the day the Union surrendered Fort Sumter. On the same day in Lexington, Unionists and Secessionists demonstrated in the streets. The cadets were eager to join the fracas, but Jackson and others stepped in and ordered them back to campus. Later that day, in an address that the soon-to-be Confederates would never forget, Jackson proclaimed: *"Be slow to draw the sword in civil strife, but when you draw it, throw away the scabbard."* One impressionable cadet, William M. Polk, son of Leonidas Polk, remembered that "the enthusiasm created by this speech was beyond description." Several years later, Leonidas Polk communicated to British military observer Arthur Fremantle how his son was influenced by this

---

[34] James I. Robertson, Jr., *Stonewall Jackson: The Man, the Soldier, The Legend* (New York: Macmillan, 1997) xi–xii, 121, 119, 125, 132.

event. Indeed, Jackson's peroration overshadowed his previous ten years of service at VMI, and cadets such as the young Polk interpreted the speech as a sign of the professor's ardent Southern nationalism and his advocacy of the Confederate cause.[35]

However, after the war, the Old Dominion's Lost Cause exegetes downplayed any notion that Virginians had welcomed or encouraged secession and maintained that the radical fire-eaters of their sister states forced secession on them. Moreover, they claimed that Virginians did not fight to erect a slaveocracy but to perpetuate the republican principles of the nation's founding fathers.[36] According to Stonewall's widow, Mary Anna Jackson, the general "never was a secessionist," and he advocated that the South "fight for her rights *in the Union.*" With respect to slavery, Mrs. Jackson insisted that her husband had "accepted" the labor system not because of its desirability "but as allowed by Providence for ends which it was not his business to determine." Irrespective of the accuracy of Mrs. Jackson's claims, the image that emerges is one of a hesitant secessionist and a reluctant supporter of slavery. As a result, the Jackson mystique intensified because of its compatibility with the thematic components of the Virginians' Lost Cause narrative.[37] These Confederate apologists portrayed the South as a deeply religious society, where masculine prerogatives and martial honor were compatible with the Christian faith, and they constructed an understanding of Jackson that supported such notions. For instance, Presbyterian divine Robert L. Dabney, who served as Jackson's chief of staff and spiritual advisor during the war, claimed that his "prime object" in writing the general's biography was "to portray and vindicate his Christian character, [so] that his countrymen may possess it as a precious example." Likewise, Francis H. Smith, Superintendent of the Virginia Military Institute, informed the academy's first post-Civil War class that Christian values were a large part of the institution's educational philosophy. Specifically, Smith promised that professors would "by precept and by

---

[35] The Polk account is in James Arthur Lyon Fremantle, *Three Months in the Southern States: April–June, 1863* (New York: John Bradborn, 1864) 151.

[36] Thomas Connelly and Barbara Bellows, *God and General Longstreet: The Lost Cause and the Southern Mind* (Baton Rouge: Louisiana State University Press, 1982) 42.

[37] Mary Anna Jackson, *Life and Letters of General Stonewall Jackson* (New York: Harper and Brothers, 1892) 139, 140, 143.

example, hold up the Word of Life so that the perfect man may be formed upon the model of the Christian gentleman." Not surprisingly, Smith reminded the student body that just a few years earlier Jackson had joined with cadets in search of "the blessing of a covenanted God."[38]

Furthermore, Dabney hoped to serve his own sectarian agenda by capitalizing on Jackson's popularity. Not only did he exalt Jackson as a Christian gentleman but presented him as a calculated Presbyterian. As a young adult, Jackson had been baptized by an Episcopal clergyman, but at that time he displayed little interest in organized religion and he chose not to join that church. According to Dabney, Jackson also "examined" Catholicism, only to "reject it as apostasy." Ultimately, Jackson embraced Presbyterianism and its Calvinist belief system as a result of "deliberate comparison, serious study" and prayer. Dabney reasoned, "What Christian can justify himself for acting in any other way?" In examining the role of religion in the Lost Cause, historian Charles Reagan Wilson has observed that clerics "used the Lost Cause to warn Southerners of their decline from past virtue, to promote moral reform, to encourage conversion to Christianity," and to advance "Southern traditions." However, by defining the Lost Cause as a civil religion with an ecumenical nature, Wilson seriously underestimated the sectarian designs of those ministers who participated in the Lost Cause movement.[39] Indeed, Dabney declared that "to demand the suppression" of Jackson's brand of Presbyterianism would be "more invidious" than using the general's views in an "aggressive party spirit." Moreover, Dabney recognized how valuable Jackson's adherence to Old Light Presbyterianism could be as a Calvinist-bulwark against the encroachments of Pelagianism and Arminianism. Thus, Dabney demonstrated that Lost Cause icons could serve denominational purposes that were independent of the Lost Cause movement in general.[40]

While Stonewall Jackson, along with Robert E. Lee and Jefferson Davis, formed the Lost Cause's Great Triumvirate, others, including Leonidas Polk, became supporting characters in the cultural narrative that

---

[38] Robert L. Dabney, *Life and Campaigns of Lieut-Gen. Thomas J. Jackson* (New York: Blelock and Co., 1866) vi; Francis H. Smith, *The Inner Life of the VMI Cadet: Introductory Address to the Corps of Cadets, Sept. 10, 1866* (Lexington VA: Virginia Military Institute Press,1873) 14, 16, 47.

[39] Dabney, *Life and Campaigns*, 83, 85; Wilson, *Baptized in Blood*, 11, 12.

[40] Dabney, *Life and Campaigns*, 85.

glorified the Confederate cause. Polk's incorporation into the rituals of memory resulted in part from the Herculean efforts of the Louisiana chapters of the United Confederate Veterans (UCV), the Sons of Confederate Veterans (SCV), and the United Daughters of the Confederacy (UDC). The UCV originated in New Orleans in June 1889, and Louisiana veterans were participants in the regional movement to honor Confederate soldiers. Of the various social, literary, historical, and benevolent activities, textbook endorsements became a fundamental concern of the Louisiana chapters of the UCV, and state members reacted positively to the work of Ann E. Snyder. Their endorsement of her textbook exposed Louisiana school children to an extremely favorable assessment of Polk's Civil War career. In *The Civil War: From a Southern Stand-Point*, Snyder presented Polk as an effective and aggressive military leader. She charged the Union with being "the first to violate" Kentucky's neutrality, and she argued that Polk's offer for a multilateral withdrawal confirmed the Confederacy's goodwill toward the Bluegrass State. Snyder deemed Polk's victory at Belmont to be "one of the most brilliant of the war," and she made no mention of his strife-ridden relationship with Bragg, his suspension after Chickamauga, or his role in the failure of command in the Western theater.[41]

Likewise, the SCV, an offshoot of the UCV, which held goals similar to the parent organization, contributed significantly to the public remembrance of Leonidas Polk. For the SCV, camp meetings represented an integral part of their so-called educational program. In March 1907, Louisiana's Camp Beauregard contacted former Polk aide Aristide Hopkins about serving as the guest speaker at their 10 April meeting, which coincided with the bishop's one-hundred-and-first birthday. Hopkins expressed some reluctance because he did not consider himself an effective orator, but with noticeable enthusiasm he offered to prepare a manuscript that could be read by a more accomplished speaker. As a resident of Louisiana, Hopkins spoke with first-hand knowledge of Polk's distinguished service as bishop of Louisiana, and whether on the battlefield or in the pulpit he found Polk to be "*sans peur et sans reproach.*" Hopkins described Polk as a "fatherly" figure

---

[41] Herman Hattaway, "The United Confederate Veterans in Louisiana," *Louisiana History* 16/1 (Winter 1975): 13, 11; Ann E. Snyder, *The Civil War: From a Southern Stand-Point* (Nashville: Publishing House of the Methodist Episcopal Church, South, 1890) 57, 61, 163–67.

who was "always anxious to spare the lives of his troops" but at the same time showed no "regard for his own safety."[42] The tragic death of the bishop had a lasting impact on Hopkins, and he recalled vividly the events of that depressing day. After observing morning prayers, Polk and Hopkins had ridden to the front lines, and along the way, the former aide remembered that the bishop "seemed low spirited and preoccupied." Hopkins speculated that the general was either privately reminiscing about his diocese, plantation life, or perhaps was troubled by the "fast-declining fortunes of the Confederacy." A final theory was that Polk had received a premonition of death. Interestingly, Hopkins attributed the accuracy of the fatal shot to the "hand of Providence" and not the "aim of the Federal gunner." Hopkins reasoned that death had spared Polk the "anguish" the Army of Tennessee suffered at Nashville in 1865 and shielded him from the "painful sight of his shriveled corps" at the battle of Franklin.[43] Whereas the UCV and SCV often honored the Confederate dead through military reappraisals of the Civil War, some historians have suggested that the UDC focused on glorifying the Southern way of life and "the character of Confederate men."[44] Members of the UDC participated in a number of historical enterprises associated with the Lost Cause, and they greatly influenced several generations of Southern children, particularly through their sponsorship of essay contests. In 1911, the Louisiana chapters of the UDC gave seventh and eighth grade students an opportunity to write an essay highlighting the accomplishments of the state's five Civil War generals. The list included P. G. T. Beauregard, Braxton Bragg, Henry Watkins Allen, Richard Taylor, and Leonidas Polk.

Typically, the sections covering Polk mentioned his West Point education, his clerical background, and his commitment to higher education. But the students also displayed an incredible understanding of the complex

---

[42] Aristide Hopkins to W. O. Hart, 18 March 1907, Aristide Hopkins Papers, Joseph Merrick Jones Hall, Tulane University, New Orleans, Louisiana; Aristide Hopkins to W. O. Hart, 26 March 1907, Aristide Hopkins Papers.

[43] Aristide Hopkins, untitled manuscript, 26 April 1907, Aristide Hopkins Papers.

[44] Karen Cox, "Women, the Lost Cause, and the New South: The United Daughters of the Confederacy and the Transmission of Confederate Culture" (Ph.D. diss., University of Southern Mississippi, 1997) 155. For Gaines Foster, many UDC activities were designed to restore and reinforce notions of Southern manhood. See Foster, *Ghosts of the Confederacy: Defeat, the Lost Cause, and the Emergence of the New South* (New York/Oxford, 1987).

nature of Polk's military service. One essayist commented on Polk's controversial decision to fight as a combat officer rather than serve as a chaplain and remarked that it was unusual for a "Church dignitary" to receive "so much military responsibility."[45] Others explained that Polk's "love for the South" compelled him to cast "aside the mitre of bishops to take up the sword of the patriot."[46] According to several essayists, Polk's finest moment occurred at the battle of Belmont where he defeated Ulysses S. Grant and secured for the South one of its "most glorious" victories of the war.[47] The battle of Belmont occupied a special place in the minds of the Western Confederacy, a region that witnessed few military successes. In fact, Lost Cause writers often characterized the battle in the same prideful manner that Easterners spoke of the battle of Bull Run. As a result Polk's leadership during this particular battle generated a great deal of sympathy and appreciation for the bishop's military service.[48] The students also attributed very little significance to Polk's suspension after Chickamauga, and most felt that his reinstatement by President Jefferson Davis meant that he had been declared innocent of all charges.[49]

As if to confirm that the UDC had succeeded in fulfilling its primary goals, a number of students made special references to Polk's personal character, and some produced religious explanations or interpretations of his death. For example, one essayist called Polk "a prince" among men and soldiers whose "loveable nature will always be memorable to the South."[50] Also, Polk and the other generals were remembered in poetic verse as men "whom power could not corrupt / whom death could not terrify / whom defeat could not dishonor."[51] Similarly, the themes of courage, patriotism, valor, and sacrifice appeared in countless essays. Remarkably, some of the seventh and eighth graders believed that Polk's death was the result of the

---

[45] Essay 113, United Daughters of the Confederacy Papers, Louisiana Historical Association Collection, Joseph Merrick Jones Hall, Tulane University, New Orleans, Louisiana.

[46] Essay 102, United Daughters of the Confederacy Papers. See also essays 261, 262, 184.

[47] Essay 192, United Daughters of the Confederacy Papers. See also essay 67.

[48] Sarah A. Dorsey, *Recollections of Henry Watkins Allen: Brigidier-General Confederate States Army, Ex-Governor of Louisiana* (New York: M. Doolady, 1866) 69.

[49] Essays 248, 113, in United Daughters of the Confederacy Papers.

[50] Essay 262, United Daughters of the Confederacy Papers.

[51] Essay 82, United Daughters of the Confederacy Papers.

mysterious workings of divine providence, and they framed the incident in the language of a Greek tragedy that depicted a favored son who was ultimately rescued from his earthly travails by a loving father. "The bullet with which the fatal wound was made," wrote one essayist, "was only a messenger from God, bearing the news to him that his term of duty was o'er. His worthy soul departed from earth to heaven...but he died as happily as though he had lived quietly in his little diocese."[52] Thus the Christian faith that proved to be a great consolation to Southerners in the aftermath of Confederate defeat also allowed students to view Polk's death as an act of compassion and not as a sign of retribution.

Naturally, Polk's family contributed to the development of his Lost Cause identity. Immediately after the war, his wife, Frances Devereux Polk, began to solicit materials from various participants in the war. One of the first men that she contacted was Benjamin Franklin Cheatham. The aristocratic bishop and the foul-mouthed, hard-drinking Tennessean formed one of the Army of Tennessee's oddest command partnerships, and given the paradoxical dimensions of their personalities, one might wonder why Mrs. Polk turned to Cheatham before anyone else. Her motive, however, was somewhat obvious. She wanted Cheatham's assistance in saving her "husband's memory from blame." Specifically, she intended to build a defense of the general's actions during the Kentucky campaign of 1862.[53] Mrs. Polk did not intend to publish an account of the campaign, fearing that a "controversy" might arise. Moreover, she believed that Simon Bolivar Buckner was better suited to produce a formal account of the campaign, and she simply wanted someone to protect her husband's name from "reproach."[54] Although the Lost Cause offered many Southern women their first real opportunity to become biographers and historians, Mrs. Polk deferred the primary responsibility for defending the bishop's name to her youngest son, William. If it had not been for the fact that William was a

---

[52] Essay 184, United Daughters of the Confederacy Papers.
[53] Frances Devereux Polk to Benjamin Franklin Cheatham, 12 July 1864, Benjamin Franklin Cheatham Papers, Tennessee State Library and Archives, Nashville.
[54] Frances Devereux Polk to Benjamin Franklin Cheatham, 2 August 1867, Benjamin Franklin Cheatham Papers. Mrs. Polk also contacted Simon Bolivar Buckner, Robert E. Lee, Robert W. Woollay, Joseph Jones, and many others. The letters are in the Leonidas Polk Papers, Jesse Ball duPont Library, University of the South, Sewanee, Tennessee.

veteran of the war as well as a well-educated Confederate apologist, Frances Polk may have used the Lost Cause movement as a platform for launching a successful career as a Southern writer.

When the war broke out, William M. Polk was a cadet at the Virginia Military Institute. With youthful enthusiasm, he marched double quick to the beat of secessionist drums. He drew his first assignment with Felix Zollicoffer in East Tennessee, and later he joined his father's staff, finishing the war with the rank of lieutenant. Thus, he was old enough to remember life on Leighton plantation and some of his father's activities as bishop of Louisiana, and he certainly possessed the military knowledge to produce a narrative of his father's wartime service. After the war, William moved to New York and enrolled at Columbia's medical school and later became dean of the medical school at Cornell University. In one of his first published accounts, Polk explored his father's views on race, slavery, and education. The junior Polk explained that the "curious sociological status" of the slaves was both a "fixed and organic law" of the South and a "stupendous problem" for the region. His father understood the complexity of Southern society and worked to incorporate Christian principles into the governing philosophies of the peculiar institution. Indeed, "the central idea in Leonidas Polk's mind," the bishop's son wrote, was to prepare and equip Southerners for the "exceptionally difficult and dangerous" responsibility of being "the ruling race of the South." The fulfillment of this aim was a motivating factor in the bishop's efforts to create the University of the South, a goal that could only be accomplished if the university promoted the tenets of "true conservatism" and demonstrated that the South was capable of producing a genuine and viable intellectual tradition.[55]

In 1893 William Polk published a two-volume biography of his father that followed the hagiographic conventions of the day. The portrait that emerged was one of a loyal churchman, benevolent slaveholder, Southern patriot, and a courageous and skilled general.[56] Interestingly, the biography

[55] William M. Polk, *The University of the South and the Race Problem, Commencement Oration, August 3, 1893* (Sewanee TN: University of the South Press, 1893).

[56] After the publication of the *Official Records* of the Civil War, Polk revised the work substantially and the second publication practically serves as a first edition. William M. Polk, *Leonidas Polk: Bishop and General*, 2 vols. (New York: Longmans, Green, and Co., 1915).

attracted the attention of several University of the South professors, beginning with William P. Trent, who had recently been discharged from the University of North Carolina after a controversy surrounding his critical biography of Southern novelist William Gilmore Simms. Trent actually reviewed the two-volume biography of Polk for the *Sewanee Review*. In contrast to the accusatory rhetoric that Chancellor William Mercer Green had used in 1879, the literature professor absolved Polk for his decision to accept a military command. He described the bishop's ordeal as "a pathetic but...noble picture of the struggle of the man to do his duty...toward his country and his church." Moreover, Trent celebrated Polk as a Confederate war hero and declared that "if any man, soldier or civilian, priest or layman...finds it in his heart to condemn Leonidas Polk or blame him harshly, [I] would not die in that man's company."[57] Others at the university followed Trent's lead. West Point graduate James Postell Jervey, who taught mathematics at Sewanee, defended Polk's military role, claiming that the Confederate government faced "a serious emergency" that required the former cadet's service. Jervey concluded that Polk "achieved brilliant" results during his two independent commands, the first against Grant at Belmont and the second against William T. Sherman in Mississippi. Moreover, the professor of mathematics excused Polk's seizure of Kentucky and blamed Braxton Bragg for the failure of command in the Western theater.[58] Like most Lost Cause writers, William Polk, Trent, and Jervey painted a relatively inaccurate picture of the bishop's military career in order to incorporate him into the broader scope of the Lost Cause.

Death on the battlefield compensated for Leonidas Polk's poor military record, and his martyrdom made him a viable character in the Lost Cause narrative. Although his controversial decision to discard his clerical robe in favor of a general's uniform caused the University of the South a great deal of consternation, the Louisiana chapters of the United Confederate Veterans, the Sons of Confederate Veterans, and the United Daughters of the Confederacy all glorified Polk as a military hero and a model of Christian character. Most importantly, Lost Cause practitioners honored Polk as a paternalistic slaveholder. The principal architects of this image

---

[57] William P. Trent, "A Noteworthy Biography: Leonidas Polk," *Sewanee Review* 2/2 (May 1893): 383.

[58] James Postell Jervey, "Leonidas Polk: The Confederate General," *Historical Magazine of the Protestant Episcopal Church* 7/4 (December 1938): 389–99.

were Bishop Stephen Elliott and William M. Polk. They praised Polk for speaking "boldly and fearlessly" to fellow slaveholders "about their duty to their slaves" and for being a living example of that Christian obligation, and they admired him for trying to build a biracial Christian society. Ultimately, Lost Cause enthusiasts crafted a positive image of Leonidas Polk because the bishop as general validated their contention that Southern slavery had not been immoral or exploitative but rather a means for Christianizing a less fortunate and docile race.[59]

[59] Elliott, *Funeral Services at the Burial of the Right Rev. Leonidas Polk*; Polk, *Polk*, 1:180.

CONCLUSION

The Confederate infantryman who cursed the Yankee bastards for killing "old Gen. Polk" was simply venting his rage over the tragic death of a popular military leader. The soldier could not have known that the death of the Louisiana bishop also ended a critical era in the history of the Episcopal church in the South. Metaphorically speaking, the Civil War claimed among its casualties several other Southern bishops. Nicholas H. Cobbs of Alabama, who preferred death to disunion, James H. Otey, the reluctant secessionist, and William Meade of Virginia all died during the war. Stephen Elliott of Georgia, Polk's closest friend, passed away before his state was readmitted to the Union. Their absence placed the mantle of leadership on Bishops Thomas Atkinson of North Carolina, Henry C. Lay of Arkansas, and Charles Quintard of Tennessee. For various reasons, they worked quickly to dissolve the Protestant Episcopal Church in the Confederate States of America and to reestablish ties with their Northern brothers and sisters of the faith. Because of their efforts and those of Northern bishops such as John Henry Hopkins of Vermont, the reunification of the Episcopal church was a relatively simple task.[1] However, the postwar period was a time of tremendous religious, social, and political change for Southerners as well as Episcopalians, and these changes tended to overshadow the achievement of reconciliation. The eradication of slavery not only destroyed the Old South's labor system, it also altered the nature of evangelicalism in the region as the freedmen gained control of their own religious organizations. As for Episcopalians, they faced an internal crisis in 1873, one rooted in theological and doctrinal concerns not sectional politics. The result was that a discontented faction chose to establish a separate denomination. Within this postwar context of denominational strife and regional redistricting of racial, gender, and class lines, no one stepped forward in the tradition of

---

[1] James M. Donald, "Bishop Hopkins and the Reunification of the Church," *Historical Magazine of the Protestant Episcopal Church* 47 (March 1978): 73–91.

Leonidas Polk and attempted to broaden the appeal and strengthen the influence of Episcopalianism in the New South.[2]

In the quarter century prior to the Civil War, Polk had presented to Southern Episcopalians a plan for entering the mainstream of the region's religious life. Polk's reputation greatly enhanced the appeal of his message. Anyone who graduated in the top ten of his class at the United States Military Academy enjoyed a certain degree of respect in the South, and his patrician manner also related well in the plantation society. As a seminarian and missionary bishop, Polk developed a deep concern for nonbelievers and was distressed by the lack of a formal Episcopal presence in many parts of the South. In many respects, his missionary bishopric was the turning point of his ministerial career. From that moment, he never again wavered in his commitment to spreading the gospel message, which he viewed as the fundamental purpose of the ministry. As bishop of Louisiana, Polk set forth his doctrinal positions and ministerial objectives in a clear and precise manner. His support for the St. Peter's Seaman's Bethel in New Orleans combined evangelical theology and social conservatism. Indeed, he promoted the theme of "unity in Christ" within the standard applications of religious benevolence. As a social reformer, Polk encouraged individual piety and condemned worldliness, and he understood that a correlation existed between religious virtue and social cohesion. His efforts on behalf of the St. Peter's Seaman's Bethel revealed a desire to attract a broad-based constituency to the Episcopal church, not solely for the purpose of social control but also for the advancement of the Episcopal faith.

In his capacity as master and minister to a large number of slaves, Polk demonstrated a desire to build a biracial Christian community in the South. On his Leighton plantation, Polk not only provided slaves with religious instruction, but he personally officiated at slave weddings, required slaves to live by a moralistic code of conduct, and avoided separating slave families. Also, Polk promoted the plantation chapel system in both Tennessee and Louisiana, and his endorsement of slave missions in his diocese made him

---

[2] Diana Hochstedt Butler, *Standing against the Whirlwind: Evangelical Episcopalians in Nineteenth Century America* (New York/Oxford: Oxford University Press, 1995); Allen C. Guelzo, *For the Union of Evangelical Christendom: the Irony of the Reformed Episcopalians* (University Park: Pennsylvania State University Press, 1994); R. Bruce Mullin, *Episcopal Vision/American Reality: High Church Theology and Social Thought in Evangelical America* (New Haven: Yale University Press, 1986).

one of the foremost proslavery clerics in the Episcopal denomination. Polk, however, would not allow plantation culture to corrupt his religious beliefs. Sugar planters throughout the South forced their slaves to work on Sunday during the critical rolling season, but Polk refused to violate the Sabbath, and in the face of criticism from his plantation manager and at the risk of financial loss, he suspended Sunday operations at Leighton. Ultimately, his religious beliefs nearly drove him into financial ruin. By refusing to take legal action against individuals who owed him money, Polk sank into a morass of debt. Embarrassed by this plight and convinced that he could no longer reconcile his role as a spiritual leader with being a prisoner of the culture of debt that was frequently a part of plantation economics, Polk liquidated most of his agricultural assets and turned his attention toward other matters.

The educational needs of the South became Polk's next crusade. The planter-prelate realized that slavery was the defining characteristic of the South. He also knew that any truly Southern academic institution would have to defend slavery and the Southern way of life. As an Episcopalian, he believed his denomination was the only religious group in the South that possessed the financial power and the intellectual and cultural bearing to establish a regional university. Thus, the University of the South combined his desire to advance the influence of Episcopalianism and to promote a type of Southern literary and cultural nationalism. Polk convinced the Southern upper class to support his interpretation of the educational endeavor. The endorsements of such individuals as Albert Taylor Bledsoe and John S. Preston illustrated that the sectional appeal of the university resonated with influential Southerners. After the election of Abraham Lincoln as president of the United States, Polk's Southern nationalism entered a new phase. Following Louisiana's ratification of an ordinance of secession, he stepped forward as an impassioned defender of Southern independence. When the Louisiana bishop advocated diocesan secession and proposed changes to the Book of Common Prayer, he registered his approval of the Confederate cause. Moreover, his decision to accept a battlefield command invested the Confederacy with a type of religious sanctification. By leading his Louisiana diocese out of the Protestant Episcopal Church in the United States and by choosing a military assignment, Polk demonstrated the inseparability of his religious beliefs and his political worldview.

Polk compiled a mediocre record as a military leader, but considering the performance of Braxton Bragg and other high-ranking officers, the bishop can hardly be singled out for ineffectiveness, incompetence, or insubordination. Many of the Army of Tennessee's problems stemmed from the Confederacy's poor understanding of the political situation in Kentucky, as in the cases of the neutrality controversy and the failed campaign of 1862. Moreover, Polk cannot be held solely responsible for inspiring the anti-Bragg movement when such soldiers as John C. Breckinridge, Simon Bolivar Buckner, and James Longstreet developed a distrust and contempt for the commander independent of the bishop's influence. Despite a suspect military record, Polk remained unusually popular among his men and with fellow officers. His contributions to the religious culture of the Army of Tennessee helped sustain troop morale, and his personal reputation as the militant Christian knight celebrated Southern notions of God and honor. His death did not cause a crisis of faith for Southerners, but his passing did produce a sense of personal loss among many soldiers and citizens of the Confederacy. In the minds of many Southerners, death on the battlefield compensated for any deficiencies that Polk had demonstrated as a military leader. Through the efforts of such organizations as the Louisiana chapters of the United Confederate Veterans, the Sons of Confederate Veterans, and the United Daughters of the Confederacy, the bishop became part of the pantheon of Lost Cause icons, as mythmakers portrayed him as a benevolent slaveholder and Christian warrior who died defending an institution and a way of life that they considered a sacred trust from God.

Leonidas Polk was one of the most complex religious leaders of the antebellum period. Clearly, he attempted to adapt Episcopalianism to the evangelical culture of the mid-nineteenth-century South. His evangelical tendencies surfaced in a variety of circumstances and were manifested in different ways, but he maintained a desire to preach the gospel, convert sinners, and promote social conservatism. As a proponent of religious benevolence and as an advocate of a biracial Christian community, the bishop sought to reconcile Episcopalianism with the defining elements of Southern evangelical culture. Similarly, his sponsorship of the University of the South combined denominational objectives with sectional consciousness. Finally, Polk's service as a Confederate officer and his inclusion in the Lost Cause movement symbolized the complementary nature of Episcopalianism and Confederate identity. Thus, when considering Leonidas Polk's evangelical experiment from a sociological rather than a narrowly construed theological or ideological perspective, one can see that the bishop constructed for Southern Episcopalians a viable strategy for entering the mainstream of Southern religious life.

BIBLIOGRAPHY

Manuscript Collections

Aristide Hopkins Papers. Tulane University, Joseph Merrick Jones Hall, New Orleans, Louisiana.

Baylor Family Papers. Virginia Historical Society, Richmond, Virginia.

Benjamin Franklin Cheatham Papers. Tennessee State Library and Archives, Nashville, Tennessee.

Brian Grimes Papers. Southern Historical Collection. University of North Carolina at Chapel Hill.

Butler Family Papers. Historic New Orleans Collection. New Orleans, Louisiana.

Charles P. Leverich Papers. Mississippi Department of Archives and History, Jackson, Mississippi.

Clayton Torrence Papers. Virginia Historical Society, Richmond, Virginia.

Devereux Family Papers. Duke University, William R. Perkins Library, Durham, North Carolina.

Historical Records of the Episcopal Church. Tulane University, Joseph Merrick Jones Hall, New Orleans, Louisiana.

James Hervey Otey Papers. Southern Historical Collection. University of North Carolina at Chapel Hill.

John McDonogh Papers. Tulane University, Joseph Merrick Jones Hall, New Orleans, Louisiana.

Leonidas Polk Biographical File. Archives of the Episcopal Church USA, Austin, Texas

Leonidas Polk Family Papers. Historic New Orleans Collection. New Orleans, Louisiana

Leverich Correspondence. Louisiana and Lower Mississippi Valley Collections. Louisiana State University, Hill Memorial Library, Baton Rouge, Louisiana.

Louisiana and Lower Mississippi Valley Collections. Louisiana State University, Hill Memorial Library, Baton Rouge, Louisiana.

Record of Delinquencies, 1822–1828. USMA Archives. United States Military Academy, West Point, New York.

Register of Merit, 1817–1835. USMA Archives. United States Military Academy, West Point, New York.

Reports of the Board of Visitors, 1826. USMA Archives. United States Military Academy, West Point, New York.

Samuel P. Heintzelman Diary. USMA Special Collections. United States Military Academy Staff Records, 1818 to 1835. United States Military Academy, West Point, New York.

"Scrapbook of Louisiana History." Tulane University, Joseph Merrick Jones Hall, New Orleans, Louisiana.

United Daughters of the Confederacy Papers. Tulane University, Joseph Merrick Jones Hall, New Orleans, Louisiana.

Vertical file: Sewanee Description, 1900–1940. Leonidas Polk Papers. Board of Trustees Collection. University of the South, Jesse Dupont Library, Sewanee. Tennessee.

Newspapers and Religious Periodicals

Appeal (Memphis TN). 1861.

Church Intelligencer (Raleigh NC). 1860–1861.

De Bow's Review (New Orleans LA). 1859–1860.

Sewanee Daily Purple (Sewanee TN). 1884.

Southern Churchman (Alexandria VA). 1844–1845.

The Daily Picayune (New Orleans LA). 1849, 1853.

The Spirit of Missions (New York NY). 1839–1841.

University News (Sewanee TN). 1876.

University Record (Sewanee TN). 1874.

Government Publications

Official Registers of the U.S.M.A., 1818–1850. West Point: US Military Press, 1850.

Population Schedule, Washington DC: Government Printing Office, 1843.

Regulations of the United States Military Academy. West Point: US Military Press, 1823.

Slave Schedule. Washington DC: Government Printing Office, 1853.

United States Census Office. *Seventh Census of the United States*, 1850.

United States Census Office. *Sixth Census of the United* States, 1840.

Pulished Sources

Abernethey, Thomas P. *From Frontier to Plantation in Tennessee: A Study in Frontier Democracy.* Chapel Hill: University of North Carolina Press, 1932.

Agnew, James. *Eggnog Riot: The Christmas Mutiny at West Point.* San Rafael CA: Presidio Press, 1979.

Allardice, Bruce S. *More Generals in Gray.* Baton Rouge: Louisiana State University Press, 1995.

Ambrose, Douglas. *Henry Hughes and Proslavery Thought in the Old South.* Baton Rouge: Louisiana State University Press, 1996.

Ambrose, Stephen E. *Duty, Honor, Country: A History of West Point.* Baltimore: Johns Hopkins University Press, 1966.

Angellotti, Mrs. Frank B. *The Polks of North Carolina and Tennessee.* Easley SC: Southern Historical Press, 1984.

Armentrout, Donald S. *James Hervey Otey: First Episcopal Bishop of Tennessee.* Knoxville TN: The Episcopal Diocese of Tennessee, 1984.

Ash, Stephen V. *Middle Tennessee State Society Transformed 1860–1870: War and Peace in the Upper South.* Baton Rouge: Louisiana State University Press, 1988.

Banner, Lois W. "Religious Benevolence as Social Control: A Critique of an Interpretation." *Journal of American History* 60/1 (June 1973): 23–41.

Barnwell, John. *Love of Order: South Carolina's First Secession Crisis.* Chapel Hill: University of North Carolina Press, 1982.

Basler, Roy P., editor. *Collected Works of Abraham Lincoln.* 9 volumes. Brunswick: Rutgers University Press, 1953–1955.

Bauer, Jerald. "Regionalism and Religion in America." *Church History* 54/3 (September 1985): 366–78.

Bellows, Barbara L. *Benevolence among Slaveholders: Assisting the Poor in Charleston 1670–1860.* Baton Rouge: Louisiana State University Press, 1993.

Bercovitch, Sacvan. *The American Jeremiad.* Madison: University of Wisconsin Press, 1978.

Bettersworth, John K. "Protestant Beginnings in New Orleans." *Louisiana Historical Quarterly* 21/3 (July 1938): 823–45.

Boudreaux, Julianna Liles. "A History of Philanthropy in New Orleans, 1835–1863." 2 volumes. M.S.W. thesis, Tulane University, 1961.

Bouwsma, William J. *John Calvin: A Sixteenth-Century Portrait*. New York: Oxford University Press, 1988.

Boyette, Gene W. "Money and Maritime Activities in New Orleans during the Mexican War." *Louisiana History* 17/4 (Fall 1976): 413–30.

Bragg, Jefferson Davis. *Louisiana and the Confederacy*. Baton Rouge: Louisiana State University, 1941.

Brandon, Edgar Ewing. *A Pilgrimage of Liberty: A Contemporary Account of the Triumphal Tour of General Lafayette through the Southern and Western States in 1825, as Reported by the Local Newspapers*. Athens OH: Lawhead Press, 1944.

Brown, Lawrence L. "Richard Channing Moore and the Revival of the Southern Church." *Historical Magazine of the Protestant Episcopal Church* 35 (March 1966): 3–63.

Brydon, G. Maclaren. *The Episcopal Church among the Negroes of Virginia*. Richmond: Virginia Diocese Library, 1937.

Butler, Diana H. *Standing against the Whirlwind: Evangelical Episcopalians in Nineteenth Century America*. New York: Oxford University Press, 1995.

Cantrell, Gregg. *Kenneth and John B. Rayner and the Limits of Southern Dissent*. Urbana: University of Illinois Press, 1993.

Castel, Albert. *Decision in the West: The Atlanta Campaign of 1864*. Lawrence: University Press of Kansas, 1992.

Censer, Jane Turner. *North Carolina Planters and Their Children, 1800–1860*. Baton Rouge: Louisiana State University Press, 1984.

Champomier, Pierre A. *Statement of the Sugar Crop Made in Louisiana*. New Orleans: Cook, Young, and Company, 1844–1862.

Chitty, Arthur Benjamin, Jr. *Reconstruction at Sewanee: The Founding of the University of the South and Its First Administration*. Sewanee TN: The University Press, 1954.

Chorley, E. Clowes. *Men and Movements in the American Episcopal Church*. New York: Scribner, 1946.

Church, Albert E. *Personal Reminiscences of the United States Military Academy*. West Point: US Military Press, 1879.

Clement, Priscilla Ferguson. "Children and Charity: Orphanages in New Orleans, 1817–1914." *Louisiana History* 27/4 (Fall 1986): 337–52.

Connelly, Thomas L. *Army of the Heartland: The Army of Tennessee, 1861–1862*. Baton Rouge: Louisiana State University Press, 1967.

———. *Autumn of Glory: The Army of Tennessee, 1862–1865.* Baton Rouge: Louisiana State University Press, 1971.

Connelly, Thomas L., and Barbara Bellows. *God and General Longstreet: The Lost Cause and the Southern Mind.* Baton Rouge: Louisiana State University Press, 1982.

Connelly, Thomas L., and Archer Jones. *The Politics of Command: Factions and Ideas in Confederate Strategy.* Baton Rouge: Louisiana State University Press, 1973.

Cooke, J. W. "Albert Taylor Bledsoe: An American Philosopher and Theologian of Liberty." *Southern Humanities Review* 8 (Spring 1974): 215–28.

Cooling, Benjamin Franklin. *Forts Henry and Donelson: The Key to the Confederate Heartland.* Knoxville: University of Tennessee Press, 1987.

Coulter, E. Merton. *The Civil War and Readjustment in Kentucky.* Chapel Hill: University of North Carolina Press, 1926.

Cox, Karen. "Women, the Lost Cause, and the New South: The United Daughters of the Confederacy and the Transmission of Confederate Culture." Ph.D. dissertation, University of Southern Mississippi, 1997.

Cozzens, Peter. *No Better Place to Die: The Battle of Stone's River.* Urbana: University of Illinois Press, 1990.

———. *This Terrible Sound: The Battle of Chickamauga.* Urbana: University of Illinois Press, 1992.

Crabtree, Beth G., and James W. Patton, editors. *"Journal of a Secesh Lady:" The Diary of Catherine Ann Devereux Edmonston, 1860–1866.* Raleigh: North Carolina Division of Archives and History, 1979.

Craven, Avery. *The Growth of Southern Sectionalism, 1848–1861.* Baton Rouge: Louisiana State University Press, 1953.

Crewdson, Robert L. "Bishop Polk and the Crisis in the Church: Separation or Unity?" *Historical Magazine of the Protestant Episcopal Church* 52 (March 1983): 43–51.

Crist, Lynda L., et al, editors. *The Papers of Jefferson Davis.* 11 volumes. Baton Rouge: Louisiana State University Press, 1971–2004.

Cunningham, S. A. "Religion in the Southern Army." *Confederate Veteran* 1/1 (January 1893): 11–17.

Cushman, Joseph D. *A Goodly Heritage: The Episcopal Church in Florida, 1821–1892.* Gainesville: University of Florida Press, 1965.

Dabney, Robert L. *Life and Campaigns of Lieut-Gen. Thomas J. Jackson.* New York: Blelock, 1866.

Davis, Steven. "The Death of Bishop Polk." *Blue and Gray Magazine* 6/3 (June 1989): 12–18.

Davis, Varina Howell. *Jefferson Davis, Ex-president of the Confederate States of America.* 2 volumes. New York: Belford Company, 1892.

Davis, William C. *Breckinridge: Statesman, Soldier, Symbol.* Baton Rouge: Louisiana State University Press, 1974.

———. *Diary of a Confederate Soldier: John S. Jackman of the Orphan Brigade.* Columbia: University of South Carolina Press, 1990.

Denton, Edgar III. "The Formative Years of the United States Military Academy, 1775–1833." Ph.D. dissertation, Syracuse University, 1964.

Donald, James M. "Bishop Hopkins and the Reunification of the Church." *Historical Magazine of the Protestant Episcopal Church* 47 (March 1978): 73–91.

Dorsey, Sarah A. *Recollections of Henry Watkins Allen: Brigidier-General Confederate States Army, Ex-Governor of Louisiana.* New York: M. Doolay, 1866.

Dubose, William Porcher. "Ellison Capers." *Sewanee Review* 16/2 (April 1908): 368–73.

———. "The Romance and Genius of a University." *Sewanee Review* 13/4 (October 1905): 500–502.

———. *Turning Points in My Life.* New York: Longmans, Green and Company, 1912.

Duffy, John. *Sword of Pestilence: The New Orleans Yellow Fever Epidemic of 1853.* Baton Rouge: Louisiana State University Press, 1966.

Duke, Basil. *A History of Morgan's Cavalry.* 1867. Reprint, Bloomington: University of Indiana Press, 1960.

Duncan, Herman C. *The Diocese of Louisiana: Some of Its History, 1838–1888.* New Orleans: A. W. Hyatt, 1888.

Eaton, Clement. *A History of the Old South: The Emergence of a Reluctant Nation.* New York: Macmillan, 1975.

———. *The Mind of the Old South.* Baton Rouge: Louisiana State University Press, 1967.

Elliott, Stephen. *A High Civilization: The Moral Duty of Georgians, a Discourse Delivered before the Georgia Historical Society on the Occasion of the Fifth*

Anniversary, Monday, 12th, February 1944. Savannah: Georgia Historical Society, 1844.

―――. *Funeral Services at the Burial of the Right Rev. Leonidas Polk, D. D.:Together with the Sermon Delivered in St. Paul's Church, Augusta, Georgia, on June 29, 1864.* Columbia SC: Evans & Cogswell, 1864.

Faust, Drew Gilpin. "Christian Soldiers: The Meaning of Revivalism in the Confederate Army." *Journal of Southern History* 53/1 (February 1987): 63–90.

―――. *The Creation of Confederate Nationalism: Ideology and Identity in the Civil War South.* Baton Rouge: Louisiana State University Press, 1988.

Fleming, Walter L. "Jefferson Davis at West Point." *Publications of the Mississippi Historical Society* 10/3 (1909): 247–67.

Folmsbee, Stanley J., Robert E. Corlew, and Enoch L. Mitchell. *History of Tennessee.* 4 volumes. New York: Lewis Historical Publishing, 1960.

Ford, Lacy K. *The Origins of Southern Radicalism: The South Carolina Upcountry, 1800–1860.* New York: Oxford University Press, 1988.

Foster, Gaines. *Ghosts of the Confederacy: Defeat, the Lost Cause, and the Emergence of the New South, 1865 to 1912.* New York: Oxford University Press, 1987.

Fox-Genovese, Elizabeth, and Eugene D. Genovese. "The Divine Sanction of the Social Order: Religious Foundations of the Southern Slaveholders' World View." *Journal of the American Academy of Religion* 55/2 (Summer 1987): 211–33.

Franklin, John Hope. "Negro Episcopalians in Ante-Bellum North Carolina." *Historical Magazine of the Protestant Episcopal Church* 13/3 (September 1944): 216–34.

Fremantle, Arthur Lyons. *Three Months in the Southern States: April–June, 1863.* New York: John Bradborn, 1864.

Gallay, Alan. "Planters and Slaves in the Great Awakening." In *Masters and Slaves in the House of the Lord: Race and Religion in the American South, 1740–1870.* Edited by John B. Boles. Lexington: University Press of Kentucky, 1988.

Genovese, Eugene D. *Roll, Jordan, Roll: The World the Slaves Made.* New York: Pantheon, 1974.

―――. *The Slaveholders' Dilemma: Freedom and Progress in Southern Conservative Thought, 1820–1860.* Columbia: University of South Carolina Press, 1992.

Genovese, Eugene D., and Elizabeth Fox-Genovese. "The Religious Ideals of Southern Slave Society." *Georgia Historical Quarterly* 70/2 (Spring 1986): 1–16.

Gillette, Charles. *A Few Historic Records of the Church in the Diocese of Texas, during the Rebellion Together with a Correspondence between the Right Rev. Alexander Gregg and the Rev. Charles Gillette.* New York: John A. Gary and Green Printers, 1865.

Goen, C. C. *Broken Churches, Broken Nation: Denominational Schisms and the Coming of the American Civil War.* Macon GA: Mercer University Press, 1985.

Goodwyn, Lawrence. *The Populist Moment: A Short History of the Agrarian Revolt in America.* New York: Oxford University Press, 1978.

Grant, Ulysses S. *Personal Memoirs of U. S. Grant.* 2 volumes. New York: Charles L.Webster, 1885.

Gray, Lewis C. *History of Agriculture in the Southern United States to 1860.* 2 volumes. 1933. Reprint, Gloucester MA: Peter Smith, 1958.

Green, William Mercer. *Address Delivered before the Board of Trustees, University of the South, Sewanee, Tennessee, August 4, 1879.* Charleston SC: Walker, Evans and Cogswell, 1879.

Gregg, Alexander. *The Duties Growing out of It and the Benefits to Be Expected, from the Present War.* Austin TX: Office of the State Gazette, 1861.

————. *The Sin of Extortion, and its Peculiar Aggravations at a Time Like the Present.* Austin: Texas Almanac Office, 1863.

Gregg, Wilson, and Arthur H. Noll. *Alexander Gregg: First Bishop of Texas.* Sewanee TN: The University Press, 1912.

Griffin, Clifford S. "Religious Benevolence as Social Control, 1815–1860." *Mississippi Valley Historical Review* 44/3 (December 1957): 423–44.

Guelzo, Allen C. *For Union of Evangelical Christendom: The Irony of the Reformed Episcopalians.* University Park: Pennsylvania State University Press, 1994.

————. "Ritual, Romanism, and Rebellion: The Disappearance of the Evangelical Episcopalians, 1853–1873." *Anglican and Episcopal History* 62/4 (December 1993): 535–60.

Guerry, Moultrie. *Men Who Made Sewanee.* Sewanee TN: The University Press, 1932.

Haiman, Miecislaus. *Kosciuszko in the American Revolution.* 1943. Reprint, Boston: Gregg Press, 1972.

Hallock, Judith Lee. *Braxton Bragg and Confederate Defeat*. Tuscaloosa: University of Alabama Press, 1991.

Hamilton, J. G. de Roulhac, editor. *The Papers of Thomas Ruffin*. 4 volumes. Raleigh NC: Edward and Broughton, 1920.

Harrison, Lowell H. *The Civil War in Kentucky*. Lexington: University Press of Kentucky, 1975.

Harwell, Richard Barksdale, editor. *Kate, The Journal of a Confederate Nurse*. Baton Rouge: Louisiana State University Press, 1959.

Hattaway, Herman. "The United Confederate Veterans in Louisiana." *Louisiana History* 16/1 (Winter 1975): 5–37.

Hayden, J. Carleton. "Conversion and Control: Dilemma of Episcopalians in Providing for the Religious Instruction of Slaves, Charleston, South Carolina, 1845–1860." *Historical Magazine of the Protestant Episcopal Church* 40/2 (June 1971): 143–71.

Heyrman, Christine Leigh. *Southern Cross: The Origins of the Bible Belt*. Chapel Hill: University of North Carolina Press, 1997.

Hildreth, Peggy Bassett. "Early Red Cross: The Howard Association of New Orleans, 1837–1878." *Louisiana History* 20/1 (Winter 1979): 49–76.

Hollifield, E. Brooks. *The Gentlemen Theologians: American Theology in Southern Culture, 1795–1860*. Durham: Duke University Press, 1978.

Hood, R. E. "From Headstart to Deadstart: The Historical Basis for Black Indifference toward the Episcopal Church, 1800–1860." *Historical Magazine of the Protestant Episcopal Church* 51/3 (September 1982): 267–98.

Horn, Stanley F. *The Army of Tennessee*. Indianapolis: Bobbs and Merill, 1941.

Howell, Isabel. "John Armfield of Beersheba Springs." *Tennessee Historical Quarterly* 3/1 (1944): 46–64.

Hoyt, William H., editor. *The Papers of Archibald D. Murphey*. 2 volumes. Raleigh NC: E. M. Uzzell, 1914.

Hughes, Nathaniel C., Jr. *The Battle of Belmont: Grant Strikes South*. Chapel Hill: University of North Carolina, 1991.

———, editor. *The Civil War Memoir of Philip Daingerfield Stephenson, D.D.: Private, Company K, 13th Arkansas Volunteer Infantry, Leader, Piece No.4, 5th Company, Washington Artillery, Army of Tennessee, CSA*. Baton Rouge: Louisiana State University Press, 1995.

Hughes, Nathaniel C., Jr., and Roy P. Stonesifer, Jr. *The Life and Wars of Gideon Pillow*. Chapel Hill: University of North Carolina Press, 1993.

Jackson, Mary Anna. *Life and Letters of Stonewall Jackson*. New York: Harper and Brothers, 1892.

Jervey, James Postell. "Leonidas Polk: The Confederate General." *Historical Magazine of the Protestant Episcopal Church* 7/4 (December 1938): 389–404.

Johnson, Michael P. "Planters and Patriarchy: Charleston, 1800–1860." *Journal of Southern History* 46/1 (February 1980): 45–72.

Jones, Archer. *Civil War Command and Strategy: The Process of Victory and Defeat*. New York: Free Press, 1992.

Jones, Charles Colcock. *The Religious Instruction of the Negroes in the United States*. Savannah: Thomas Purse, 1842.

Keller, H. A., editor. *Solon Robinson, Pioneer and Agriculturalist*. 2 volumes. Indianapolis: Indiana Historical Bureau, 1936.

Kershner, James W. "Sylvannus Thayer: A Biography." Ph.D. dissertation, West Virginia University, 1976.

Lefler, Hugh T., and Albert Ray Newsome. *The History of a Southern State: North Carolina*. Chapel Hill: University of North Carolina Press, 1954.

Lemmon, Sarah McCulloh. "Dissent in North Carolina during the War of 1812," *North Carolina Historical Review* 49/2 (April 1972): 103–18.

Losson, Christopher. *Tennessee's Forgotten Warrior: General Frank Cheatham and His Confederate Division*. Knoxville: University of Tennessee Press, 1989.

Loveland, Anne C. *Emblem of Liberty: The Image of Lafayette in the American Mind*. Baton Rouge: Louisiana State University Press, 1971.

————. *Southern Evangelicals and the Social Order, 1800–1860*. Baton Rouge: Louisiana State University Press, 1980.

McCardell, John. *The Idea of a Southern Nation: Southern Nationalists and Southern Nationalism*. New York: W. W. Norton, 1979.

McDonough, James L. *Shiloh-in-Hell before Night*. Knoxville: University of Tennessee Press, 1977.

————. *Stone's River-Bloody Winter in Tennessee*. Knoxville: University of Tennessee Press, 1980.

————. *War in Kentucky: From Shiloh to Perryville*. Knoxville: University of Tennessee Press. 1994.

McFeely, William S., *Grant: A Biography*. New York: Norton, 1981.

McIlvaine, Charles P. "Leonidas Polk: The Bishop-General Who Died for the South, Interesting Reminiscences of Life at West Point of the Gallant Churchman and Soldier." *Southern Historical Society Papers* 18/3 (1890): 371–81.

———. *The Apostolic Commission. The Sermon Preached at the Consecration of the Rt. Rev. Leonidas Polk, D. D., Missionary Bishop for Arkansas, in Christ Church, Cincinnati, December 9, 1938.* Gambier OH: Myers, 1838.

McIver, George W. "North Carolinians at West Point before the Civil War." *North Carolina Historical Review* 7/1 (January 1930): 15–45.

McKenzie, Robert Tracy. *One South or Many? Plantation Belt and Upcountry in Civil War-Era Tennessee.* New York: Cambridge University Press, 1994.

McMurry, Richard M. *John Bell Hood and the War for Southern Independence.* Lexington: University Press of Kentucky, 1982.

McPherson, James M. *Battle Cry of Freedom: The Civil War Era.* New York: Oxford University Press, 1988.

McWhiney, Grady. *Braxton Bragg and Confederate Defeat.* New York: Columbia University Press, 1969.

Malone, Henry Thompson. *The Episcopal Church in Georgia, 1733–1957.* Atlanta: The Protestant Episcopal Church in the Diocese of Atlanta, 1960.

Mathews, Donald. *Religion in the Old South.* Chicago: University of Chicago Press, 1977.

———. "Charles Colcock Jones and the Southern Evangelical Crusade to Form a Biracial Community." *Journal of Southern History* 41/3 (August 1975): 299–320.

May, Robert L. *John A. Quitman: Old South Crusader.* Baton Rouge: Louisiana State University Press, 1985.

Miles, Edwin A. "The Old South and the Classical World." *North Carolina Historical Review* 48/3 (July 1971): 258–75.

Monroe, Haskell. "Bishop Palmer's Thanksgiving Day Address." *Louisiana History* 4/2 (Spring 1963):105–18.

Mooney, Chase C. *Slavery in Tennessee.* Bloomington: Indiana University Press, 1957.

Moore, Frank, editor. *The Rebellion Record: A Diary of American Events.* 12 volumes. 1861–1868. Reprint, New York: Arno Press, 1977.

Morrison, James L., Jr. *"The Best School in the World": West Point, the Pre-Civil War Years, 1833–1866*. Kent OH: Kent State University Press, 1986.

Mullin, R. Bruce. *Episcopal Vision/American Reality: High Church Theology and Social Thought in Evangelical America*. New Haven: Yale University Press, 1986.

Nicolay, John G., and John Hay. *Abraham Lincoln: A History*. 10 volumes. New York: The Century Company, 1886–1890.

Noll, Arthur H. *History of the Church in the Diocese of Tennessee*. New York: James Pott, 1900.

Noll, Arthur L., editor. *Doctor Quintard: Chaplain C. S. A. and Second Bishop of Tennessee, Being His Story of the War, 1861–1865*. Sewanee TN: The University Press, 1905.

Olmsted, Frederick Law. *The Cotton Kingdom: A Traveller's Observations on Cotton and Slavery in the American Slave States*. 1861. Reprint, New York: Knopf, 1953.

Otey, James H. *Preaching the Gospel: A Charge, Delivered to the Clergy of the Protestant Episcopal Church in the State of Tennessee at the Twelfth Annual Convention of the Diocese*. Nashville: S. Nye, 1840.

——. *Proceedings of a Convention of the Trustees of a Proposed University for the Southern States, under the Auspices of the Protestant Episcopal Church*. Atlanta: C. R. Hanleiter, 1857.

——. *The Duty of the Ministers of the Gospel, to Their People, Considered in Their Civil Relations: Set Forth in a Primary Charge to the Clergy of the Diocese of Tennessee*. Nashville: S. Nye, 1837.

——. *The Triennial Sermon, before the Bishops, Clergy, and Laity, Constituting the Board of Missions of the Protestant Episcopal Church in the United States of America, Preached in St. Stephens Church, Philadelphia, September 6, 1838*. Philadelphia: C. Sherman, 1838.

Owen, Christopher H. *The Sacred Flame of Love: Methodism and Society in Nineteenth-Century Georgia*. Athens: University of Georgia Press, 1998.

Palmer, Benjamin Morgan. *The South: Her Peril and Her Duty. A Discourse Delivered in the First Presbyterian Church, New Orleans, on Thursday, November 29, 1860*. New Orleans: Office of the True Witness and Sentinel, 1860.

Paludan, Phillip Shaw. *The Presidency of Abraham Lincoln*. Lawrence: University Press of Kansas, 1994.

Pappas, George S. *To the Point: The United States Military Academy, 1802–1902.* Westport CT: Praeger, 1993.

Parks, Joseph H. *General Leonidas Polk, C. S. A.: The Fighting Bishop.* Baton Rouge: Louisiana State University Press, 1962.

Polk, Leonidas. *A Letter to the Right Reverend Bishops of Tennessee, Georgia, Arkansas, Texas, Mississippi, Florida, South Carolina, and North Carolina from the Bishop of Louisiana.* New Orleans: B. M. Norman, 1856.

————, and Stephen Elliott. *Address of the Commissioners for Raising the Endowment of the University of the South.* New Orleans: B. M. Norman, 1860.

Polk, William M. *Leonidas Polk: Bishop and General.* 2 volumes. New York: Longmans, Green, and Company, 1915.

————. *The University of the South and the Race Problem, Commencement Oration, August 3, 1893.* Sewanee TN: The Sewanee Press, 1893.

Powell, William S. *Dictionary of North Carolina Biography.* 6 volumes. Chapel Hill: University of North Carolina Press, 1979–1996.

Preyer, Norris W. *Hezekiah Alexander and the Revolution in the Backcountry.* Charlotte NC: Heritage Printers, 1987.

Prichard, Robert W. *The Nature of Salvation: Theological Consensus in the Episcopal Church, 1801–73.* Urbana: University of Illinois Press, 1997.

Randall, James G. *The Civil War and Reconstruction.* Boston: D. C. Heath, 1937.

Rankin, Hugh F. *The North Carolina Continentals.* Chapel Hill: University of North Carolina Press, 1971.

Rankin, Richard. *Ambivalent Churchmen and Evangelical Church Women: The Religion of the Episcopal Elite in North Carolina, 1800–1860.* Columbia: University of South Carolina Press, 1993.

Rawley, James A. *Turning Points of the Civil War.* Lincoln: University of Nebraska Press, 1966.

Reilly, Timothy F. "Parson Clapp of New Orleans: Antebellum Social Critic, Religious Radical, and Member of the Establishment." *Louisiana History* 16/2 (Spring 1975): 167–91.

Remini, Robert V. *Andrew Jackson and the Course of American Empire.* New York: Harper & Row, 1977.

Rice, Katharine S. "A Study of the Children's Home of the Protestant Episcopal Church of the Diocese of Louisiana." M.S.W. thesis, Tulane University, 1937.

Robertson, James I., Jr. *Soldiers Blue and Gray*. Columbia: University of South Carolina Press, 1988.

———. *Stonewall Jackson: The Man, the Soldier, the Legend*. New York: Macmillan, 1997.

Roland, Charles P. *Albert Sidney Johnston: Soldier of Three Republics*. Austin: University of Texas Press, 1964.

———. "Louisiana and Secession." *Louisiana History* 19/4 (Fall 1978): 389–99.Rolle, Andrew. *John C. Fremont: Character as Destiny*. Norman: University of Oklahoma Press, 1991.

Scarborough, William K. "Lords or Capitalists? The Natchez Nabobs in Comparative Perspective." *Journal of Mississippi History* 54/3 (Summer 1992): 239–67.

———. "Science on the Plantation." In *Science and Medicine in the Old South*, edited by Ronald L. Numbers and Todd L. Savitt, 79–106. Baton Rouge: Louisiana State University Press, 1989.

———, editor. *The Diary of Edmund Ruffin*. 3 volumes. Baton Rouge: Louisiana State University Press, 1972–1989.

Schafer, Judith Kelleher. "The Immediate Impact of Nat Turner's Insurrection on New Orleans." *Louisiana History* 21/4 (Fall 1980): 361–76.

Schaff, Morris. *The Spirit of Old West Point, 1858–1862*. Boston: Houghton, Mifflin, and Company, 1907.

Schmitz, Mark. *Economic Analysis of Antebellum Sugar Plantations in Louisiana*. New York: Arno Press, 1977.

Schultz, Harold S. *Nationalism and Sectionalism in South Carolina, 1852–1860*. Durham: Duke University Press, 1950.

Shippe, Lester B., editor. *Bishop Whipple's Southern Diary, 1843–1844*. New York: Oxford University Press, 1937.

Showman, Richard K., editor. *The Papers of Nathanael Greene*. 11 volumes. Chapel Hill: University of North Carolina Press, 1976–1999.

Silver, James W. *Confederate Morale and Church Propaganda*. Tuscaloosa: Confederate Publishing Company, 1957.

Sitterson, J. Carlyle. *Sugar Country: The Cane Sugar Industry in the South, 1753–1950*. Lexington: University Press of Kentucky, 1953.

———. "The William J. Minor Plantations: A Study in Antebellum Absentee Ownership." *Journal of Southern History* 9/1 (February 1943): 59–74.

Smith, Francis H. *The Inner Life of the V. M. I. Cadet: An Introductory Address to the Corps of Cadets, Sept. 10, 1866.* Lexington: Virginia Military Institute Press, 1873.

Snay, Mitchell. *The Gospel of Disunion: Religion and Separatism in the Antebellum South.* New York: Oxford University Press, 1993.

Snyder, Ann E. *The Civil War: from a Southern Stand-Point.* Nashville: Publishing House of the Methodist Episcopal Church, South, 1890.

Startup, Kenneth M. *The Root of All Evil: The Protestant Clergy and the Economic Mind of the Old South.* Athens: University of Georgia Press, 1997.

Stroupe, Henry S. *The Religious Press in the South Atlantic States, 1802–1865.* Durham: Duke University Press, 1956.

Symonds, Craig L. *Joseph E. Johnston: A Civil War Biography.* New York: W. W. Norton, 1992.

———. *Stonewall of the West: Patrick Cleburne and the Civil War.* Lawrence: University Press of Kansas, 1997.

Taylor, Georgia Fairbanks. "The Early History of the Episcopal Church in New Orleans, 1805–1840. *Louisiana Historical Quarterly* 22/2 (April 1939): 428–478.

Taylor, Joe Gray. *Negro Slavery in Louisiana.* Baton Rouge: Thomas J. Moran and Sons, 1963.

Thomas, Arthur Dickens, Jr. "O That Slavery's Curse Might Cease." *Virginia Seminary Journal* 45/1 (December 1993): 56–61.

Thompson, Thomas Marshall. "National Newspapers and the Legislative Reactions to Louisiana's Deslondes Slave Revolt." *Louisiana History* 33/1 (Winter 1992): 5–29.

Tise, Larry E. *Proslavery: A History of the Defense of Slavery in America, 1701–1840.* Athens: University of Georgia Press, 1987.

Touchstone, Blake. "Planters and Slave Religion in the Deep South." In *Masters and Slaves in the House of the Lord.* Edited by John B. Boles. Lexington: University Press of Kentucky, 1988.

Trent, William P. "A Noteworthy Biography: Leonidas Polk." *Sewanee Review* 2/2 (May 1893): 377–84.

US War Department. *The War of the Rebellion: A Compilation of the Official Records of the Union and Confederate Armies.* 128 volumes. Washington DC: Government Printing Office, 1880–1901.

Vandiver, Frank E. *Their Tattered Flags: The Epic of the Confederacy*. College Station: Texas A & M University Press, 1970.

———. *Ploughshares into Swords: Josiah Gorgas and Confederate Ordinance*. Austin: University of Texas Press, 1952.

Villard, Henry. *Memoirs of Henry Villard: Journalist and Financier, 1835–1862*. 2 volumes. Westminister England: A. Constable, 1904.

Wakelyn, Jon L. *Biographical Dictionary of the Confederacy*. Westport CT: Greenwood Press, 1977.

Walker, Peter Franklin. "Building a Tennessee Army: Autumn 1861." *Tennessee Historical Quarterly* 16/3 (June 1957): 99–116.

Warner, Ezra. *Generals in Blue: Lives of the Union Commanders*. Baton Rouge: Louisiana State University Press, 1964.

———. *Generals in Gray: Lives of the Confederate Commanders*. Baton Rouge: Louisiana State University Press, 1959.

Watkins, Sam. *"Co. Aytch," Maury Grays First Tennessee Regiment*. 1882. Reprint, Jackson TN: McCowat-Mercer Press, 1952.

Watson, Harry L. *Jacksonian Politics and Community Conflict: The Emergence of the Second American Party System in Cumberland County, North Carolina*. Baton Rouge: Louisiana State University Press, 1981.

White, Greenough. *A Saint of the Southern Church: Memoir of the Right Reverend Nicholas Hamner Cobbs*. New York: James Pott, 1897.

Wiggins, Susan Woolfolk, editor. *The Journals of Josiah Gorgas, 1857–1878*. Tuscaloosa: University of Alabama Press, 1995.

Wilmer, Joseph P. B. *General Robert E. Lee: An Address Delivered Before the Students of the University of the South, October 15, 1870*. Nashville: Paul & Tavel, 1872.

Witcher, Robert C. "The Episcopal Church in Louisiana, 1805–1861." Ph.D. dissertation, Louisiana State University, 1969.

Woodworth, Steven E. "Indeterminate Qualities: Jefferson Davis, Leonidas Polk and the End of Kentucky Neutrality, September 1861." *Civil War History* 38/3 (December 1992): 289–97.

———. *Jefferson Davis and His Generals: The Failure of Confederate Command in the West*. Lawrence: University Press of Kansas, 1990.

———. *Six Armies in Tennessee: The Chickamauga and Chattanooga Campaigns*. Lincoln: University of Nebraska, 1998.

Wooster, Ralph A. *The Secession Conventions of the South*. Princeton: Princeton University Press, 1962.

Wyatt-Brown, Bertram. "Church, Honor, and Secession." In *Religion and the American Civil War*. Edited by Randall M. Miller, Harry S. Stout, and Charles Reagan Wilson. New York: Oxford University Press, 1998.

———. "God and Honor in the Old South." *The Southern Review* 25/2 (April 1989): 283–96.

———. *The House of Percy: Honor, Melancholy, and Imagination in a Southern Family*. New York: Oxford University Press, 1994.

Yeatman, Trezevant P. Jr. "St. John's—A Plantation Church of the Old South." *Tennessee Historical Quarterly* 10/4 (December 1951): 334–43.

Ziesler, J. A. *Pauline Christianity*. New York: Oxford University Press, 1983.

INDEX